PROMISE AND PERIL

Thanks for
reading.

HBW.

PROMISE AND PERIL

Justin Trudeau in Power

AARON WHERRY

HarperCollins*Publishers*Ltd

Published by HarperCollins Publishers Ltd

First edition

HarperCollins books may be purchased for educational, business, or sales promotional use through our Special Markets Department.

HarperCollins Publishers Ltd
Bay Adelaide Centre, East Tower
22 Adelaide Street West, 41st Floor
Toronto, Ontario, Canada
M5H 4E3

www.harpercollins.ca

Library and Archives Canada Cataloguing in Publication information is available upon request.

ISBN 978-1-4434-5827-6

Printed and bound in the United States of America
LSC/H 9 8 7 6 5 4 3 2 1

For Sharon and Ivy

CONTENTS

PROLOGUE

THAT DREAM WHERE YOU'RE BACK IN HIGH SCHOOL

By coincidence, Justin Trudeau was back at Montreal's Collège Jean-de-Brébeuf on the night of February 27, 2019.

Brébeuf—named for the French missionary and martyr—was founded by the Jesuits in 1928, built on farmland at the foot of Mount Royal. Its motto became *Viam veritatis elegi*, or "I chose the path of truth." "Almost from the start, it was considered the most prestigious college in Quebec," historians Max and Monique Nemni later wrote in a biography of its most famous alumnus.

Pierre Trudeau started there in 1932, at the age of twelve, and graduated eight years later with top marks in arts and science. In 1984, after retiring from a career in politics, Pierre moved back to Montreal and enrolled his eldest son, Justin. It was there Justin learned Latin, debated sovereignty for Quebec, was teased about his parents' divorce, made lifelong friends, became an awkward teen, struggled to stay disciplined and began to contend with the weight of his last name.

More than three decades later, space at the school was rented to host a celebration of the Liberal Party's success in the recent by-election in the riding of Outremont. That win, two nights earlier, had avenged a symbolically powerful by-election loss there to the New Democratic Party and Thomas Mulcair in 2007. Mulcair's victory presaged the Orange Wave that very nearly drowned the Liberal Party in 2011. But Trudeau's Liberals had bested Mulcair's NDP in 2015, and now Rachel Bendayan, the Liberal candidate, had taken back Outremont. To mark the accomplishment, Trudeau was scheduled to greet and thank Liberal volunteers at 7 p.m. on this Wednesday night. His daughter had come along to check out her father's alma mater. For members of the media, it was to be a photo opportunity only.

Then, shortly after 6 p.m., a note went out from the Prime Minister's Office. Trudeau would be speaking to reporters at 8 p.m. As had become readily apparent, there was something he needed to address.

"Good evening, everyone. What a pleasure to be back in Outremont this evening," the prime minister began, standing in front of a podium set up inside the school's renovated old chapel. "I have some very good memories of this place. I'm very pleased to be able to show my former school to my daughter, who is here this evening." After some kind words for Bendayan and the Liberal volunteers in Outremont, some of whom stood in rows behind him, Trudeau moved to the matter at hand.

"My friends, this has been a difficult few weeks. And it's been difficult because we've had internal disagreements."

This was putting it mildly.

There was a lot going on for Justin Trudeau's government in that fourth week of February 2019. On Tuesday, for instance, Statistics Canada reported that the overall poverty rate had declined to 9.5 percent in 2017. As compared to 2015, 278,000 fewer children were living in poverty, a development credited, in part, to the Trudeau government's move to reform and bolster the system of federal child benefits.

On Thursday, the Liberal government would table legislation to allow for the transfer of child welfare services to Indigenous communities, a response to concerns that infants were being unnecessarily and recklessly separated from their Indigenous mothers; Alberta premier Rachel Notley would appear before a Senate committee to register her concerns about federal plans to overhaul the environmental assessments of major resource projects; and Trudeau would announce Canada's participation in a new space station that would orbit the moon. On Friday, as part of the government's move to legalize cannabis, legislation would be introduced to expedite pardons for Canadians who had been previously convicted of possessing marijuana.

These were big things, hard things, things that can shape a country and define the legacy of a prime minister and his government.

But seemingly none of it mattered as much as what had happened in the late afternoon and early evening of that Wednesday, between 3:50 and 7:20 p.m. It was then that Jody Wilson-Raybould, the former justice minister and attorney general of Canada, finally testified publicly before the House of Commons justice committee, the star witness in a series of hearings launched amid allegations of attempted political interference in the prosecution of SNC-Lavalin, the Montreal-based engineering firm. Over the course of those three and a half hours, she implicated a half-dozen of the most senior officials in the Trudeau government, including Gerald Butts, Trudeau's former principal secretary and close friend; Katie Telford, Trudeau's chief of staff; and Michael Wernick, the clerk of the Privy Council. Trudeau himself had been involved in one of the meetings Wilson-Raybould recounted.

Wilson-Raybould had resigned from cabinet eleven days earlier. Butts had quit six days after that. Minutes after Wilson-Raybould finished her testimony to the justice committee, Conservative leader Andrew Scheer strode into the foyer of the House of Commons and solemnly declared that Trudeau should resign. The *Globe and Mail*'s lead political columnist would declare Trudeau had lost the "moral mandate" to govern. NDP leader Jagmeet Singh, showing relative restraint, called for a public inquiry.

A political career born of great potential now faced a moment of great peril.

"It was important for Jody Wilson-Raybould to speak openly at the justice committee today, and I'm glad she had the chance to do so," Trudeau said at Brébeuf. "I strongly maintain, as I have from the beginning, that I and my staff always acted appropriately and professionally. I therefore completely disagree with the former attorney general's characterization of events."

A reporter asked Trudeau if he thought he should resign.

"Canadians," he said, "will have a very clear choice in a few months' time about who they want to be prime minister of this country and what party they want to form government."

Nearly four years earlier, their choice had been Trudeau. A candidate of great promise had become a prime minister of a great many promises. And then Donald Trump became president of the United States, the entire world order seemed to be upended and suddenly everything felt precarious. All the while, the planet kept burning.

The boy with the famous last name became a prime minister whose story—this story—would be framed by promise and peril; by big questions, lofty ideals, complicated answers, odd failures and high stakes.

The following pages are an attempt to take stock of all that might be said to have weighed on that moment at Brébeuf on the last Wednesday in February 2019.

———

SIX AND A HALF years earlier, on a stage in a different part of Montreal: "Make no small dreams," he said, "they have not the power to move the soul."

Maybe only the first-born son of Pierre Trudeau would have chosen to start this way. Maybe only the first-born son of Pierre Trudeau would have dared. It was confident, ambitious, perhaps a bit cheesy, more than a little ostentatious and potentially silly.

Justin Trudeau had added the line to the speech himself. It was a quote he had come across several years earlier, when he was pursuing a master's degree in environmental geography. His thesis supervisor was a professor named Peter Brown, and Brown had been looking to establish an international institute for the environment in Montreal.

Trudeau remembers reading the quote at the top of the prospectus that Brown prepared for the project. "And it just stuck with me," he says, snapping his fingers. "I really . . . I really liked that idea."

Trudeau didn't finish that degree in environmental geography. His studies were put aside when he decided to seek public office as the MP for Papineau. But Trudeau at least came away from the program with a bit of inspiration.

(Ten years later, Brown was among the signatories on a letter from Quebec environmentalists objecting to Trudeau's decision to approve the Trans Mountain expansion.)

Pat Martin, an NDP MP, would suggest Trudeau's opening line sounded like something Tommy Douglas used to say: "Dream no little dreams." But in the official text of Trudeau's remarks, the quote was attributed to Johann Wolfgang von Goethe, the eighteenth-century German poet, playwright and novelist. Unfortunately, it is not clear Goethe ever actually wrote or said that. At the behest of a *Maclean's* reporter, an academic at McGill University later searched an archive of Goethe's work and found no record of the phrase.

The likeliest source is Daniel Burnham, the great American architect and planner, who is credited with saying something like it: "Make no little plans; they have no magic to stir men's blood, and probably themselves will not be realized. Make big plans; aim high in hope and work, remembering that a noble, logical diagram once recorded will never die, but long after we are gone will be a living thing, asserting itself with ever-growing insistency."

Whatever the provenance of Trudeau's opening line, this was how—on the evening of October 2, 2012—a forty-year-old politician with barely four years of experience as a backbench MP began his campaign for leadership of the Liberal Party and, in so doing, formally declared his interest in becoming the next prime minister of Canada.

"For me the essence of it is, if you're going to do something, do it," Trudeau says in 2019, seated in an armchair in the new Office of the Prime Minister in Parliament's West Block, an office his father had occupied when Pierre was minister of justice for Lester B. Pearson. "I mean, if we're going to work to try and create a government that is reflective of our values, our priorities, the team, the vision we have, then let's max it out. Let's not just try and stretch out our time in office and try to do a couple of nice things. No. There are big things that need doing, and if we're going to go through the personal family sacrifices, the hassles, the difficulties—everything that comes automatically with this, whether you're doing big things or small things—well, let's gather the most brilliant possible people, let's look at the real problems, whether it's reconciliation or climate change or the fundamental challenge of making sure that the middle class is still benefiting from the economic models we have. These are big things, not small things. These are problems that the entire world is facing. These are things that Canada is perhaps better suited, if it feels like it, to address. So let's just go for it."

Trying to do big things can be inspiring. It can also raise expectations.

Expectations for—and suspicion of—Trudeau had been building for years before that moment in the fall of 2012. For the pursuit of a career in politics, Trudeau was blessed with the sort of advantages that can't be easily acquired or learned: good looks, nice hair, youthful vigour, a sunny disposition, name recognition. What's more, he had a romantic story and a lifelong relationship with the public. Indeed, it is not hyperbole to say there had never been a Canadian politician quite like Justin Trudeau. There have been sons of famous fathers and there have been men and women who were famous before they were politicians, but Trudeau was something else: a public figure since his birth on Christmas Day in 1971, and the first son of this country's most captivating prime minister.

A lifetime of appearing on television screens and in photographs began the moment he was carried out of the hospital. He travelled the world and mingled with presidents and monarchs. His life played out in public: his parents' divorce, his mother's struggles with fame and her mental health, his youngest brother's death in 1998, his father's death in 2000 and his wedding to Sophie Grégoire in 2005. For comparisons, one would have to look abroad: to members of the Kennedy family in the United States or the royal family in Britain.

It was the eulogy at the televised funeral of his father on October 3, 2000—a eulogy that he opened with a line from Shakespeare's *Julius Caesar*—that ignited speculation about Justin Trudeau's political future. From then on, he was publicly measured in terms of potential. Would he run for office? Did he want to be prime minister? Could he live up to his last name?

On the evening of October 2, 2012, the first question was whether he could save the Liberal Party of Canada. John A. Macdonald, a Conservative, famously got Canada started, but it was Liberals who mostly ran the country after that. Between 1896 and 2006—from the election of Wilfrid Laurier to the resignation of Paul Martin—Liberal prime ministers were in office for a little over seventy-eight years. The Liberal Party was the great centrist institution of the twentieth century in Canada, and one of the most successful political organizations in the Western world.

But it was no longer the twentieth century. The government of Stephen Harper, arguably the most ideologically conservative prime minister in Canadian history, was now into its seventh year. And the Liberals were not even the Official Opposition. For the first time in the party's history it had been knocked down to third place. The NDP, under the sunny leadership of Jack Layton, had vaulted ahead and was now the presumed government-in-waiting. Federal politics in Canada seemed to have finally moved beyond Liberal centrism to adopt a more conventional right-left split. The party's day was arguably past. There were even suggestions that the Liberals and New Democrats should join forces.

But Layton's death in the fall of 2011 left an opening. Forced to find a new leader, the NDP anointed the prickly Mulcair at a convention in March 2012 ("Smart. Tough. Nasty. Stephen Harper Has Finally Met His Match" was how *Maclean's* put it). Then, a week after Mulcair was chosen, Justin Trudeau bloodied the nose of Conservative senator Patrick Brazeau in a charity boxing match. That odd spectacle had the odd effect of improving Trudeau's stature as a potential leader.

Trudeau had ruled out the possibility of being a leadership candidate shortly after the 2011 election. But in May 2012, *Maclean's* dared suggest Trudeau was worthy of consideration. "Justin Trudeau should be the next leader of the Liberal Party," the magazine declared on its cover. "No, seriously." Whether Trudeau should be taken seriously would remain in question for another three years (among Conservatives, it is probably still an open question). Given those natural advantages it was all the easier to wonder whether he was just a pretty face or a famous name. What *really* had he done to prove himself? What was there to justify the public's interest?

Trudeau himself wasn't ready in May to give it a shot. But he was by the fall. On that night in October 2012, his hair was a bit too long and his suit didn't fit particularly well. But the basic outline of an agenda was there. Interspersed were merely some of the greatest challenges of the twenty-first century.

Standing on a stage in Montreal's Parc Ex, a working-class neighbourhood known for the waves of immigrants who have moved through it and part of the federal riding of Papineau, he began with a nod to the people and cultures of his riding, enthusing about the importance and value of diversity. "This magnificent, unlikely country was founded on a bold new premise. That people of different beliefs and backgrounds, from all corners of the world, could come together to build a better life for themselves and for their children than they ever could have alone," he said. "This new idea that diversity is strength."

This would be a defining and precious notion, to be championed, celebrated and wrestled with. In 2012, these words might have seemed perfunctory. Within four years, this basic idea would seem in desperate need of defenders.

"We need to match the beauty and productivity of this great land with a new national commitment to steward it well," Trudeau said. "My generation understands that we cannot choose between a strong and prosperous economy and a healthy environment."

This was a very simple statement about a very hard thing, foreshadowing a future discussion about carbon pricing and pipelines and federalism. In full, it would mean figuring out how to confront an existential threat in a politically feasible manner while holding a country together.

He described what would come to be understood broadly as reconciliation. "To our First Nations, the Canadian reality has not been—and continues to not be—easy for you. We need to become a country that has the courage to own up to its mistakes and fix them together, people to people. Your place is not on the margins. It is at the very heart of who we are and what we are yet to become." This was to contend with more than 150 years of history and injustice.

And there was much about the middle class. "We need to learn what we have forgotten," he said. "That the key to growth, to opportunity, to progress, is a thriving middle class. People with good jobs. Families who are able to cope with modern life's challenges."

This he set up as the problem. "Canadian families have seen their incomes stagnate, their costs go up, and their debts explode over the past thirty years," he said. This was the great challenge at the root of everything: to ensure shared prosperity and security lest anxieties lead to suspicion and strife.

In solving that problem, he explained, he would reject the "tidy ideological answers" of the NDP and the Conservatives. For a couple years he would not offer very many answers at all. The leadership would be won on popularity, appeal and organization. To that, Trudeau would periodically add a dramatic flourish. He proposed that marijuana should be legalized. He kicked senators out of the Liberal caucus. He declared that all Liberal members of Parliament would be expected to take a pro-choice position in Parliament.

"I do not present myself as a man with all the answers," he said in October 2012. "In fact, I think we've had quite enough of that kind of politics."

Given the suspicion with which many observers regarded the young candidate with the famous last name, probably no one would have believed him if he *had* claimed to have all the answers. But in that doubt there was a chance to style himself as a different kind of leader from Stephen Harper: more open, more collaborative, more willing to listen to expertise. Later, he would build a slate of men and women with formidable resumés—a CEO, a police chief, an Indigenous chief, a journalist—that further buttressed him against the charge of unseriousness.

"I do know I have a strong sense of this country," he said. "I feel so privileged to have had the relationship I've had, all my life, with this country, with its land, and with its people. From my first, determined steps as a toddler to my first, determined steps as a politician: we've travelled many miles together, my friends. You have always been there for me. You have inspired me, and supported me in good and more difficult times. And you have made me the man and the father I have become."

Any number of politicians have cast themselves as a native son of someplace or another. Surely few, if any, have positioned themselves as a nation's son. Few, if any, could have plausibly qualified.

Nearing the end of this speech, he spoke of growing up and generational change. "It is time for us, for this generation of Canadians, to put away childish things," he said, referring to the Letter of St. Paul to the Corinthians, as read by his father at his brother's funeral. "More, it is time for all of us to come together and get down to the very serious, very adult business of building a better country." The son was declaring himself ready to do that work.

It was, in many ways, a simpler time.

The previous spring, in the finale of the fifth season of *Celebrity Apprentice*, Donald Trump had chosen former talk show host Arsenio Hall as the winner over former *American Idol* runner-up Clay Aiken. Barack Obama was now a few weeks away from winning his second term as president of the United States, with Hillary Clinton serving as his secretary of state. The United Kingdom was a committed member of the European Union. The Syrian civil war had only just begun to take shape. No one feared for the future of liberal democracy or the international rules-based order. Populism was a marginal concern, a folksy relic of the past. Trudeau had not yet promised to fundamentally change Canada's electoral system. And the RCMP was still two and a half years away from charging SNC-Lavalin with fraud and corruption related to the company's work in Libya.

The future was unknown and thus uncomplicated.

———

TRUDEAU SET OFF FROM Montreal to campaign for the job of prime minister. He was viewed with both great expectation and sneering doubt. All that made him uniquely suited to politics also made him easy to dismiss. He was either an exciting new figure or an airy lightweight. Sounding a little like Burnham, he spoke of "hope and hard work." Support for the Liberal Party surged and then dwindled. He promised "real change." His opponents dismissed him as "just not ready."

On the eve of the first televised debate of the long election campaign in 2015, an official from the Conservative Party attempted to pre-empt any analysis that Trudeau would end up winning the night by merely exceeding expectations. No leader, the official said, had ever faced lower expectations. "I think that if he comes on stage with his pants on, he will probably exceed expectations," was the memorable quip.

Trudeau managed to show up in pants. And then, when it was nearly over, he looked directly into the camera and, with a noticeably slower pace than he had used in the preceding two hours, delivered a concluding appeal. Butts would invoke that closing statement years later as "pretty much the unfiltered Justin Trudeau." Butts himself had initially been unsure about it, but Trudeau had decided this was what he wanted to say.

"Mr. Harper has spent millions of dollars on attack ads trying to convince you that I'm not ready for this job," Trudeau began. "As silly as they are, they do pose an important question. How can you decide whether someone is ready to be your prime minister? Here's what I think. In order to know if someone is ready for this job, ask them what they want to do with this job, and why they want it in the first place."

This was at least an interesting premise. Trudeau was not going to win a comparison of CVs. Maybe he could present a more appealing vision.

But next he was talking about more than just a plan for the future. "I'm a forty-three-year-old father of three kids, and I love them deeply, and I want them to grow up in the best country in the world, one that we can all be proud of. What I learned from my father is that to lead this country, you need to love this country, love it more than you crave power. It needs to run through your veins. You need to feel it in your bones."

Love is an odd metric for choosing a leader. But Stephen Harper, standing a few spots over to Trudeau's left, might have felt a twinge of memory.

Nearly ten years earlier, on the first day of the 2006 federal campaign, the Conservative leader had been hit with a question about his feelings for the country. "Do you love Canada?" a reporter wondered. When Harper failed to use the word "love" in his response—"Well, I've said Canada is a great country"—Paul Martin's Liberals poked fun. Harper responded by saying Liberals believed that "people who don't vote Liberal don't love this country. This is what we've got to expect. It's mean and it saddens me. I believe Liberals do love this country, but they love power too much."

Stephen Harper probably does love Canada. But, by all accounts, he doesn't love all the ideas and people that were used to define Canada during the seventy-eight years that the Liberal Party was in charge. Once in office, the Harper government championed different things. The War of 1812 was enthusiastically celebrated. John Diefenbaker and John A. Macdonald got their names on official buildings in downtown Ottawa. The thirtieth anniversary of the Charter of Rights and Freedoms, on the other hand, went unmarked.

Justin Trudeau was promising change, but part of that change was to go back to the pre-Harper version of Canada: progressive, peaceful, co-operative, bureaucratic, nice. And there would turn out to be an audience for that idea.

"Canadians clearly told us they had grown tired of now-defeated Prime Minister Stephen Harper and were yearning to return to the values that they believe traditionally defined Canada and Canadian society," Ensight, a public relations firm, reported after the 2015 election, basing its conclusions on polling and focus groups.

Trudeau's own name harkened back to "a time that many people feel was the Golden Age of Canada and its values, with the patriation of the Constitution, the development of the Charter of Rights and Freedoms, bilingualism, multiculturalism and compassion." The Liberal leader, Ensight argued, had campaigned "on a return to the values that many feel have traditionally defined Canadian society—civility, kindness, inclusion, consultation, collaboration and community."

He wore a young, fresh face, but came wrapped in nostalgia.

Having established just how much he loved this country, Trudeau then drew a philosophical distinction between himself and Harper. "Mr. Harper and I part ways on many issues, but our differences go deeper than just policy. Mr. Harper is dead wrong about one thing. He wants you to believe that better just isn't possible," he said. "Well, I think that's wrong. We are who we are, and Canada is what it is, because in our hearts we've always known that better is always possible."

This assertion—that "better" is "possible"—was a vague ideal to rest on. But it suggested ambition. It is, on one level, how a liberal or a progressive might differentiate himself from a conservative. The conservative generally aims to limit, maintain or defer. The liberal thinks about what more they can do. But Harper had also been an incrementalist. It had arguably been his defining trait. He wanted to make small, gradual changes. He wanted to firmly establish conservative principles within the national debate. He wanted to reduce the capacity of the federal government. But he didn't want to scare anyone while he was doing any of that. He was waging a non-threatening insurgency, premised on sticking around until his ideas felt familiar.

Trudeau was very nearly the opposite. This Liberal leader wanted to do all sorts of things and big things and different things: legalizing marijuana, adopting a new electoral system, running a deficit. He was also apparently not worried about promising too much. By one count, the Liberal platform in 2015 contained 353 commitments, nearly double the number of promises made by Harper's Conservatives in 2006.

Ambition was part of the appeal. It was what separated the Liberals not only from the Conservatives, but also from the New Democrats, another party that seemed worried about scaring voters. And that appeal to ambition was not tempered once the campaign was over. Looking upon the results of the election on the night of October 19,

2015, Trudeau said Canadians had shown they wanted "a government with a vision and an agenda for this country that is positive and ambitious and hopeful." A few weeks later, in the Throne Speech, the governor general declared on the government's behalf that "the agenda outlined today is an ambitious one."

"Our prime minister, he doesn't aim for bunts and singles," Scott Brison, president of the Treasury Board in Trudeau's first cabinet, would later say. "He swings for the bleachers." The thing about swinging hard, of course, is that it increases the chances you'll miss. But perhaps some significant number of Canadians wanted a leader who was looking beyond the fence.

With the time remaining for him to finish his concluding statement at that first debate, Trudeau tried to broadly sketch what he saw when he thought about the better that was possible. "An economy that works for the middle class means a country that works for everyone, a country that is strong not in spite of our differences but because of them. The world needs more of both those things. And after ten years of Mr. Harper, so do we."

It was, in its entirety, in danger of being a bit much, particularly in its delivery. On Twitter, there was virtual eye-rolling. And that reaction made its way to Trudeau directly. "Your closing remarks, they were kind of horrible," a television reporter told him in the post-game scrum.

But, as reported by Paul Wells of *Maclean's* a few months later, the Liberals had been running a focus group during the debate, and within that room those who liked it outnumbered those who didn't by a ratio of two to one.

In addition to wearing pants, Trudeau had also not looked like a goof that night. The Conservatives had expended great amounts of energy and money telling Canadians that Trudeau was a goof—pretty and nice and likeable, but ultimately callow and unqualified. Now he had stood with Harper and Mulcair, two unquestionably serious-looking men, and held his own. His opponents had set a very low bar, and he would spend the campaign mostly exceeding it.

======

JUSTIN TRUDEAU WAS SWORN in as Canada's twenty-third prime minister on November 4, 2015. "Make no small dreams" would soon be matched with a new saying: "hard things are hard." Big dreams, it turns out, can be difficult to realize.

There's another saying Trudeau has picked up: that there are people who get into politics to *be* something and there are people who get into politics to *do* something. He probably got it from Butts, who heard it from his aunt. "It never even really occurred to me that I had to be something, because that just was always around me, right? No matter what I was doing, people would have me being something," Trudeau says. "It's what am I doing with it that is all that matters. And what are we doing with it as a government."

The following story is about what happened when Justin Trudeau tried to do something, and the stakes of it all. He has led a government of successes and failures, ideals and shortcomings, faced with massive problems and offering imperfect solutions. The strength of his positions has been tested, as have the tensions between those positions. He has been measured against his hopeful words, by what has changed and what hasn't. He has been pursued by doubts and doubters. He has moved the country forward and he has screwed up. It has been four years of wrestling with big and important things: economic security, reconciliation, resource development, gender equality, climate change, Donald Trump.

At the time of this writing, the spring of 2019, he and his government are less than six months away from an election that will pass judgment on these four years. So this is necessarily a story without a tidy ending that neatly endorses or condemns everything that came before. There will be another four years. Or there will be a sudden stop. Indeed, as of this writing, public polling suggests a bit of a toss-up, not least because of that perilous moment in February.

But it is not too early to start reckoning with all that has already occurred. And to do so at considerably more length and depth than a tweet allows. Given everything that has happened, a reckoning of some kind seems necessary.

For four years, a uniquely suited but imperfect prime minister has thrown himself at a selection of the thorniest challenges of this era, attempting to chart and champion a path for liberalism at an anxious moment for the country and the world. He also took a bad vacation.

The following is an account of all that.

CHAPTER 1

THINGS FALL APART

"When the Congress of Vienna took place two hundred years ago and the modern rules of diplomacy were established—the *note verbale*, the *demarché*, the *bout de papier*, and all that—no one had conceived of 'le Tweet,'" says Peter Boehm.

From July 2017 to September 2018, Boehm was the personal representative for the prime minister of Canada and "sherpa" in the preparations, organization and follow-through of the forty-fourth summit of the G7 nations, held in Charlevoix, Quebec. It was the last assignment of a thirty-seven-year career in the foreign service. He had been posted to Cuba, Costa Rica and Washington and was Canada's ambassador to Germany from 2008 to 2012. Before Charlevoix, Boehm also served as a sherpa for Paul Martin and Stephen Harper. Such an emissary is appointed by each of the participating leaders in advance of any significant meeting of nations. The sherpas then spend some number of months preparing the ground for an agreement, effectively guiding their leaders to the achievement of a successful summit. For Charlevoix, there was the added burden of hosting and chairing the discussions.

Such has been the pace and timbre of these times that the meeting in Charlevoix—a moment when the world order seemed to be unravelling before our eyes—now seems like a distant memory, overtaken by new crises and different dramas. But, one way or another, history will surely record it, either as an odd reflection of this era or as some hint of what was to come. In the middle of it all was Justin Trudeau—a politician derided by his opponents as callow and unready—just trying to hold it together.

"We are about to conclude a very successful G7 summit here in Charlevoix," Trudeau told the assembled reporters and TV cameras on the afternoon of June 9, 2018, when the main event seemed to be over. "I'm happy to announce that we've released a joint communiqué by all seven countries."

Boehm, seated in the front row for Trudeau's closing news conference, could be forgiven for dozing off. He hadn't slept much in the previous forty-eight hours.

The issuing of a joint communiqué—a unanimous declaration relaying the shared principles, positions and intentions of the participants—is the ideal and preferred conclusion to this sort of thing. In some cases, when agreement cannot be found, the host will issue a "chair's statement," a second-best option that summarizes the discussion and lays out the conflicting points of view. But a consensus had been achieved in Charlevoix. And this was no small feat. Because, in this case, any consensus had to involve Donald J. Trump, the forty-fifth president of the United States of America.

There had been speculation Trump might not even attend. That he did make the trip was of limited solace. In the year since the last meeting of the G7, Trump had moved to withdraw his country from the Paris Agreement on climate change and abandoned an international arrangement to monitor Iran's nuclear activities. A week before arriving in Charlevoix, he imposed new tariffs on steel and aluminum products originating in Canada and the European Union, igniting a trade war between the United States and its closest allies.

It seemed possible Charlevoix would host the realization of a G6+1, with the United States standing outside the consensus. "Maybe the American president doesn't care about being isolated today, but we don't mind being six, if needs be," French president Emmanuel Macron had said, standing beside Trudeau at a news conference in Ottawa on the eve of the summit.

As he departed the White House to fly to Quebec, Trump told reporters that Vladimir Putin's Russia should be readmitted to the G7. It was, at the very least, an odd time to be considering Russia's return to the fold.

Russia had been a member of what was the G8 from 1997 until 2014, when it was expelled in response to the forcible annexation of Crimea by Russian forces. In 2018, Russia was still in possession of Crimea, and North Atlantic Treaty Organization (NATO) forces were still stationed in Latvia and Ukraine to deter further incursions.

Putin and Russia had also since emerged as a startling new threat to Western democracy. Russian agents had interfered in the American presidential election campaign, stealing private emails from the Democratic campaign and attempting to use social media to inflame divisions within the public. Trump's own campaign was being investigated for possible collusion with Russian agents, and Russia was implicated in similar efforts to disrupt elections in France, Germany and the United Kingdom. Then, in March, the British government expelled Russian diplomats in response to the poisoning of a former Russian agent and his daughter in Salisbury, England.

Official photos from inside the Charlevoix meetings, quickly distributed online, seemed to show just how unsettled the free world now was. In the most iconic image, Trump is seated opposite German chancellor Angela Merkel, the two of them surrounded by a crowd of other leaders and officials. Merkel, with a hint of impatience, is leaning forward with her hands on the table between them. Trump's arms are folded across his chest and the look on his face suggests petulance. An enterprising artist would later alter the image to put Trump in a toddler's high chair with a bowl of pasta on his head.

But when it was over, there was a 4,400-word communiqué.

Still, on his way out of town, Trump sounded as bellicose as ever. And the first question for Trudeau went at that incongruity: What use was a statement of consensus if the American president was talking like a man at odds with the other six countries?

"The president will continue to say what he says, at various occasions," Trudeau artfully responded. "What we did, this weekend, was come together and roll up our sleeves and come up with consensus language that we could all agree to, on a broad range of issues."

Okay, but what about those American tariffs and Trudeau's threat of retaliation?

In hindsight, maybe Trudeau should have given this a pass. He could have, for instance, offered a few innocuous words on those tariffs and then redirected the discussion to what had been achieved that weekend. Knowing what followed, it is tempting to conclude that discretion would have been the better part of valour. But blaming Trudeau for what ensued risks excusing the abnormality of Trump's reaction.

"I highlighted directly to the president that Canadians did not take it lightly that the United States has moved forward with significant tariffs on our steel and aluminum industry, particularly did not take lightly the fact that it's based on a national security reason that, for Canadians, who either themselves or whose parents or community members have stood shoulder to shoulder with American soldiers in far-off lands and conflicts from the First World War onwards, that it's kind of insulting," the prime minister said. "And I highlighted that it was not helping in our renegotiation of NAFTA and that it would be with regret, but it would be with absolute certainty and firmness, that we move forward with retaliatory measures on July 1, applying equivalent tariffs to the ones that the Americans have unjustly applied to us. I have made it very clear to the president that it is not something we relish doing, but it is something that we absolutely will do. Because Canadians, we're polite, we're reasonable, but we also will not be pushed around."

However colourful that response, none of it was particularly remarkable. Trudeau had made similar statements before, including during an appearance on American television six days earlier. Canadian sources insist he had said the same thing to Trump in private.

After another thirty minutes of questions, the prime minister exited the news conference, and that was seemingly that for another annual meeting of the world's leading democracies.

At least until 7:03 p.m. Eastern Standard Time, when Donald Trump hit the tweet button.

=====

THE G7 WAS BORN out of the economic shocks of the early 1970s: the Nixon shock of 1971, when the United States suddenly walked away from the fixed exchange rates that had governed international currencies since 1944, and the oil shock of 1973, when petroleum-producing Arab countries launched an embargo against the Western countries that had supported Israel in the Yom Kippur War. Hoping to better work through their differences in advance of larger international meetings, the finance ministers of the United Kingdom, France, Germany and the United States met as the "Library Club" in March 1973 (so named for the fact that the meeting took place in the White House library). Japan was later added to make the Group of Five.

"This close exposure to European leaders and their readiness to work informally and cooperatively impressed on me that I could deal directly with them, that small and frank discussions were desirable, and that people of vision and breadth could be found who could understand positions far wider than those of their own country," George P. Shultz, the U.S. secretary of the treasury at the time, later wrote.

The leaders of those five countries, plus Italy, then met as the G6 in Rambouillet, France, in 1975. Canada was added a year later. "The interdependence of our destinies makes it necessary for us to approach common economic problems with a sense of common purpose and to work toward mutually consistent economic strategies through better cooperation," the leaders declared in the communiqué that was issued after the 1976 summit.

The two or three days that the leaders of the free world spend together are now preceded by months of discussion and negotiation aimed at putting together both a communiqué and any number of other statements, commitments and action plans. For Charlevoix, public consultations with civil society and interest groups began in October 2017.

That fall Boehm travelled to meet with each of his counterparts, beginning with the American sherpa. The seven sherpas then met four times in advance of the summit, while their deputies—the "sous sherpas"—met on three other occasions. Separate sets of cabinet ministers from the seven countries met in Montreal, Toronto and Whistler between March and May, and environment and energy ministers then met in Halifax in September. Trudeau's chosen themes included "investing in growth that works for everyone," "preparing for jobs of the future," "working together on climate change, oceans and clean energy" and "advancing gender equality and women's empowerment." Gender equality, one of the Trudeau government's favourite preoccupations, was integrated across all subject areas, and the prime minister appointed a gender equality advisory council that offered recommendations.

Building on those themes, the summit produced not just a communiqué, but also seven other documents: four commitments, one declaration, one "common vision" and one blueprint. The total output was more than 11,000 words.

Such stuff can seem like just a bunch of nice words. But those nice words might help hold the Western world together.

Given the potential for disagreement, Boehm had tried to avoid committing to a communiqué. But the Europeans and Japanese were keen to get one, he says, believing a communiqué would show solidarity, common purpose and the values that set the G7 apart. "My view is, knowing that we were going to have an impasse on trade, knowing that we were going to have an impasse on climate change and maybe one or two others, why negotiate down to the lowest common denominator and then not have very much?" Boehm says. "Then you're condemned by stakeholders, by the media, by the opposition and your governments and whatnot."

Trump's tariffs on steel and aluminum landed just as the G7's finance ministers were gathering in Whistler. That meeting ended with a chair's statement. Two days earlier, a meeting of Organisation for Economic Co-operation and Development trade ministers in Paris was similarly stymied by American disagreement, angering the French hosts. "So the mood was already a little bit sour," Boehm says. "In looking at this, I told the prime minister, 'Look, everybody wants a communiqué, I'm going to give it my best shot.' And he said, 'Fine, go for it.'"

Trudeau's first G7 summit had been in Japan in 2016. At that meeting, Trudeau recalls, the complaint was that the leaders were too much of one mind. "Everyone's like, 'Look at all this production of a summit, you all agree on things. What's the point of a G7?'"

At that summit, he joked with Barack Obama and Britain's David Cameron that if they messed things up they were going to leave him to deal with Boris Johnson and Donald Trump.

By 2018, Trudeau was the third-longest serving leader at the table. And 2016 seemed like a long time ago. Obama, of course, had been replaced by Trump. Cameron, the moderate British prime minister, had been undone by his disastrous decision to allow a referendum on the United Kingdom's membership in the European Union. Fuelled by anti-immigrant and anti-European sentiment, a slim majority of Britons voted to leave, and Cameron, who had opposed an exit, resigned. Boris Johnson, who had championed a split with the EU, promptly announced he wouldn't seek to lead the U.K. Tories through the upheaval he'd sought. Cameron was instead succeeded by the unfortunate Theresa May.

A similar fate had befallen Italy's Matteo Renzi. He and Trudeau had been hailed, for a brief moment, as the new pillars of Western liberalism. But then Renzi proposed a series of political reforms and submitted those measures to a referendum. He lost and duly resigned, and Italy was now governed by a coalition of two populist parties: the Five Star Movement, an anti-establishment party founded in 2009 by a comedian and blogger, and the League, a far-right party that promised to deport many of the migrants who had recently arrived in Italy from the Middle East and Africa.

Trudeau was nonetheless not without allies. Emmanuel Macron's victory in May 2017—his campaign was assisted by Tom Pitfield, a friend of Trudeau's since childhood, who had overseen the Liberal campaign's digital operation in 2015—had given the G7 another handsome, left-of-centre fortysomething. And the dean of the G7 was still

Germany's Merkel, the sturdy and serious centre-right chancellor who was now being hailed as the leader of the free world.

In Charlevoix, Trudeau would be chairing the official discussions, something he is apparently quite good at. "I must say, I mean he's my boss and everything, but the PM really knows how to chair a meeting," Boehm says. "He does that very well. Keeps it going, ensures that there is participation by everyone."

Boehm is not alone in his assessment. "He runs a fantastic meeting," says Jane Philpott (in an interview conducted before her departure from Trudeau's cabinet). "He is one of the best people at saying, 'This is what has to happen, this is the time I've roughly allocated for every agenda item.' And he keeps people to a timeline." Sometimes at cabinet, when time is short, Trudeau will tell the room who is at the end of his speaking list as a warning to the other ministers that they will be costing that person a chance to speak if they take up too much time.

The seven leaders began meeting on Friday afternoon with a working lunch on economic growth. This afforded each a chance to comment on the general state of affairs in the global economy. According to a source familiar with the closed-door discussions, Donald Tusk, the president of the European Union, commented that while each of the countries represented was experiencing relatively strong growth and low employment, there was tremendous dissatisfaction amongst citizens who felt that they were being left behind or that others were coming in and taking advantage. Trump said immigration was the source of Europe's problems. Trudeau pushed back, noting the contributions of refugees to growth and the need to create pathways to success for newcomers.

After the leaders stepped outside to pose for the traditional family photo, a second session on the economy turned into a lively exchange on trade. Trump contended the United States was acting as the world's piggy bank. He complained about European tariffs on American products, criticized the North American Free Trade Agreement and raised the case of Wisconsin dairy farmers who, he argued, were being punished by Canada's policy of supply management. Macron was particularly forceful in response, challenging Trump's statistics and referencing American tariffs on Canadian softwood lumber.

During a break, Trudeau and Trump met for a scheduled sit-down. By this point, the United States, Canada and Mexico had been formally negotiating a new trade deal for ten months. The room was crowded—each leader was accompanied by a half-dozen officials—and the meeting ran long. Usually, Trudeau says, a bilateral meeting such as this would be dominated by the two leaders, with officials speaking up if called upon. This was not like that. "At one point, Bob Lighthizer and I were directly back and forth on issues around dairy or something-or-other," Trudeau says, referring to the U.S. trade representative. "And then Gerry [Butts] got involved and then me and Donald back together. It was very animated."

Trudeau emphasized the harm that would be done by American tariffs on Canadian-made vehicles and auto parts, which Trump had threatened to impose. Trump, according to a source, tried to assure Trudeau that Trudeau would eventually agree to Trump's demand for a sunset clause. Trudeau assured Trump that he would not. Trump again raised the alleged plight of the Wisconsin dairy farmer.

Nonetheless, the meeting was a bit like all of Trudeau's other conversations with the president. "There's a combination of genuine—I don't know if warm is the right word but, you know, genuine human moments of interaction between the president and me. There are moments of disagreement or strong rhetoric from him," Trudeau says. "One of the things I say to people is, the way he is in public is the way he is in private. And you get a mix of all that and you figure out how to move through it."

There was some sense, though, that it had been a positive meeting and a useful airing of the issues.

Over dinner, the G7 leaders discussed international affairs. Trudeau wanted to talk about Russia. "We wanted to be very categorical that there was no room for Russia at the G7," Trudeau says. He turned the floor over to May to discuss the Salisbury poisoning as well as Russia's role in cyber attacks and disinformation campaigns. Merkel shared her thoughts on dealing with Putin directly and warned of his support for various political movements in Europe. Trudeau, the source says, argued that Putin had shown a disregard for the law and that there must be consequences.

Trump was apparently unmoved. "Some people like the idea of bringing Russia back in. This used to be the G8, not the G7. And something happened a while ago, where Russia is no longer in. I think it would be an asset to have Russia back in. I think it would be good for the world," Trump told reporters afterwards, later arguing that it was Obama's fault Russia had seized Crimea and suggesting Russia had spent "a lot of money" to rebuild Crimea.

Life, as they say, comes at you fast.

Four years earlier, during an appearance on Radio-Canada's popular chat show *Tout le monde en parle*, Trudeau attempted to make a hockey joke while discussing Russia's possible role in the violent response to anti-government demonstrators in Ukraine. "It's very worrying, especially because Russia lost in hockey, they'll be in a bad mood," he said, a reference to the fact the Russian men's hockey team failed to win a medal at the Sochi Olympics.

This did not go over well. Indeed, it was probably the lowest point of Trudeau's time as Liberal leader. After a day of indignation, Trudeau made a public apology.

Comedy is not Trudeau's strong suit. In 2018, he caused a minor furor when he attempted a quip about saying "peoplekind" instead of "mankind." Domestic and international critics, taking him seriously, gasped at his apparent desire for extreme political correctness. Trudeau eventually conceded it was a "dumb joke" and "a little reminder that I shouldn't be making jokes even when I think they're funny." His lack of comedic timing is itself something of a running gag among his advisors. "He's got a mischievous side," says Gerry Butts. "Our joke with him, for a long time, is, 'Prime Minister, you are not funny.'"

But Trudeau's greater problem in 2014 and 2015 was being taken seriously. During an election debate on foreign policy, members of the audience audibly chuckled when Trudeau was asked how he'd deal with Putin. "Mr. Trudeau, you can't even stand up to Stephen Harper on C-51," the NDP's Thomas Mulcair taunted shortly thereafter. "How are you going to stand up to Putin?"

Less than two weeks after he was sworn in as Canada's twenty-third prime minister, Trudeau went to Turkey for a meeting of the G20. As later recounted by Roland Paris, a former advisor, Trudeau made a point of approaching Putin and telling him that Canada's support for the people of Ukraine would continue.

What couldn't have been grasped in 2015 was that a moment like June 2018 would ever come to pass. That Trudeau, chairing a meeting of the G7, would be looking across the table at Donald Trump, who, having allegedly benefited from Russian interference in the American presidential election, was now calling for Putin's return to the fold.

However surreal, it was not particularly funny.

———

THE SHERPAS HAD CONVENED on the Thursday morning at 8:30, before the leaders arrived, and worked until 3:30 the next morning to advance negotiations on both the commitments and a possible communiqué. On Friday night, after an evening entertainment program featuring Cirque du Soleil, the leaders gathered to deal with their outstanding differences. "It was all of us sort of digging in and wordsmithing a little bit and trying to figure out a way where we could talk about the need to reform the WTO [World Trade Organization] but also recognize the rules-based system that we have in place," Trudeau says.

Larry Kudlow, the colourful former Wall Street analyst and TV host now serving as Trump's senior economic advisor, got involved, and Trudeau wound up negotiating directly with him on certain points. "The sherpas were in the back row pulling their hair out because the last thing they ever want is their bosses to be wordsmithing a communiqué at ten o'clock at night around a series of couches," Trudeau says.

The leaders eventually went to bed and the sherpas took over again, meeting until 5:30 on Saturday morning to redraft the communiqué.

The Americans and Japanese were uncomfortable with what the other leaders wanted to promise about removing plastic from the world's oceans. The United States didn't want to reference the Paris Agreement; the other leaders did. The other leaders wanted to reference the joint plan of action on Iran from which the United States had withdrawn. And the United States was uncomfortable with references to "the rules-based international order," preferring that any communiqué refer to "a" rules-based international order instead.

The United States and Japan would dissent from the G7's "ocean plastics charter," but the issue of plastics would make it into the final communiqué, as would both the Paris Agreement and a reference to the American position on energy. To solve the Iran impasse, Boehm suggested the communiqué refer to United Nations Security Council resolution 2231, effectively covering the Iran plan of action without explicitly referencing it.

When the sherpas finished in the early hours of Saturday, only the relative existence of an international rules-based order remained to be resolved.

Boehm was due to brief the prime minister at 7 a.m., so he went to his room to shower and shave and then went down to breakfast, where he ran into Greta Bossenmaier, Trudeau's national security advisor. "Oh, you're an early riser, Peter," she said.

Trump arrived late to that morning's discussion on gender equality, but it also became clear that he was planning to leave even earlier than expected. From the G7, Trump was travelling to Singapore for a much-hyped summit with North Korean dictator Kim Jong Un. Boehm informed Trudeau and it was decided that the leaders would have to come together again for an unscheduled meeting. "Well, Donald, you're leaving a little earlier, we still have to settle this," Trudeau said.

That impromptu gathering, Boehm says, was not as hostile as the photos would suggest, but it does seem to have been lively. Boehm, who speaks both French and German, found himself between Merkel and Macron. "So she's asking me stuff in German, and Macron is asking me stuff in French in my right ear and behind me I've got Theresa May saying, 'I know you speak English as well, what the hell's going on?'" Boehm recalls.

"Angela and Emmanuel were really pushing on certain things. And I remember a couple of times seeing where both of them were coming at a problem in real opposite ways, but there was a way to sort of bring it up the middle and I sort of weigh in on this and then I'd step back," Trudeau says. "But that's really—my job at the G7 was just to hold together the G7."

At some point, Boehm engaged with John Bolton, Trump's moustachioed national security advisor. "So Bolton then says, 'The problem ... with the international rules-based order is we don't know what it is.' And I said, 'Well, it's what we've all created, including with your leadership over the years. It's the international multilateral institutions, the Bretton Woods institutions, all of that.' And he says, 'Well, we still don't know what it is.' And then we discuss a bit more and then he said, 'Well, of course the international rules-based order doesn't work.' And I said, 'So you're acknowledging that it exists?'" Boehm recalls. "He didn't like that."

At another point, there was a dispute over how to refer to Iran. Merkel and Trudeau tried to maintain focus. "She is very Germanic and orderly: 'We have to finish this. We have to get this done,'" Boehm recounts, affecting a German accent. "The PM was standing and he was saying, 'Okay, enough chit-chat. Okay guys.' And he'd keep people on task."

In the end, the first sentence of the Charlevoix communiqué refers to "a" rules-based international order. But further down the document there are two references to "the" rules-based international order.

"I can remember once that was done we were feeling tremendously relieved that we'd actually managed to pull this together in a way that was constructive and cordial and reasonable," Trudeau says. "And, yeah, that's a positive feeling. Wow, we managed to be successful in demonstrating collective leadership from the G7 on big issues in the world."

Afterwards, Trudeau's senior advisors gathered to toast that success at the lobby bar of Le Manoir Richelieu, the grand eighty-nine-year-old hotel that hosted the summit.

The first person to notice Trump's tweet was Cameron Ahmad, the prime minister's director of communications. He handed his phone over to Butts and Katie Telford to show them. At first, Butts thought the tweets must have come from a parody account.

"Based on Justin's false statements at his news conference, and the fact that Canada is charging massive Tariffs to our U.S. farmers, workers and companies, I have instructed our U.S. Reps not to endorse the Communique as we look at Tariffs on automobiles flooding the U.S. Market!" Trump posted at 7:03 p.m.

A minute later, he elaborated. "PM Justin Trudeau of Canada acted so meek and mild during our @G7 meetings only to give a news conference after I left saying that, 'US Tariffs were kind of insulting' and he 'will not be pushed around.' Very dishonest & weak. Our Tariffs are in response to his of 270% on dairy!"

In a separate room, Trudeau's assistant showed the prime minister. "My first thought was, Oh my god, what did I say in the press conference?" Trudeau says. "Where did I say more than I had before? What was it? 'Cause I thought I did okay, I thought I walked the line." Trudeau's advisors that assured that him he had. His next thought was whether Canadians were going to end up suffering some kind of consequence and whether something needed to be done to remedy the situation.

After nearly two years of stepping carefully around the president's temper, Trudeau had finally become a subject of Trump's tweeted wrath. A discussion about how to respond ensued. Ultimately, it was decided that the best course was to avoid escalation. The entirety of the government's response would be two sentences sent out by Ahmad: "We are focused on everything we accomplished here at the G7 summit. The Prime Minister said nothing he hasn't said before—both in public, and in private conversations with the President."

Trump's apparent retraction of support for the communiqué was actually tweeted before the communiqué could be distributed. With Canada acting as host, the document had to be translated into French before it could be released. Boehm, wanting to get the communiqué out before anything else could be done, pressured his team to finish as quickly as possible.

There is no precedent for the retroactive revoking of support for a G7 communiqué and thus no established process for doing so. Though subsequent news reports suggested otherwise, the leaders don't actually sign a copy of the document. It is simply agreed to and then presented by the chair. The only thing Trump officially signed while he was in Charlevoix was a scroll that was presented to the local mayor.

Beyond Trump's tweets, nothing was formally done to acknowledge American dissent. Officially, the Charlevoix communiqué stands, unaltered and unamended.

"I don't know whether technically they're still in the communiqué or they're out of it or what," Trudeau says. "But, we just sort of shrug and keep moving."

The next day, two of Trump's lieutenants competed to see who could most extravagantly up the rhetorical ante.

Appearing on CNN, Kudlow said Trudeau's comments were a "betrayal," "a double-cross" and a "sophomoric, political stunt." On Fox News, Peter Navarro, an economist whose fierce views on China and global trade had found a home in Trump's administration, translated international relations into the language of professional wrestling. "There's a special place in hell for any foreign leader that engages in bad-faith diplomacy with President Donald J. Trump and then tries to stab him in the back on the way out the door," Trump's trade advisor declared. "And I'll tell you this, to my friends in Canada, that was one of the worst political miscalculations of a Canadian leader in modern Canadian history."

Navarro later conceded his language was "inappropriate."

This was by no means the first time a Canadian prime minister had angered his American counterpart. Richard Nixon, for instance, once called Pierre Trudeau a "pompous egghead" and ordered his chief of staff to plant an unflattering story about the Canadian leader with a reporter. But Nixon at least had the decency to do such things in private.

Interestingly, Navarro also lashed out at the Trudeau government's approach to NAFTA—specifically a much-scrutinized campaign to lobby American lawmakers beyond the White House. "We'd have a great deal with NAFTA, by now, if the Canadians would spend more time at the bargaining table and less time lobbying Capitol Hill and our press and state governments here," he said.

It was Kudlow who suggested that Trump's meeting with Kim Jong Un was the real reason for the president's attack on Trudeau. "He is not going to permit any show of weakness on the trip to negotiate with North Korea," he said. That lines up with Boehm's recollection from the summit. "To me, it was very clear that the president had his mind on the summit in Singapore," he says. "That's what he was thinking about. In the discussions that took place, there was not, for me, a really deep reflection on some of this detailed stuff that we had been negotiating. The others were up to speed."

The Canadian response was, per usual, restrained. "We had a general habit of not reacting to the grandiose statement or the big statements that get made from time to time that are challenging," Trudeau says. "And that was something that we sort of got into as a pattern. So it was always, 'Okay, let's see what actual substance comes of this.'" On Sunday, Foreign Affairs Minister Chrystia Freeland was sent out to respond. "Canada does not believe that ad hominem attacks are a particularly appropriate or useful way to conduct our relations with other countries," she said.

The next day, members of Parliament from all parties unanimously adopted an NDP motion that condemned the American remarks and pledged solidarity with the Trudeau government's decision to impose retaliatory tariffs. "Mr. Speaker, over the weekend, Canadians witnessed, with shock and dismay, the U.S. administration hurl insults, verbal attacks, and threats of more tariffs at us," Conservative House leader Candice Bergen said at the outset of that day's Question Period. "We are all Canadians first, and we will stand with Canadian workers and the families impacted by this escalating trade war."

This mood wouldn't last. But, for the moment, Trudeau was something like a wartime prime minister, basking in the patriotic support a leader enjoys only in the immediate aftermath of an actual attack on the nation.

One of Boehm's mementos from the summit is a photo of the famous huddle on Saturday morning, Merkel looking down at Trump, Trudeau standing to Trump's left. The framed photo hangs in his office, with an inscription from Trudeau: "Thanks for a hell of a summit, Peter, my friend."

On Boehm's last day as a civil servant, September 28, 2018, the prime minister asked him if he'd like to be a senator. Boehm had actually applied two years earlier. He was still interested. And so his retirement came to a quick end on October 3, when he was appointed to the upper chamber as an independent senator.

After disparaging the democratically elected leader of America's closest ally, Trump came out of his summit with North Korea's Kim Jong Un and praised the dictator as a "very talented man" and a "smart negotiator" who "loves his country very much." The two had apparently formed a "special bond."

Trudeau and Trump crossed paths again a month later, at a NATO meeting in Brussels. "I went over and chatted with him and tried to show that I don't carry grudges that way, there's no hard feeling, it is what it is," Trudeau recalls.

But Trump caused chaos there too, attacking the other members of an alliance that has stood for decades as a bulwark against Russian aggression. Robert Kagan, a former speechwriter for George P. Shultz and a senior fellow at the Brookings Institution, was moved to ring the alarm.

"Any student of history knows that it is moments like this summit that set in motion chains of events that are difficult to stop," Kagan wrote in the *Washington Post*. "The democratic alliance that has been the bedrock of the American-led liberal world order is unravelling. At some point, and probably sooner than we expect, the global peace that that alliance and that order undergirded will unravel, too. Despite our human desire to hope for the best, things will not be okay. The world crisis is upon us."

A FEW DAYS after Charlevoix, Chrystia Freeland went to Washington. It was her twenty-seventh trip to the American capital since Trump's election. On this visit she'd be picking up an award: the editors of *Foreign Policy* magazine had named her diplomat of the year. It was an honour that, by this point, seemed as much an expression of empathy as admiration.

The honour also offered Freeland a chance to say a few things about the state of the world. A year earlier, Freeland had stood in the House of Commons and delivered a speech that dared to suggest an end to American leadership in the world. Canada, she said at the time, would have to step up. Now, less than three kilometres from the White House, she went further.

"Tonight," Freeland said, "I would like to speak about a challenge that affects us all: the weakening of the rules-based international order and the threat that resurgent authoritarianism poses to liberal democracy itself."

Lest there be any confusion about what constituted the rules-based international order, Freeland mentioned the World Trade Organization, the United Nations, the International Monetary Fund, the G7, the G20 and the World Bank. To that could be added NATO and the European Union—the patchwork of multilateral acronyms, institutions and agreements that had come into existence since the end of the Second World War, binding nations to each other in commerce, communiqués and shared efforts. However imperfect those institutions, their existence has coincided with seventy years of relative peace and expanding prosperity.

Recalling her time as a journalist, Freeland spoke of being a correspondent in the former Soviet Union as it transitioned, seemingly, into a fledgling democracy. This was supposed to have been the triumph of liberal democracy. The end of history, as Francis Fukuyama famously put it. But countries like Venezuela and Russia were now slipping back into authoritarianism. China was stubbornly clinging to communism.

"And within the club of wealthy Western nations, we are seeing home-grown anti-democratic forces on the rise," Freeland said. "Whether comprising neo-Nazis, white supremacists, incels, nativists or radical anti-globalists, such movements seek to undermine democracy from within."

This was not just Freeland's analysis. In its annual report for 2017—entitled "Democracy in Crisis"—Freedom House, an American think tank, warned that "political rights and civil liberties around the world deteriorated to their lowest point in more than a decade in 2017, extending a period characterized by emboldened autocrats, beleaguered democracies, and the United States' withdrawal from its leadership role in the global struggle for human freedom." In its own survey, the *Economist* downgraded the United States from a "full democracy" to a "flawed democracy" in 2016 and reported another year of global decline in 2017.

The American publishing industry offered another barometer. Any future historian trying to understand the tenor of these times will only have to peruse the titles of books released in 2017 and 2018, a list that included *How Democracies Die*; *How Democracy Ends*; *The People vs. Democracy*; *Fascism: A Warning*; *How Fascism Works*; *Can It Happen Here? Authoritarianism in America*; *On Tyranny*; *The Retreat of Western Liberalism*; *Why Liberalism Failed*; and *A World in Disarray*.

These were not texts produced by partisan cranks or provocateurs, but by Harvard professors, respected analysts and a former U.S. secretary of state. Another book, *The Death of Democracy: Hitler's Rise to Power and the Downfall of the Weimar Republic* by Benjamin Carter Hett, published in April 2018, was received as not only an important work of historical scholarship, but as a bracingly relevant book that could be used to process the present.

"Why are our liberal democracies vulnerable at home? Angry populism thrives where the middle class is hollowed out, where people are losing ground and losing hope, even as those at the very top are doing better than ever," Freeland continued. "When people feel their economic future is in jeopardy, when they believe their children have fewer opportunities than they had in their youth, that's when people are vulnerable to the demagogue who scapegoats the outsider, the other—whether it's immigrants at home or trading partners abroad."

In broad strokes, Freeland was attempting to broaden the Trudeau government's "middle class" mantra to the world at large and the great challenge of the moment.

The middle class had been at the centre of the Liberal campaign in 2015, as both a political and an economic imperative. For too long, the Liberals argued, the middle class had been stuck and squeezed while prosperity accumulated at the top of the income scale. For the Canadian economy to grow, the middle class needed to be supported and expanded. This required direct government intervention (a small tax increase for the richest, an expanded child benefit aimed at families with lower incomes) and higher levels of government investment in infrastructure (to both stimulate the economy and make life easier for the general public).

The degree to which the current outbreak of global turmoil could be traced to the struggles of the middle class was debatable. "Economic anxiety" had been the initial theory to explain Donald Trump's appeal and success in 2016. White, working-class Americans, it was argued, were turning against the politicians and the ideas that had let them down. They were worried about their jobs and their future and so they had become hostile toward free trade and immigration. Trump, sounding nothing at all like those phonies in Washington, promised to renegotiate the bad deals, close the border and put Americans first.

But subsequent waves of research suggested a different, and more disturbing, problem: that Trump's victory was actually propelled by racial and cultural resentments, particularly among white male voters. "It's much more of a symbolic threat that people feel," the author of one study told the *New York Times*. "It's not a threat to their own economic well-being; it's a threat to their group's dominance in our country over all."

Another argument proposed that it was, in fact, the "identity politics" of the left—the priority put on recognizing and correcting the systemic disadvantages faced by women and minority groups—that was at the root of this new phenomenon. To that, one could add a number of other possible factors, particularly in the American context: political polarization, tribalism, the discourse of social media, cynicism toward traditional institutions, the decline of mainstream media, the emergence of partisan news sources, legislative dysfunction, a lack of meaningful regulation to limit the power of money in political campaigns, the lasting shock of 9/11 or the spectre of uncontrolled immigration.

Some combination of those things might explain what is happening in Europe—far-right and nationalist parties in various countries have, for instance, exploited concerns about the arrival of hundreds of thousands of migrants fleeing instability and war in the Middle East.

Maybe it was too much to imagine that a growing and prosperous middle class would necessarily solve all that. But a sense of prosperity and hope for the future could at least take the edge off humanity's darkest impulses.

"Authoritarianism is also often justified as a more efficient way of getting things done," Freeland continued, pointing to those who chafe at the checks and balances of democracy. "We need to resist this corrosive nonsense. We need to summon Yeats's oft-cited 'passionate intensity' in the fight for liberal democracy and the international rules-based order that supports it."

Here Freeland was quoting from William Butler Yeats's "The Second Coming." Its oft-cited first verse is well known among those who have had reason to fear that the world is coming undone: "Things fall apart; the centre cannot hold; / Mere anarchy is loosed upon the world, / The blood-dimmed tide is loosed, and everywhere / The ceremony of innocence is drowned; / The best lack all conviction, while the worst / Are full of passionate intensity."

Yeats wrote that in 1919, shortly after the end of the First World War and in the wake of revolutions in Ireland and Russia. It is thought by some to have prophesied the Second World War. Joan Didion, the great American essayist, took inspiration from it when she went to San Francisco in 1967 to write about the hippies, the last time the United States seemed to be coming undone. "It was the first time I had dealt directly and flatly with the evidence of atomization, the proof that things fall apart," Didion later wrote.

Writers, critics and despondent observers revived Yeats's stanzas again in the wake of Trump's emergence. "Political Establishments worthy of the name and middle-ground politicians who care about more than power understand the dangers of a Yeats moment—to social harmony, to tolerance and, if things go really badly, to democracy and freedom," E.J. Dionne Jr. wrote for the *Washington Post* in 2015. "The next decade will test whether the political classes of the world's democracies are up to the challenge."

It was because of all these concerns—the nationalism, the xenophobia, the authoritarianism, the struggles of the world's great democracies—that both the Trudeau government and Canada seemed to matter to the world in 2018. The handsome prime minister and his nice country were, amid the tumult, a relatively successful example of liberalism, tolerance and sanity.

Supporting liberal democracy, Freeland continued, meant "resisting foreign efforts to hijack our democracies through cyber-meddling and propaganda," a clear reference to Russia. "And it means governing with integrity," she declared. "Facts matter. Truth matters. Competence and honesty, among elected leaders and in our public services, matter."

It might be fairly impossible to read those words and not think of the forty-fifth president of the United States, a man whose propensity for falsehood and lying has exceeded all previous standards and inspired a cottage industry of journalists dedicated to cataloguing his deceptions. But Freeland never said Donald Trump's name.

Freeland pivoted to the American tariffs on Canadian steel and aluminum. Never mind that Trudeau's complaints had upended the G7, Freeland proceeded to reissue those objections, at length. The American tariffs, she said, were "absurd" and "hurtful," not to mention "illegal under WTO and NAFTA rules." It was a "a naked example of the United States putting its thumb on the scale." Canada had "no choice but to retaliate."

"No one will benefit from this beggar-thy-neighbor dispute. The price will be paid, in part, by American consumers and by American businesses," Freeland said. "The price will also be paid by those who believe that a rules-based system is something worth preserving. Since the end of the Second World War, we have built a system that promoted prosperity and prevented smaller and regional conflicts from turning into total wars. We've built a system that championed freedom and democracy over authoritarianism and oppression. Canada, for one, is going to stand up in defence of that system when that system is under attack. We will not escalate—and we will not back down."

The alternative to that multilateral order, Freeland suggested, would be a "Metternichian world defined not by common values, mutually agreed-upon rules and shared prosperity, but rather by a ruthless struggle between great powers governed solely by the narrow, short-term and mercantilist pursuit of self-interest." That, she argued, would be to the detriment of both the United States and the world at large.

"You may feel today that your size allows you to go mano-a-mano with your traditional adversaries and be guaranteed to win. But if history tells us one thing, it is that no one nation's pre-eminence is eternal."

America, she concluded, could still be the shining city on the hill, helping to lead the world's democracies, "but whatever this great country's choice will turn out to be, let me be clear that Canada knows where it stands and we will rise to the challenge."

The next day, when Freeland met with Robert Lighthizer, she presented him with a printed copy of the speech.

Freeland's remarks were perhaps the most provocative a Canadian minister had delivered in the United States since Lester B. Pearson visited Temple University in 1965 and suggested the United States should suspend, for a limited time, its bombing of Vietnam. Pearson was promptly summoned to Camp David where Lyndon Johnson is said to have grabbed the prime minister by the lapels and advised him, "You don't come here and piss on my rug."

But Freeland's speech was, in one telling, a deliberate show of strength. "It was a calculated risk. We knew if they read Chrystia saying something like that, in their kitchen, they would know we were not afraid of them," says a Liberal source. "Whatever else they said about it, they would know we were not afraid of them. And there was no way to do a deal with that guy if he thinks you're afraid of him."

It would later emerge Trump had already been treated to a similar lecture by members of his own cabinet. According to Bob Woodward's *Fear*, an account of Trump's first two years in the White House, Defense Secretary Jim Mattis and Gary Cohn, the president's top economic advisor, convened a meeting in July 2016 in hopes of impressing upon the president the importance of international allies and trading partners. "The great gift of the greatest generation to us," Mattis said, "is the rules-based, international democratic order." "This is what has kept the peace for seventy years," explained Rex Tillerson, then secretary of state. They apparently got nowhere. (It was at the end of this meeting, after Trump left, that Tillerson is said to have referred to Trump as a "fucking moron.")

Trump's feelings about Freeland would not become known for several more months.

Whatever else Canada might do to preserve the global rules-based order, the Trudeau government had first to resolve the continental order. Indeed, Trudeau's chances of remaining a figure on the global scene— of getting re-elected in 2019—depended mightily on his ability to hold NAFTA together. To be a counterbalancing force for the long term, he had to successfully make a deal with Donald Trump. But, like the G7, NAFTA would hang in the balance for several more months, seemingly in danger of being upended, at any moment, by a tweet.

CHAPTER 2

TRUDEAU INC.

Even if he or she never ends up on the receiving end of a presidential tweet, even if they never have to preside during a uniquely fractious moment for the Western world, a prime minister is an inherently fascinating creature. He exists at the centre of a grand human endeavour, surrounded by concentric circles of advisors, ministers, officials and staff. He is the great glowing orb around which everything else moves. At least until he quits or is forcibly replaced.

No prime minister has come to that place with quite the same prologue as Justin Trudeau. He was an object of fascination long before he was prime minister, and his life, or at least large portions of it, has been lived publicly. But there are still things to learn about this prime minister. And things only become more interesting when the humans involved are in conflict, as was the case for Trudeau and the characters in his orbit during the difficult spring of 2019.

Ask people who know him and you will inevitably hear Justin Trudeau described as disciplined. But it still surprises Trudeau to hear himself described with that adjective.

"It was drilled into me by my father that I was not disciplined," he says. He puts on the voice of his father to re-enact a lecture. "Now Justin, you're just floating along and everything comes easy to you in school so you sit back and you're not focused on doing your homework and you're not focused on studying. You write everything at the last minute. And there's a lack of personal discipline there that really worries me, Justin. I don't know what you're going to make of yourself."

His father was famously a man of discipline and order—reason over passion and all that. For Justin Trudeau, the discipline came later, when he got into politics. "I wasn't motivated to actually do that until something with sufficient stakes came along," he says.

He typically wakes up between six and seven each morning, sometimes earlier if Hadrien, his youngest child, gets up. He tries to get eight hours of sleep every night. He is also fairly rigorous about what he eats and how often he exercises. He doesn't drink coffee, but will have a can of Coca-Cola from time to time when he needs a boost, say at the end of an international trip. He runs regularly. Every couple of weeks he goes boxing, which helps him burn off excess energy.

"The rules I laid down early on: I need to sleep enough every night, I need to eat well—don't just give me sandwiches for every lunch 'cause that's not going to work—and I need to exercise regularly," he says, recalling a conversation in 2012 with his nascent campaign team for the Liberal leadership. "If you could give me those things, I'll do ten events a day and be happy to do it." His stamina is another thing that comes up.

He can be counted on to read the briefing notes and memos he receives, but he likes to have a conversation afterwards to talk things through and ask questions. He doesn't mind being corrected in front of other people, apparently a somewhat uncommon trait among politicians. He can be persuaded to change his proposed approach if someone makes a good case.

"In a typical cabinet meeting you will have a large number of what they call annex items, it may be fifteen or some such number of small items that are on the agenda but usually not up for discussion," says John McCallum, the former immigration minister. "One thing that struck me about Justin Trudeau is that once in a while one of those items would come up—most people wouldn't have a clue what any of them were about—and the prime minister would give a very detailed description of what the issues are, the pros and cons and why we were doing a certain course of action." This, McCallum suggests, runs counter to the negative caricature that has dogged Trudeau since he announced his candidacy. By way of comparison, McCallum doesn't remember the two previous prime ministers he worked for—Jean Chrétien and Paul Martin—displaying such knowledge of obscure matters.

Trudeau is not a particularly passionate partisan, but he is competitive. And he likes a fight. "If there's a choice of doing something that might be safer or just going full on, they know me well enough [to know] that I'm more likely going to go full on," Trudeau says of discussions with his top advisors. "If this is going to be a fight, let's make it a fight."

Those who know him say Trudeau has a certain fearless streak. "Sometimes I think he doesn't have enough fear," says Marc Miller, the Liberal MP who has known Trudeau since high school. "Fear is a good thing."

Trudeau recognizes that fearlessness in himself. "I think one of the roles of folks around me is to make sure I have all the different elements in my mind before I sort of leap into a decision, and I have a natural tendency to be a bit of a contrarian."

"Justin is typically the first person to jump in—usually with both feet," says Tom Pitfield (Pitfield's father, Michael, was clerk of the Privy Council and a close aide to Pierre Trudeau). "His self-awareness and confidence are a large part of his success, but when we started the leadership campaign, his confidence was also sometimes a liability. He might germinate and explore an idea in public or debate a protester, for example. We eventually recognized that it was better to support his instincts rather than to try to work them out of him. In return, Justin became extremely disciplined."

In his own assessment, and in the judgment of others, Trudeau is not an ideologue. "Whenever someone presents me with an ideological argument, I'll strip it down to, okay, so what does it mean in terms of principles and values? And then what does it mean tangibly in people's lives?" he says. "There is no frame that we could have set up in the past intellectually that is going to answer all solutions. Whereas fundamental principles and values—respect for the individual, individual rights, empowerment of the individual, the inherent value in every individual—these are things that for me provide you a bedrock upon which to then make decisions."

Empowering individuals to "be able to control their destiny and their future . . . truly inhabiting and driving their own democracy" seems, in particular, to be a strongly held idea, something Trudeau uses to connect disparate topics such as reconciliation, the Canada Child Benefit and even fighting the internet's dens of disinformation and fear.

His government is certainly more activist than the last Liberal government to hold power for a significant period of time—Jean Chrétien's from 1993 to 2003. It has also aligned itself with social justice issues and found common cause with labour unions. And, in those ways, it has taken up more space on the left of the political spectrum. But in various other ways, Trudeau has split the difference between right and left: on the environment and resource development, on taxes, on working with the private sector. A conservative would say he's a left-leaning progressive. A social democrat would say he's a squishy centrist.

Trudeau has been known to send his advisors back for further study if he doesn't think he's heard enough or if he feels they haven't fully thought something through. But he is purportedly a confident decision maker. "He can make a decision. And that decision can last for longer than three minutes," says Peter Harder, the senator and former public servant who advised Trudeau during the post-election transition period in 2015, contrasting Trudeau with unnamed others.

Harder says Trudeau also has an "ability to onboard negative information"—that is, to deal with bad news. Gerry Butts says Trudeau is capable of treating himself like he's an "object in the room," recalling meetings in which Trudeau assured those around the table that their criticism would not faze him. "I think he learned to separate himself from other people's observations of him from a very early age," Butts says.

He is also a hugger. "He's a millennial. A lot of hugging. A lot of personal stuff, right?" Harder says of Trudeau. "And there's not a hint of sarcasm in my saying that. They're millennials. They have an ease of social interaction that I admire." Trudeau is actually a member of Generation X—the first prime minister of that generation—but, regardless, there was probably a lot less hugging when Harder was coming up through the public service in the eighties.

Trudeau's advisors believe he is most vulnerable when he is doing well: that, however self-aware and disciplined, he has a tendency to put a foot wrong when he is walking tallest. "It's an odd tic," Butts says. "I keep saying I hope we go into the campaign tied or behind because I don't know what the hell he'd do if we had a ten-point lead." (Butts says this in 2018, months before Trudeau and the Liberals successfully eliminated any chance of entering the 2019 campaign with an overwhelming lead.)

There are several examples that apparently support this theory, including his wayward elbow in the House of Commons in May 2016. In that incident, a group of troublemaking New Democrats were preventing the Conservative whip from getting down the aisle to his seat, and that seemed to be preventing the House from proceeding with a vote. Trudeau, with his approval rating hovering around 60 percent, apparently decided it was his problem to resolve and, perhaps lacking in fear, charged across the aisle to break it up. In the confrontation, Trudeau's elbow inadvertently struck NDP MP Ruth Ellen Brosseau in the chest. Multiple apologies followed.

In an ad that ran in 2011, the Conservative Party proudly promoted the idea of Stephen Harper working alone at his desk until late into the night, reading memos, writing notes and working his way through a stack of documents. However staged the scene, it was apparently close to the truth of how Harper liked to spend his time and how he saw the job. One senior official raises it as a point of comparison. "That is not how Trudeau conceives of his job," the official says. "It's much more about public engagement and direction setting and strategic communication and meeting with people and mobilizing support and building partnerships, mobilizing diverse communities and stakeholders around common goals."

Which is apparently not to say Trudeau won't do the solitary work that Harper was most fond of. Trudeau is said, for instance, to have spent hours at home poring over the speeches and records of the leading candidates when it came time to appoint a new chief justice of the Supreme Court.

Trudeau says he is a learned extrovert. That if he had a choice of what to do for three hours—either hang out with friends or go read a book—he'd go read. He also had to learn how to be a politician. His former assistant, Louis-Alexandre Lanthier, had to push Trudeau to approach people and introduce himself when he was first seeking office in Papineau. To slow Trudeau down when he was walking around in public, Lanthier would walk in front of him. After Trudeau was elected, Lanthier had him sending out 10,000 Christmas cards and 22,000 birthday cards each year to constituents. Trudeau came up with the idea to add a personalized note to the cards that marked a milestone birthday.

Now it is said that he gets antsy, maybe even a little grumpy, if he goes a while without being out among the public. He draws energy from interaction. Trudeau says that if he's in Ottawa for long he starts thinking that what's going on in Ottawa matters too much. But talking to people is also what he's always done. "My whole life has been conversations with Canadians. Wherever I was going backpacking across the country, travelling as a kid, as a teenager, as a young man, small talk with me quickly turned to the country as soon as someone figured out who I was," he says. "I got to be part of these conversations where in someone's daily life, maybe once every month or so they might talk about the nature of their country and high-level politics. I would tend to trigger that in people because of my dad."

His father was not known as a retail politician—"My dad was never much of a small talker or a glad-hander; he hated that stuff"—but Trudeau says he still learned from Pierre's example, both from watching his father take time to speak with those who approached him and then, later, hearing stories from members of the public who'd met the former prime minister.

"People come up to me and they'll say, 'I got a picture with your father on a train station in the late seventies.' And that's their story, right? It's, 'I shook his hand, and he said hi, and I said hi back.' And

I've heard that story many, many times, but it is extraordinarily valuable to them," he says. "Taking that moment to connect to someone, to allow that connection and to pause everything else is something that I learned is very valuable to them but is really good for me too."

Miller says Trudeau has only ever offered him a couple pieces of advice about being a politician, one of which was to try to get something out of every interaction you have. For one thing, that will show the person you're listening. But it also helps you maintain your energy.

"Meeting people, at that level and at that scale, is actually extremely exhausting," Miller says. "It's that person's moment to get everything they've got out. And they're probably extremely nervous. So you're focusing and you're trying to parse through a lot of nerves and emotions. Getting something out of it is a self-defence mechanism so far as it takes a lot of out of you. If you're not focusing on trying to get something out of that conversation, you're being drained as a person. It's an important mechanism to cope with the extreme demand that people have on him."

Chrystia Freeland has joked that if aliens ever land on Earth, it is Trudeau, with his capacity for empathy, who should be put forward to greet them. Another senior Liberal, comparing Trudeau to the two previous Liberal leaders, Stéphane Dion and Michael Ignatieff, puts it this way: "The retail element of politics was a necessary evil to do the job that they wanted to do. Whereas for Trudeau, he wants to do that job because of that experience of doing the retail politics."

In 2016, the correspondence unit of the Prime Minister's Office—the department that deals with the tens of thousands of emails and letters that Trudeau has annually received—began forwarding a selection of letters and emails directly to Trudeau for him to read. The practice was inspired by a similar habit in Barack Obama's White House: at the end of each day of his presidency, Obama was given ten letters to read.

Near the end of 2016, Katie Telford and Dan Arnold, the director of research, discussed taking it a step further: maybe Trudeau could start calling some of the people who wrote him. The first concerted attempt was made the following February. A large number of people had written to Trudeau about Donald Trump's travel ban. A sample were selected for Trudeau to call.

Since then, it has become a semi-regular practice. About once each month, schedule permitting, Trudeau makes another round of calls. Trudeau often has to first convince the person he's calling that it actually is him and not someone pulling a prank. He is said to like being challenged, so letters that criticize the government's decisions are often set aside for follow-up.

Inasmuch as the practice is known to the general public—the calls have generated a few media stories—it is surely good for Trudeau's image. But Trudeau explains it another way: that it gives him something he can't get from polling and focus groups.

"The Omar Khadr calls were unbelievably useful for me," Trudeau says. "They said, 'I'm really mad,' and I said, 'I'm mad too. I'm really mad too and you should be mad. We shouldn't be in this.' And I actually developed the heart of my public narrative in tangible conversations with a real person who had real feelings who wasn't trying to win an argument, was just trying to share how they felt, and I had to try to figure out how to reassure them that I was still the person they wanted me to be. And that dynamic is different from any conversation with an opposition politician or a member of the media. They don't have an agenda that they're trying to win, they're just saying, 'Look, I really don't get it. Why did you do this? I'm really mad and I voted for you and I support you but this, you know.' And those real conversations— it's amazing how rarely they happen."

He likens it to a conversation with a neighbour or a brother-in-law at a backyard picnic. "Suddenly you're explaining things in a different way than the sort of the common lingo and the common accepted realities that we all have within this bubble." This would seem to be a conscious preoccupation. Butts often stressed the need to talk like regular people talk. Outside the adjoining offices of Telford and Butts hung three frames, arranged vertically, each with the word "people" inside, a reminder of a mantra Butts had once scrawled on a whiteboard: "people, people, people."

Trudeau is, by any measure, a much more public figure than his predecessor. Between November 4, 2015, and January 7, 2019, Trudeau gave 242 interviews to local, national or international journalists. He tends to enter and exit the House of Commons through the front door, giving himself a chance to offer a quick comment to the cameras and reporters that congregate in the foyer (Harper preferred to come and go via a back exit that allowed him to avoid the waiting hordes). He also typically stops to say something to reporters before the weekly meeting of the Liberal caucus on Wednesday mornings, and he semi-regularly visits the National Press Theatre for extended news conferences (Harper never did the former and largely avoided the latter).

In 2017, 2018 and 2019, Trudeau participated in a series of open town hall forums across the country. A prime minister being readily available to the public likely has some intrinsic value for Canadian democracy, but at one of the first of those town halls in 2016, a woman praised him simply for being there. "It takes tremendous courage to come into a room where we were not screened," she said. "Courage" overstated matters. But Trudeau no doubt derives some political benefit from simply putting himself in such situations.

For one thing, it contrasts nicely with the last guy. Harper tended to campaign within a carefully constructed bubble. More than that, the worst thing a politician can be is out of touch with the common man, and Trudeau has never scanned as common. But he is now regularly seen hearing directly from citizens, periodically getting yelled at. And it is harder to accuse a prime minister of being remote when he is literally standing in the middle of an auditorium full of his fellow citizens.

Harper generally kept his public appearances to a minimum. "Harper works hard to take himself out of many pictures," Paul Wells wrote in *The Longer I'm Prime Minister*. It gave his detractors less fodder for criticism and afforded his supporters a cleaner slate on which to draw a flattering picture of him. In either case, Harper seemed keen to avoid wearing out the public's tolerance for him. "Canadians know—actually know for a fact, from the evidence of his own testimony—less about Stephen Harper than about any other prime minister who has lasted as long as he has," Wells explained. "This helps explain why he has lasted. He lies low because he wants to last." Eventually, Harper did wear out his welcome. But it took a lot longer than it might have.

That difference in profile between Trudeau and Harper could be connected to various other distinctions: between an activist liberal and an incremental conservative, a learned extrovert and a committed introvert, someone who was born a public figure and someone who wasn't, someone who was blessed with a certain amount of the public's goodwill and someone who wasn't. But Trudeau also does not act or sound like someone who is biding his time.

For all this effort to stay engaged and connected, there is perhaps some irony in the fact that Trudeau's greatest crisis would involve, by his own admission, a breakdown in trust and communication between his office and his justice minister.

———

FROM THE FIRST SERIOUS discussions about pursuing the Liberal leadership in 2012 through until the spring of 2019, Trudeau's most senior advisors were an integral duo: Katie Telford and Gerry Butts. Other senior advisors filled important roles, but Telford and Butts were the co-CEOs of Trudeau Inc. With Trudeau as chairman of the board, they formed a triumvirate. The Trudeau project built outward from them as they recruited candidates and staff.

Butts was famously a friend before he was an official advisor. He and Trudeau met as undergraduates studying English literature at McGill in the early 1990s. Butts recruited Trudeau to join the school's debate team (he was also Trudeau's tutorial assistant in a course on the works of James Joyce). They share ideals and interests, and Butts has shaped significant pieces of the Trudeau agenda, including the pre-eminent focus on the middle class. In *Common Ground*, his 2014 autobiography, Trudeau wrote that nearly twenty-five years after their first meeting, Butts is "not just still a best friend; he is my closest advisor as leader of the Liberal Party of Canada." In a conversation in March 2019, a few weeks after Butts's departure from his office, Trudeau's eyes teared up when asked about his friend's resignation.

They were born six months apart in 1971. Butts was the youngest son of a coal miner and a nurse in Cape Breton, Nova Scotia. He was influenced by the politics of his aunt, Sister Peggy Butts, a nun, social activist and university professor. In 1997, she became the first religious sister ever appointed to the Senate, and she sat as a Liberal until reaching the mandatory retirement age in 1999.

For a while, Butts wanted to be a writer. But through Sister Peggy he got a job after university as a researcher for another senator, Allan MacEachen, a former minister in Lester B. Pearson's cabinet and the legendary House leader who guided Pierre Trudeau's government and then engineered his return in 1979. To help MacEachen prepare an autobiography, Butts and another researcher were hired to go through MacEachen's archives and prepare short essays on the major themes. MacEachen never got around to writing the book—he died in 2017— but Butts got an education in a pivotal era of Liberal politics.

Butts moved on to Toronto and then Queen's Park, eventually becoming an advisor to Ontario Liberal leader Dalton McGuinty. Within a few years, Butts was working in the premier's office and McGuinty was leading a government that invested heavily in education and moved aggressively on the environment. Butts departed in 2008 to become president of World Wildlife Fund's Canadian office. He remained there until the fall of 2012, when his friend decided to run for the Liberal leadership.

Telford, the daughter of two public servants, is from Toronto. Bob Rae was a neighbour (she used to take care of his dog), and she was a legislative page at Queen's Park during high school. She and Butts first crossed paths on the university debating circuit, but became friends at Queen's Park. After university, Telford volunteered for the Ontario Liberals, and then worked as an assistant to Gerard Kennedy, the party's education critic. After McGuinty's Liberals formed a government in 2003, Kennedy was named education minister. A year later, shortly before her twenty-sixth birthday, Telford became his chief of staff.

By 2006, Telford was managing Kennedy's campaign for leader of the federal Liberal Party. Kennedy, the youngest of the serious contenders, was running something of a proto-Trudeau campaign, based on themes of change and renewal. Butts was officially neutral, but supportive. Trudeau became interested and Butts connected him with Telford. Trudeau's decision to endorse Kennedy led to a star turn at the Liberal leadership convention—Trudeau's first real step into the political arena after eulogizing his father six years earlier.

Unfortunately for Kennedy, he finished fourth on the first ballot. But his subsequent move to support Stéphane Dion helped Dion leap over Michael Ignatieff to win on the fifth ballot. Telford moved into a position in Dion's office. Trudeau went looking for a riding to run in.

Five years later, the Liberal Party was in shambles. Under Dion and then Ignatieff the party had crashed to seventy-seven and then thirty-four seats. Trudeau was among the survivors, but he initially dismissed the possibility that he might lead the party back from oblivion.

When he started to rethink that position, he told Butts and then they sat down with Telford. Telford ran Trudeau's leadership campaign, then the Liberal election campaign in 2015 and then became chief of staff in the office of the new prime minister. Butts, a senior advisor throughout, became the principal secretary. "It just became absolutely obvious that the way the three of us worked together—it just really fit," Trudeau says. "We were complementary in all the right ways and so aligned in our values and our dreams and our vision for this country that it was like, 'Okay, this is the dynamic right here.' And then it just sort of stayed."

Butts, the taller and chattier of the two, was a networker, a frequent correspondent with journalists and a willing combatant on social media. Telford, shorter and quieter, enjoyed a slightly lower profile. But they both became public figures, a departure from traditional Canadian practice, but similar to what's seen with modern American strategists. Butts appeared onstage at a Liberal convention in April 2018 to interview David Axelrod, a former advisor to Barack Obama. Telford is a regular public speaker on women's advancement and agreed to an extended, televised interview with *Maclean's* in May 2018. Each has been profiled several times by newspapers and magazines. "I'm a big believer that one of the ways we get people to trust in government is for people to believe that there are not these dark, shady, awful backrooms," Telford says.

Their unique significance and public stature might have also made it that much easier to blame them when the government ran into trouble in the spring of 2019.

The typical shorthand explanation for their working relationship drew a somewhat basic distinction between the two. Butts was more inclined toward narrative, strategic communication and policy (a *Globe and Mail* profile in 2016 suggested that he was "unusually gifted at figuring out what lies at the core of the politicians he serves, and how to connect that with what voters care about"). Telford was the more linear thinker, concerned with organization and logistics. "I think there are occasions where he might have some sort of gaps in things because he passionately believes in them and sometimes can perhaps lose perspective. And I think she helps bring him back," says David MacNaughton, the ambassador to the United States who worked with both of them at Queen's Park. Trudeau once said that "Katie is the grown-up around me and Gerry. She's the one who is exceedingly well-organized and she thinks things through in a really far-seeing and broad way. She thinks about the deeper consequences when Gerry and I are trying to outsmart each other."

One or the other might have also taken more of an active role on a particular file: Butts, for instance, on carbon pricing or the Trans Mountain pipeline expansion. Telford, just the second woman to be chief of staff to a prime minister, is perhaps best known for her championing of gender equality and played a leading role in the renegotiation of NAFTA.

But Telford and Butts were also more of a symbiotic pair than two distinct officials. Members of the public service were known to refer to them as "GerKat." They operated what amounted to a two-key system, in which all important paper flowed through both of them. They attended many of the same meetings and regularly ate lunch together. They listened in on many of the prime minister's briefings and sat in on meetings of the cabinet and Liberal caucus. They were sparring partners and gut checks. In the final weeks of negotiating NAFTA, both went to Washington.

Whenever a decision was needed from the prime minister, Telford and Butts would typically go to Trudeau with a set of options or scenarios to consider, and the three of them would talk it through. "They come at things differently," Trudeau says. One or the other might raise their misgivings about a particular path. "The three of us together coming to a particular position gives us a fairly high degree of confidence that we're in the right direction," Trudeau explains (in a conversation before Butts's departure).

The triumvirate ended with the announcement of Butts's departure on February 18, 2019. For the three weeks following, until after Butts testified at the justice committee on March 6, Butts was completely out of touch with his former colleagues. In his absence, more work fell to Telford and other senior advisors, including managing the various relationships and points of contact that Butts had maintained in and around government. As plans came together, advisors found themselves thinking about what Butts might have been saying or doing. Insofar as he might never again be a full-time member of the team, it remains to be seen what Butts's departure means for the political career and government of his close friend.

In the midst of the SNC-Lavalin affair, there were four other advisors who featured prominently in the internal deliberations. Two had nearly as much tenure as Telford. Kate Purchase, the executive director of communications and planning, had become an advisor in 2013 after working for Bob Rae. Mike McNair, the executive director for policy, had been an early recruit in 2012. Both were now mainstays of Trudeau's career as a political leader, though both also had the distinction of actually being skeptical of Trudeau before getting to know him. Brian Clow, a more recent arrival, was now in charge of "issues management," a fancy term given to the task of dealing with the day-to-day controversies of politics. He had run the Liberal war room in 2015 and then became chief of staff to Chrystia Freeland when she was minister of international trade. He moved to the PMO in January 2016 to lead a new team assigned to deal with Canada–United States relations after Donald Trump's arrival. After NAFTA, he was promoted.

That team within the PMO was helped by Jeremy Broadhurst, the chief of staff to Chrystia Freeland as foreign affairs minister. Broadhurst, formerly chief of staff to Rae, had been made national director of the Liberal Party in 2013 and then served in the PMO as a deputy to both Butts and Telford. Also providing counsel was David MacNaughton, who spent a day and a half in meetings at the PMO while Butts was out of touch.

There was an effort too to reach out beyond the existing inner circle. Trudeau spoke with three of his predecessors: Jean Chrétien, Paul Martin and Brian Mulroney. His advisors consulted with some of their predecessors, including former advisors to Chrétien and Martin, as well as Andrew Bevan, a former chief of staff to Kathleen Wynne and Stéphane Dion. Such outreach might have insulated Trudeau's office from any accusations that it was too insular or too unwilling to consider the counsel of older generations of Liberals (until his departure, Butts was the eldest of Trudeau's most senior advisors). But those efforts might also simply speak to an office that found itself in the middle of an unprecedented drama and in need of all the advice it could get.

The efficiency of the organization Telford and Butts oversaw was not beyond debate. From within and around the government, it has been said that the PMO was a bottleneck when it came to moving things along. That too much depended on two people. That not enough people beyond Telford and Butts had the authority to make decisions. That not enough attention was paid to keeping the trains running on time. That decisions and plans tended to come together at the last minute.

Complaints about "the centre" have likely existed for as long as there have been officials around the prime minister with any authority. And it's not perfectly obvious that any of the major problems of the first four years can be traced directly back to such concerns—that any of the significant controversies the government stumbled into, including the SNC-Lavalin affair, would have been avoided with different people or a different structure.

But, from the outside, the Trudeau government did not always resemble a model of smooth and relentless execution. Vacancies in federal appointments piled up in the early going while a new process was being developed to broaden and diversify the field of candidates. The first attempt to appoint a new official languages commissioner collapsed in controversy when a former Ontario Liberal cabinet minister was selected. It took more than a year to appoint a new chief electoral officer after Marc Mayrand resigned in December 2016. It took nearly a year for the new infrastructure bank to get a chief executive officer.

A government that was a bit more rigorous, or just a bit more fearful, might have perhaps avoided some of the least flattering stumbles of the first two years. Inexperienced ministers, some with inexperienced advisors, walked into avoidable expense scandals. So did Butts and Telford. The prime minister took an unfortunate vacation around Christmas in 2016 (more on that later).

The Liberals were periodically chided for not passing legislation at the same rate as Stephen Harper's majority government, but the government had also built in processes that the Conservatives didn't have to worry about. As promised, the Liberals consulted broadly—at an "unprecedented scale," according to a summary prepared by the public service in 2018—but that necessarily led to slower action. The newly independent Senate also wasn't as easy to stage-manage. That was something like the intent of Trudeau's reforms, but it still took the government a while to fully grasp the extent of the change it had initiated.

That things sometimes looked a bit messy was perhaps inevitable—this was a government that had promised to do a great number of things. And the government was managing to get a number of things done. But when things did bog down it was tempting to wonder whether the organization needed to be improved. And when things really went sideways, in the spring of 2019, the attention eventually landed squarely on Telford and Butts with a 6,000-word story in the

Globe and Mail under the headline "System breakdown." That investigation couldn't quite establish that some systemic flaw had directly produced the crisis, but it was inevitable that the focus would fall on the co-CEOs.

In the wake of the SNC-Lavalin affair, Trudeau and his office did make changes. There was already an official in the PMO who was responsible for liaising with caucus, but a second advisor, George Young, one of the few individuals in the Trudeau government whose experience extends back to the Chrétien years, was assigned to that task as well. The PMO also established a new forty-eight-hour rule: a commitment that any Liberal MP who asked to speak with Trudeau would get a meeting or a phone call within two days.

"I pride myself on being accessible to and close to members of caucus and certainly cabinet and that anyone who wants to come and talk to me about this, that or the other thing should feel comfortable about everything," Trudeau says. He recalls Telford and Butts sometimes counselling him to not immediately share his opinion when opening a discussion because his opinion would have an impact on everyone else's view. But, he says, "I sometimes underestimate both the weight of what I say and the barriers in getting to me.

"Since this issue came up, I've spent a lot more time having one-on-one meetings and group meetings. If I'm out to Manitoba, instead of, after a long day, going back to watch Netflix in my hotel room, I actually sat down and had a dinner with the local Manitoba caucus. And those opportunities to have just real interactions, I sort of took them for granted. But they really do matter," he continues. "In my mind I'm just one of the guys. I happen to be prime minister, but I'm no more different or inaccessible than anyone else. But there are barriers there that this process particularly has had me think about. And we've done a much better job of both creating formalized processes for people to come in and connect with me, but also really pushing me."

One addition to the office was made in May 2019: Ben Chin, the chief of staff to Finance Minister Bill Morneau, was brought in as a senior advisor. Chin, a former advisor in the McGuinty government, was among the group invited to Mont Tremblant in the summer of 2012 to discuss Trudeau's possible bid for the Liberal leadership, but he came to the PMO now with a useful mix of experience and perspective. As Morneau's chief, he had been involved in the negotiations that culminated in the government's purchase of the Trans Mountain pipeline and, having previously advised Christy Clark when she was premier of British Columbia, he added valuable knowledge of an important political battleground to Trudeau's senior team. As a former advisor to both Clark and McGuinty, he had experience with re-election campaigns. And, as a former journalist and communications advisor, he brought some of the narrative-shaping skills that Butts had contributed.

A larger rearranging of Trudeau's PMO has not occurred, at least as of this writing. Butts was not immediately replaced—the timing, so close to the next election, might not have been ideal for a new principal secretary. Though she oversaw the 2015 campaign, Telford stayed in place at the PMO, while Broadhurst was sent to the Liberal Party to lead the next campaign.

Trudeau has operated before without either Butts or Telford in his immediate vicinity. Lanthier and Cyrus Reporter, two experienced aides, were officially his top assistants when he was a backbench MP and opposition leader, respectively. But a truly post-GerKat Trudeau would still likely be instructive, both for whatever would change about Trudeau and his government and what wouldn't. That's a conversation that won't be had unless Trudeau and his government first survive the vote in October.

========

As a reward for winning a leadership campaign and then a general election, Trudeau, Telford and Butts got to build a cabinet. And the cabinet that Trudeau unveiled in November 2015 was a sight to behold. Yes, it was composed of an equal number of men and women. But it was also full of new faces: thirteen ministers were rookie MPs who had not previously been elected to office at any level. And among those new faces were interesting people with exemplary backgrounds.

The new minister of defence, Harjit Sajjan, was a lieutenant colonel who fought in Afghanistan. An Indigenous woman and former chief, Jody Wilson-Raybould, was minister of justice and attorney general. A young woman and former refugee, Maryam Monsef, was minister of democratic institutions. The new health minister, Jane Philpott, was a family doctor who had worked in Africa. The new finance minister, Bill Morneau, was the CEO of a major human resources firm. There was also an astronaut (Marc Garneau), a well-connected journalist (Chrystia Freeland), an economist (Jean-Yves Duclos), the director of a homeless shelter (Patty Hajdu) and an oboist (Jim Carr).

It was the platonic ideal of a Liberal cabinet—like something out of a Canadian version of *The West Wing*. And the team seemed to speak to Trudeau's ability and eagerness to surround himself with bright and talented people.

At various points, the most impressive minister in the shiny new cabinet was still an old-fashioned career politician: the sturdy, if unexciting, Ralph Goodale. Goodale was first elected in 1974, before three of his current cabinet colleagues were born, and had been a young backbencher during Pierre Trudeau's last run as prime minister. After being defeated in 1979, he returned to Parliament in 1997, joined Jean Chrétien's cabinet and then became Paul Martin's finance minister.

He was considered a contender to be Justin Trudeau's finance minister, and so Public Safety seemed at first to be a consolation prize. But then Goodale seemed to be everywhere the government needed him to be: rewriting the Harper government's controversial anti-terror laws with a minimum of fuss, chairing a special cabinet committee struck to deal with the mess created by the Phoenix pay system for public servants, and speaking for the government on an array of tricky matters: marijuana legalization, the return of "foreign fighters" from Syria and Iraq, the arrival of asylum seekers at the southern border, and the financial settlement with Omar Khadr. And while many of his less-experienced colleagues seemed merely to want to survive or endure each afternoon's Question Period, Goodale was a confident and willing combatant—one of the few who could give the Liberal backbench something to get excited about.

Amongst the new generation, there was a predictable mix of stumbles and successes. Monsef, for instance, struggled with the impossible task of delivering on Trudeau's fatally flawed promise of electoral reform. Mélanie Joly, as heritage minister, couldn't convince her fellow Quebecers to accept the government's decision to not tax Netflix. Both were given new jobs and a chance to rehabilitate their careers. Philpott was investigated by the ethics commissioner after her office paid a seemingly exorbitant price for a car service run by someone who had volunteered for her campaign in Markham–Stouffville (though the minister was ultimately exonerated). Sajjan made an odd boast that overstated his contribution to an important mission during the Afghanistan campaign, but remained at Defence.

Beyond such headlines, there were emergent contributors. Duclos became a valued figure around the cabinet table and a dependable source of social and economic policy. Hajdu emerged as an important voice for social justice and was promoted from Status of Women to Labour. Later, after being promoted to cabinet in 2017, Karina Gould became a reliable spokeswoman for the government, both on her own file (democratic institutions) and more generally when the SNC-Lavalin affair took hold of the press gallery's attention.

In addition to Goodale's steady aptitude, the two most obvious stars of the Trudeau cabinet were rookies from that initial group of fifteen women: Philpott and Freeland.

Philpott, a confident communicator who could explain the government's position without sounding scripted, proved adept at getting things done as health minister: co-managing the legislation for medical assistance in dying and advancing federal efforts to deal with the epidemic of opioid addiction. When Trudeau later decided to dissolve the Department of Indigenous Affairs, he picked Philpott to lead a new department focused on delivering services for Indigenous communities and peoples. She again won plaudits for her ability to get things done and then was promoted once more, this time to Treasury Board, the organizational backbone of the federal government, to fill the gap left by Scott Brison's departure.

Unfortunately for everyone involved, her stay at Treasury Board lasted just seven weeks.

Freeland came to the fore during the final negotiations of a trade agreement between Canada and the European Union, specifically when the government in the Wallonia region of Belgium threatened to scuttle the deal. At an impasse, Freeland walked away from the table and, clearly exhausted, gave a teary-eyed interview to Belgian reporters expressing her frustration with the Walloons. A brief debate ensued about the minister's display of "visible emotion"—a Conservative MP, Gerry Ritz, suggested Freeland needed "adult supervision"—but a deal soon followed. Days later, in the middle of Question Period, she walked across the aisle to hug her Conservative predecessor, Ed Fast, in appreciation for the work he had done to advance the agreement before the Harper government was defeated.

Shortly thereafter, Donald Trump was elected president of the United States, and Freeland was moved to the front of the Trudeau government's efforts to deal with a changed world. There she proved to be a tireless and frenetic foreign minister. Whenever the moment arrives for the Liberals to think about a new leader, Freeland is likely to be promoted as one of the potential successors.

In at least the initial stages, the cabinet is said to have been possibly too agreeable. With the exception of Stéphane Dion—who was perhaps too willing to be critical—ministers did not readily challenge each other. Hajdu says that, at one point in the early going, Trudeau had to tell everyone to stop thanking each other, if only to save time. "He said, 'Okay, look, let's just pretend everybody thanks everybody else. Let's just get that out of the way,'" she recalls. "'Everybody thinks everybody did great work, we can just skip that part.'"

The most difficult debate in those early days involved medical assistance in dying, an issue that had been entirely absent from the election campaign but that had been looming as an unavoidable decision for whoever would be in government. The Supreme Court had struck down the existing prohibition in February 2015, but the Harper government had chosen to not deal with that decision before the fall election.

"Around the cabinet table, the range of views as to which way we should land on things was probably almost as broad as the range in Canada," Philpott says. "People had really different senses of what to do, and it was extremely emotional. We had people who had faced cancer diagnoses in the past and were kind of thinking through what it would be like for them in those circumstances."

The cabinet was pushed by both a special House committee, chaired by Liberal MP Rob Oliphant, and the newly independent Senate. But the result was nonetheless a relatively cautious bill, with no allowances for advance directives, minors or those facing non-terminal illnesses. Legal challenges may yet necessitate those changes, but, in taking the first step, the Trudeau government seemed conscious of not going too far.

Generally speaking, the group's disposition, according to a senior official, was to be "nice and collaborative and helpful," and the prime minister is said to prioritize consensus. But, in time, there were also disagreements. It is said, for instance, that there were lively debates over the details of legalizing marijuana and implementing pay equity legislation. Though it did not become public until after she departed cabinet, Philpott raised objections to the government's handling of Canada Summer Jobs grants and an attempt to prevent pro-life groups from accessing that funding. Carolyn Bennett, as minister of Indigenous affairs and then minister of Crown-Indigenous relations, clashed with Wilson-Raybould over the government's reconciliation agenda. "The Indigenous agenda is one where there are ministers with strong views and legitimate differences of opinion," says a senior official. One source says the dispute between Bennett and Wilson-Raybould caused other ministers to pick sides. As the SNC-Lavalin affair revealed, there had been a significant dispute over Bennett's proposal for an Indigenous rights framework.

There also seem to have been other tensions that foreshadowed the dramatic breakdown in the spring of 2019.

In a conversation in April 2019, nearly three weeks after he expelled Wilson-Raybould from the Liberal caucus, Trudeau says his relationship with his former justice minister was not ideal. "My conception of what this job is all about, from my father, is really deeply anchored in justice. The search for the just society, the Charter of Rights and Freedoms—this idea of justice and the fact that he was minister of justice, that was the one real role he had before becoming prime minister. The idea of justice, and that's sort of how he raised me, was always fundamental," Trudeau says. "And a number of times over the first years of my government, I grumbled to myself that it was difficult for me to not have a minister of justice that I was super-sympatico with."

Wilson-Raybould acknowledges that she and the prime minister had some "challenges."

Trudeau describes Wilson-Raybould as "brilliant" and a "very smart politician" who was "excellent at a lot of things." "I have huge respect for her," he says, "and if things had happened differently I would've continued to appreciate having her in cabinet." If Scott Brison had not stepped down, Trudeau says, there wouldn't have been a cabinet shuffle and Wilson-Raybould would have gone into the 2019 election as minister of justice. "But it wasn't the kind of relationship that I would've ideally imagined," he continues. "I don't think that she would have ideally imagined."

Wilson-Raybould says she had a "decent" relationship with the prime minister, but she says he was not particularly accessible. "He was difficult to be able to have conversations with," she says. "More difficult if you wanted to have a conversation with him one-on-one. But I think I had more one-on-one time with him than a lot of ministers did." (Not all sources agree that the prime minister's accessibility to ministers has been an issue.)

In a news conference in March 2019, Trudeau blamed the SNC-Lavalin affair on an "erosion of trust" between his office and Wilson-Raybould, in particular between Butts and the former minister. "I was not aware of that erosion of trust," he said. "As prime minister and leader of the federal ministry, I should have been."

There were policy differences, even beyond the reconciliation file. And some of those disagreements spilled out into the public domain in the wake of Wilson-Raybould's resignation. She had recommended that a Manitoba judge become the next chief justice of the Supreme

Court—Trudeau instead went with Richard Wagner, a member of the high court since 2012—and there was a dispute over the management of judicial appointments. But there was also a conflict over justice reform. Wilson-Raybould proposed a wide repeal of mandatory minimum penalties. Others in government balked at going as far as she suggested.

"I had always been clear from day one, both publicly and internally, that I think that judicial discretion is paramount in terms of making good decisions. Mandatory minimum penalties get in the way of that," Wilson-Raybould says, speaking generally about her view. "I think for the most serious of offences, like murder and treason and impaired driving, that it's proven that mandatory minimums are appropriate in those cases. The rest of them, I think there needs to be serious consideration about the removing of those and putting in place judicial discretion, so a judge can take into account the person that's before them."

During its decade in office, the Harper government embraced mandatory minimum sentences as an easy way to signal that it was "tough on crime." Legal experts have lamented that such provisions are ineffective at reducing crime and expensive to enforce, while judges have repeatedly struck down such sentences as excessive and disproportionate in certain cases. But a wide repeal of those provisions would be a significant political challenge. There are now mandatory minimums attached to more than seventy offences in Canada, including drug trafficking, firearms offences and offences against children. Conservatives would be happy to criticize anything that could be portrayed as a softer approach to such crimes. And the general public might not be inclined to believe that withdrawing minimum sentences is the wisest course.

Wilson-Raybould is also said to have frustrated some Liberal backbenchers whose private members' bills on justice issues she opposed. In March 2017, 105 Liberal MPs broke with the cabinet and voted to support a Liberal MP's bill to ban genetic discrimination. Wilson-Raybould publicly opposed the bill and, reportedly, both she and Trudeau argued against the bill during a meeting of the Liberal caucus before the vote. Wilson-Raybould declines to comment now, saying caucus discussions are confidential.

Trudeau suggests the issues between himself and the former minister of justice had more to do with "process," "personality" or "team" differences. "Any time we come to a budget, for example, there will be things that Bill [Morneau] will put forward that I know he feels really passionately about that I just don't think is a right idea, and I will push back and he'll argue really stringently that, 'No, I think this is the way to go,'" Trudeau says. "And I will end up having the last word and I say, 'No, you know what, we're not going this way or we are going this way even though you're not crazy about it.' And then he will say, 'Okay, you know, I gave it my best shot but I know there is a big picture here that you see because you're in this job and that's totally fine.' Right? And most if not all of the ministers are like that."

Wilson-Raybould was apparently not like that. "Jody was so sure of her own rightness in a very specific way, particularly in regards to Indigenous justice, where she does have a level of expertise that very few other people in the country could get at; it made it almost like a threat to her identity or her expertise to suggest that maybe that wasn't the best way to go forward in the big picture."

That "friction" made it "difficult to have a genuine and deep relationship."

Another Liberal source says Wilson-Raybould could be unmovable once she had taken a position, and that disagreements either ended in stalemates or required work-arounds. The former justice minister, this source suggests, could act like a dissenting judge, a notion that does not easily line up with the idea of cabinet solidarity.

"I trusted her competence, her intelligence. I just . . . it wasn't the kind of team dynamic that I'd like to have throughout the rest of cabinet," Trudeau says. "Of course if I'm playing devil's advocate from the other perspective, there is a total argument to make that said, 'Well, because I have my own mind it didn't make me as good of a team player.' But that is not to say that Bill Morneau or Chrystia Freeland or any of the others do not very clearly have their own mind about things and still manage to respect that the big picture is my job.

"So there was always a bit of a challenge around that, that just meant that the relationship I had [with other ministers] of easy trust and faith in each other that was deeply felt and not just intellectualized wasn't really there with her to the same degree."

Wilson-Raybould acknowledges that there could be "difficult conversations." But, from her perspective, the certainty of her positions on various issues was based on robust consultation and due diligence. "Having taken into account a whole bunch of different views ... once I did make my decision then I was pretty firm and it would be very difficult for me to move from that," she says. "And that resulted in friction. I think that's why some people characterized me as 'difficult.'"

That adjective was used in a Canadian Press report after her departure from cabinet—a description that was quickly perceived as gendered and possibly misogynist.

Wilson-Raybould also suggests there was a fundamental split between herself and Trudeau's office. "I am confident that the Prime Minister's Office, specifically, had a difficult time dealing with me because—and this is only my view; they probably have a different view—I actually put policy and making very good policy choices ahead of political expediency. And I felt that I was trying to be non-partisan or less political, and that wasn't necessarily the flavour of the day or our interactions."

Indeed, one imagines Trudeau, his advisors and other members of the government might quibble with that portrayal—either because they too were interested in making good policy or because the business of governing in a democracy necessarily requires the consideration of politics and public opinion.

There were internal discussions within the PMO about moving Wilson-Raybould, but she was still justice minister after Trudeau completed what was to be his last pre-election shuffle in July 2018. Less than two months later, the director of public prosecutions notified Wilson-Raybould's office that it had decided to not negotiate a deferred prosecution agreement with SNC-Lavalin.

A difficult issue thus arrived into a bad situation. The result was a mess.

Only after Brison told Butts and Telford about his intention to resign, and after it became clear that he couldn't be convinced to stick around, did Trudeau move to find himself a new justice minister. In a conversation recorded in late January 2019, before the internal machinations behind that move were made public, Trudeau explained Wilson-Raybould's move to Veterans Affairs on two fronts. First, it would give her a chance to show more of her abilities in a role that was more directly involved with the public. Second, it would put a strong minister on an issue that he expected the Conservatives to try to attack.

In April 2019, with it now known that she was first given the chance to take on Indigenous Services, he makes a similar case about the opportunity it could have been for her. "I still wanted her in cabinet. I still had confidence in her as part of the team," he says.

"It gave us a little bit of an opening to say, 'Okay, how could we shift things a little bit and give an opportunity to Jody to grow as a politician?' Because the one thing she did and the one thing we saw in her weeks as veterans affairs minister but also we see now in her riding, is she has retail political skills. But minister of justice is not a retail role. So I said, 'Here's an opportunity—as we're approaching an election campaign where we're given an opportunity to get one of our strong, visible, respected players out there actually announcing tangible things and connecting with people: here's an ending of a boil-water advisory; here's a delivery of a new school.'

"So there was that whole side of things. But there also obviously was that sense of, you know, it'd be nice to have a really strong, comfortable relationship with a new justice minister as well."

In an odd way, the departures of Wilson-Raybould and Philpott could be viewed as the ultimate evidence that Trudeau successfully created a cabinet of fresh-thinking and individually important ministers. Maybe only a rookie minister who viewed herself as a political entity in her own right, with principle and capital to her name, would have gone so far as to resign. More deferential ministers or career partisans might have been less likely to disagree with the government or insist on walking away.

But that is an academic point. Politically, the losses of Wilson-Raybould and Philpott were grievous, both serious and spectacular. The flip side of having individually important ministers is that it hurts all the more if they resign in protest. Within the government it was sometimes said that Wilson-Raybould was "too big to fail"—that her appointment as justice minister and attorney general had been so meaningful that she needed to succeed. But that only makes it harder to excuse the prime minister or his office for the unravelling that ultimately occurred.

For Trudeau, the departures became attacks on his leadership and his government. And for two months, in the lead-up to a re-election campaign, he and his government struggled to talk about anything else. Those were days that could have been spent on other things. And there were many other things that Justin Trudeau would have rather been talking about.

CHAPTER 3

THE MIDDLE-CLASS DREAM

On the occasion of the country's sesquicentennial, Justin Trudeau stood onstage on Parliament Hill and told a story about how Canada had made it that far and what it had to do next. It was a story about citizenship, diversity, reconciliation, equality and the middle class.

"Our job now," he said, "is to advance equal opportunity to ensure that each and every Canadian has a real and fair chance at success. We must create the right conditions so that the middle class, and those working hard to join it, can build a good life for themselves and their families."

This was the mantra of the Trudeau era—"the middle class and those working hard to join it," an oft-repeated statement of empathy and aspiration, a guiding principle and an assurance that these Liberals were on your side (provided your income wasn't too far above the median). It was a thread the Liberals used to stitch together an agenda that included ideas like gender equality, reconciliation and combating climate change. It was unquestionably a tool of political marketing. But it was also, at least in theory, a weapon against the darkest impulses of populism.

"Our plan offers real help to Canada's middle class and all those working hard to join it," the Liberals explained in their 2015 platform, which itself was entitled "A New Plan for a Strong Middle Class." Both the Throne Speech that followed and the mandate letters that Trudeau issued to each of his new ministers made prominent use of the phrase.

In its entirety, it has been written into official announcements on trade, innovation, tourism and even food policy. It rolls off the prime minister's tongue with casual ease. In September 2016, the middle class was the focus of Trudeau's first speech to the general assembly of the United Nations. In order to address the current fears and anxieties of the public, he told the world, leaders needed to be able to answer questions like "What will strengthen and grow the middle class, and help those working hard to join it?"

Included within an internal government status report in the summer of 2018—one of the regular summaries of polling figures and other metrics prepared by Dan Arnold, the prime minister's director of research—was a graph showing that Liberal MPs had uttered the phrase "middle class" 381 times during debate in the House of Commons in the first six months of that year. That was far more than either the Conservatives (146 references over the same period) or New Democrats (41 mentions). But those 381 invocations actually represented a new low point for the Liberal side. They had peaked in the first six months of 2017, when Liberal MPs made 753 references to the middle class. During the fall sitting of 2017, they registered 558 mentions.

An argument for the middle class (and those working hard to join it) had been building for months, even years, before Trudeau stepped forward in the fall of 2012. The galvanizing moment had arguably occurred twelve months earlier. It was on September 17, 2011, that several hundred protesters descended on Zuccotti Park, a public square located two blocks north of Wall Street in Lower Manhattan. This was the first public demonstration of the Occupy Wall Street movement. The occupation of Zuccotti Park lasted two months and inspired similar protests in other cities and countries. The basic complaint was inequality.

Eight years earlier, two economists—Emmanuel Saez and Thomas Piketty—published a paper in the *Quarterly Journal of Economics* entitled "Income Inequality in the United States, 1913–1998." Saez and Piketty found that inequality had been rising in the United States since the 1970s, with the top one percent of earners claiming a steadily larger proportion of all income growth. "The picture that emerged was startling to those who still clung to the notion of America as a middle-class society," Paul Krugman, the economist and *New York Times* columnist, later wrote.

The inequality that Saez and Piketty identified became a point of emphasis and fascination for economists, journalists and politicians. The Great Recession and the stock market crash of 2008 only exacerbated and exemplified the gap: rich bankers had designed a house of cards, and, when it all came tumbling down, those bankers were bailed out with public funds. Included in Barack Obama's 2009 budget was a graph compiled by Saez and Piketty showing the one percent's increasing share of income. That budget aimed to raise taxes on the richest and provide more support for middle- and low-income earners.

In May 2011, American economist Joseph Stiglitz surveyed the Arab Spring uprisings in the Middle East and wondered when similar scenes would play out in the United States. "These are societies where a minuscule fraction of the population—less than 1 percent—controls the lion's share of the wealth," he wrote in *Vanity Fair*. "As we gaze out at the popular fervor in the streets, one question to ask ourselves is this: When will it come to America?"

A couple months later, *Adbusters*, the anti-consumerist magazine founded in Vancouver in 1989, printed a poster that suggested a public occupation of Wall Street. The people who showed up at Zuccotti Park declared themselves members of the "99 percent" and directed their ire at the disproportionate wealth and influence held by the richest one percent. It was a messy, leaderless movement, and its demands were vague and diffuse. But in pitting the 99 percent against the one percent, the protests helped push the issue of economic inequality to the forefront of the popular discussion.

No less a figure than Mark Carney, governor of the Bank of Canada at the time, was moved to acknowledge the concern. "I can understand the frustrations," he said in a CBC interview.

Two months after the storming of Lower Manhattan, Barack Obama went to Osawatomie, a town of 4,500 people in Kansas. A century earlier, in September 1910, Teddy Roosevelt had gone to Osawatomie and delivered a call for government intervention to restrain the privileges of wealth and ensure equality of opportunity, what would become known as his "New Nationalism" speech. "At many stages in the advance of humanity, this conflict between the men who possess more than they have earned and the men who have earned more than they possess is the central condition of progress," Roosevelt said.

At a dinner in May 2011, Obama had reportedly asked a group of prominent historians visiting the White House how he could "discuss the issue of inequality in our society without being accused of class warfare." And perhaps he'd now found an answer. In Osawatomie, Obama talked about inequality. He referenced the 99 percent and "the people who've been occupying the streets of New York and other cities." But he spent more time talking about "the middle class."

The United States had once built a strong and thriving middle class, he explained, but that middle was being hollowed out. "This is the defining issue of our time," he said. "This is a make-or-break moment for the middle class, and for all those who are fighting to get into the middle class."

The answer, Obama said, was not to cut taxes and reduce regulation and hope for the best. It was to ask the richest to pay a bit more in taxes, cut taxes for the middle class and make investments in education, innovation and infrastructure.

The president's remarks were cheered by a Reuters columnist named Chrystia Freeland. "All the doubting Thomases who wondered whether Occupy Wall Street would have lasting political impact got their answer this week," she wrote. "The movement's accomplishment is to have legitimized discussion of rising income inequality in the United States—Mr. Obama described it as 'the defining issue of our time.' That is a landmark declaration."

Less than a year later, Freeland released her second book, entitled *Plutocrats: The Rise of the New Global Super-Rich and the Fall of Everyone Else*. Seven months after that, she announced she would seek the Liberal Party nomination in a by-election for the riding of Toronto Centre, the first "star candidate" to be successfully recruited by Trudeau and his team.

The middle class was not a new focus in American politics. In 1992, Bill Clinton styled himself a champion for the "forgotten middle class." In 2004, John Kerry promised assistance for a middle class that was being "squeezed." Obama himself had struck a "Middle Class Working Families Task Force" in 2009. "America's middle class is hurting," said Joe Biden, Obama's vice-president, who chaired the task force. Third Way, a centre-left think tank in Washington, D.C., released a set of policies in 2010 that were framed as a "success agenda for the middle class." "The heart of the middle class resides in a vast public policy vacuum—a donut hole—in which most direct government support is absent," the authors wrote.

But now there were people in the streets, with a cause—inequality— that seemed urgent and powerful.

What Obama laid out in Osawatomie became the central message of his re-election campaign, eventually detailed in a twenty-page booklet entitled "The New Economic Patriotism: A Plan for Jobs and Middle-Class Security." "America does best when the middle class does best," he said. Conservatives still accused him of participating in class warfare. But the message carried him to victory against Mitt Romney, the famously wealthy Republican candidate who often seemed to be the living embodiment of the one percent—particularly when he was secretly recorded telling donors at a private fundraiser that 47 percent of American voters were guaranteed to vote for Obama because they were dependent on government and felt entitled to health care and other services.

Close analysis of that result also revealed an intriguing split in the mind of the American voter. Opinion polls conducted late in that campaign suggested Romney had an advantage over Obama when voters were asked which candidate would better manage the economy. That might have been expected to carry Romney to victory—particularly at a time when the American economy was still struggling to recover from the recession. Ever since Bill Clinton's campaign had coined the phrase, the abiding truth of most political contests seemed to be that it was "the economy, stupid."

But managing the economy wasn't exactly what voters were looking for.

"For average working-class and middle-class Americans who have believed for nearly a decade that the economic system in America had fallen out of balance for people like them, the president's personal story and policies engendered trust because they connected with voters' lives, aspirations, and beliefs about what it would take to create the future they wanted. That trust was the central economic test in this election," Joel Benenson, the Obama campaign's chief pollster, later explained in the *New York Times*. "That is why, despite the credit given to Mr. Romney for 'understanding' the economy—a phrasing that spoke to a technical understanding—Mr. Obama was always significantly more trusted on qualities that matter to working Americans. In fact, independent voters in our survey, by 54 to 40, said it was more important for a president to have 'the willingness to fight for middle-class families' rather than a 'technical understanding of the economy.'"

Though it couldn't have been appreciated at the time, Benenson was also explaining how Trudeau's Liberals were about to win the 2015 federal election. In fact, shortly after the 2012 U.S. result, Katie Telford and Gerry Butts saw Benenson speak at a conference in Washington. Afterwards, they sought him out to talk more.

———

ONE MORNING IN JUNE 2012, Butts had breakfast with Kevin Milligan, an economist at the University of British Columbia. Butts had been following Milligan on Twitter and was interested in his work on inequality and the one percent. At the end of breakfast, Butts asked Milligan if he could put together a briefing note to help inform the policy framework that was being built for a potential Trudeau campaign.

"The 'occupy' movement focused attention on growing inequality," Milligan later explained in that briefing note. "The increasing concentration of income is real, and it is large." A little more than 12 percent of all personal income in Canada was now going to the richest one percent. For the 99 percent there had been some positive developments—women were working more and earning more, workers in the resource sector were doing well, and there were fewer Canadians living below the low-income cut-off—but "the stagnation of earnings for most workers is real." Middle-class consumption was being sustained by Canadians "taking on increasingly large levels of consumer and housing debt."

Why was this important? Milligan suggested a few reasons. Economic outcomes, he argued, are the result of both hard work and luck. "So long as luck plays some role, most would agree that those who end up struggling deserve some support and those who do well should share some of the bounty of their success," he wrote. Greater equality also correlated with greater economic mobility across generations, thus preserving the great and defining dream that children can and will have it better than their parents.

There was also the possibility that addressing the problem might prevent a popular uprising. "If middle class families feel they don't benefit from growth, they won't favour the policies that support a healthy growing economy," he also posited. On this point, he invoked Otto von Bismarck, the chancellor of Germany from 1871 to 1890, who introduced social security, in part, to keep the public from turning toward communism. "Ensuring that prosperity is shared forestalls revolution," Milligan wrote.

A few months later, after announcing his bid for the Liberal leadership, Trudeau made a similar suggestion in an op-ed for the *Toronto Star*. "If we do not attend to this problem, we should not be surprised to see the middle class question the policies, and the very system, that values and encourages growth," he wrote.

For the moment, that was an interesting hypothetical.

Butts and Mike McNair, Trudeau's future director of policy, had discovered a shared interest in the economics and politics of the middle class when they met for coffee at a Starbucks on Bay Street in the spring of 2012 to discuss the possibility of McNair joining the nascent campaign. McNair had been a policy advisor to the last two Liberal leaders—Stéphane Dion and Michael Ignatieff—but after the 2011 election he had gone to work for Deloitte, the global consulting firm. The idea of focusing on the middle class was then presented by Butts and McNair when a select group of friends and advisors convened for a few days in Mont-Tremblant, Quebec, to discuss the possibility of Trudeau running for leader. "If we're going to talk about the economy, this is how we need to talk about the economy," says McNair, recalling the pitch. "Because it will be an inclusive message that Canadians will feel speaks to them. But, more important, there's actually solid policy grounds that this is what we should focus on."

The decision to focus on "the middle class" and not "economic inequality" was a conscious one. "We were pretty sure that income inequality was a much more divisive way of approaching this issue than talking about the middle class," Butts says. "Though it was really the same issue."

"It's a much broader swath of folks we want to focus on," McNair says. "If all people hear about is inequality, it implies that growth in and of itself is a bad thing. And it implies that people making money in and of itself is a bad thing. Which is actually not our approach. We actually think people should be successful. It's something to be celebrated. We want more people to be successful. But as we do that, we want to make sure that success is broadly shared."

There was, as it turns out, a deep well of public sentiment to draw on. Frank Graves, a pollster with EKOS Research Associates, had also made an appearance at Mont-Tremblant. As he later laid out in a presentation at Queen's University in 2014, the Canadian middle class was antsy and doubtful. Though 85 percent of respondents to an EKOS survey agreed that "a growing and optimistic middle class is an essential component of societal progress," a majority described the middle class as pessimistic (56 percent), falling backward (66 percent) and shrinking (69 percent). Seventy percent said middle-class families had fallen behind in the last twenty-five years. Sixty percent said the next generation would be worse off twenty-five years from now.

A plurality of Canadians—47 percent—still identified as middle-class, but that was down significantly from 2010, when 60 percent considered themselves to be of that status.

To appeal to the middle class, then, was to speak to an anxious but broad audience. And that lined up with a desire to cast a wide appeal. "The party had become a party that spoke to special interest groups, but not the broad middle," Butts argues. "And we weren't even really good at doing that. The NDP was better at it than we were."

The middle class gave the Liberal Party a chance to continue existing as the major party of the centre-left. And with that as both a foundation and an overarching theme, they could pursue a number of other goals: combating climate change, promoting gender equality and pursuing Indigenous reconciliation. "We each had, and together had, areas that we were passionate about, that would be on our bucket list of things and that we believed Canadians could get excited about too," says Katie Telford. "But we knew we had to figure out a way to talk to Canadians about what mattered to them right in front of them first. And create a linkage to that broader narrative."

The Trudeau Liberals were hardly the first Canadian party or government to aim its policies at individuals and households within the middle class, even if just implicitly. The Harper Conservatives, for instance, spoke of "everyday Canadians" and "hard-working Canadians" while targeting middle-class voters with a series of boutique tax credits. But the Trudeau Liberals would be much louder and more explicit about it.

The Liberal "red book" of 1993, the 112-page platform that Jean Chrétien campaigned on, mentioned the "middle class" just once (to note that it was "shrinking"). In 2008, the Liberal platform included five references to either "middle-class" or "middle-income" Canadians. In 2011, there were fifteen mentions of the middle class, but "families" were the predominant concern—"family" or "families" were referenced more than two hundred times in the party platform as Ignatieff's Liberals targeted that household unit with a suite of promises covering post-secondary education, child care, home care and pensions. (The NDP's platform was a more succinct appeal to the same audience—"giving your family a break.")

But not everyone lives with a family. And some of those who do probably wish they didn't.

The Liberals did not abandon the Canadian family in 2015, mind you: there were seventy-three references to families in the Trudeau platform. But there were 139 references to the middle class. In fact, the phrase appears at least once on every page.

The change was more than rhetorical. "What I would argue is that the political orthodoxy in Canada, across party lines, of what it meant to focus on economic policy, was to focus on the economic challenges of the 1990s. By that I mean slaying deficits. And looking at macroeconomics as what good economic policy was. And in a way that was also a product of how the Western world looked at economic policy, the Washington consensus: let's lower taxes to boost productivity, let's run balanced budgets, all these things which inherently do make sense and are good economic principles," McNair says.

"But as all that activity was happening, over a number of years, there was growing anxiety faced by the broad swath of the population in the Western world, that they were being left behind, that, whether through technological change or the impacts of globalization, they were less secure than they were before, and something was wrong here," McNair continues. "And what I believe is that the Liberal Party, when it thought about economic policy, for too long wasn't in touch with that reality and that anxiety. And thought we should just replicate how we thought about things in the 1990s, even though things had shifted a lot."

Trudeau, McNair says, had a sense of this. "When he'd knock on doors in Papineau, they didn't want to talk about separatism, they didn't want to talk about all the things that we in the Liberal Party always thought they wanted to talk about, they wanted to talk about their economic anxieties."

The Liberals, by this diagnosis, had to rediscover the middle-class dream of economic security for the present and hope for the future.

Not everyone was immediately impressed with the Trudeau campaign's middle-class preoccupation. "If someone says, 'I'm going to focus on a particular group,' what does that say to everybody else?" Martha Hall Findlay, a former Liberal MP, lamented during the Liberal leadership race in 2012. "Every Canadian wants a job, every Canadian wants a future for their kids and every Canadian wants to be proud of their country. So as a prime minister, the last thing I would want to say is that my focus is on a particular segment of our society."

Trudeau's Liberals would eventually expand their focus to include those "working hard to join" the middle class. But they also tended to avoid neatly defining what the "middle class" was. In truth, it is not a concept that is necessarily easy to define. Just ask an economist like Jean-Yves Duclos, the earnest professor whom Trudeau appointed minister of families, children and social development.

In March 2017, Duclos was put forward to deliver a presentation to reporters on "the state of the middle class," complete with charts and bar graphs. After the PowerPoint presentation was completed, Duclos was asked for a definition of the "middle class." He came very close to describing it as a state of mind.

"Canadians use a combination of indicators to define themselves as part of or not part of the middle class," he explained. "First, income. Second, the cost of living. And third, their level of confidence toward the future." It could depend on where you live and the cost of housing, he noted, or on the quality and security of your job. There was a "strong identification" among those earning between $50,000 and $180,000, he said, but some outside that scale might also consider themselves middle class.

That would be the last time the Liberals tried to dazzle the press gallery with Duclos's flow charts.

Beyond Hall Findlay's concerns about divisiveness, others simply questioned the Liberal diagnosis. The median income, for instance, had been rising in Canada. "It seems to me that the last thing we need is another government determined to put the middle class first," the economist Stephen Gordon, a former colleague of Duclos's at Laval University, wrote in 2013. "Why not focus on lower-income households?"

Trudeau's Liberals were undaunted by such quibbles. And the result was similar to Obama's success. Polling conducted by the Liberals in October 2015 showed that Stephen Harper still had an advantage when voters were asked which leader would best manage the economy: 33 percent picked Harper, 26 percent indicated Trudeau and 17 percent chose Mulcair. But when voters were asked who would do the most for the middle class, the result flipped: 41 percent for Trudeau, 21 percent for Mulcair and 20 percent for Harper.

———

THE CENTREPIECE OF THE Liberal agenda was Occupy-esque: a commitment to tax the rich and support the rest. The federal income tax rate for those earning $200,000 or more per year was increased from 29 percent to 33 percent, and the rate for those earning between $45,000 and $90,000 was dropped from 22 percent to 20.5 percent. More significantly, the federal system of supports for families with children was reformed to create a larger, progressive and tax-free benefit: the Canada Child Benefit (CCB).

To do so, the Liberals repealed two Conservative inventions: the Universal Child Care Benefit and income splitting for couples with children. Both policies helped some in the middle class, but they also provided lucrative benefits to those in the upper tax brackets, particularly where one spouse was the predominate earner. Money set aside for those policies was added to funding for two older measures—the National Child Benefit and the Canada Child Tax Benefit—and topped up with an additional $3.4 billion to create a $23 billion transfer, to be distributed to Canadian families with an emphasis on the lowest earners. A family with less than $30,000 in income would receive the maximum amount of $6,400 per child under the age of six. Progressively smaller cheques would go to higher earners, with nothing going to families who made $200,000 or more. The Liberals estimated that the new Canada Child Benefit would raise 300,000 kids out of poverty.

It was, in a way, a reckoning with the previous Liberal government's defeat in 2006. Going into that election, Paul Martin's Liberals had deals with the provinces to spend a total of $5 billion over four years to create a national child care system. Stephen Harper's Conservatives countered with a promise to cancel those agreements and instead give the money to parents directly—as much as $100 per month via the Universal Child Care Benefit, a refundable tax credit. Even if that much money was unlikely to make the difference between affording child care and not, the Conservatives wrapped their promise in the idea of parental choice. "We don't need old white guys telling us what to do," Conservative MP Rona Ambrose famously chided Ken Dryden, the minister who had engineered federal-provincial agreement on the Liberal plan. The Liberal retort was infamously inelegant. "Don't give people twenty-five bucks a week to blow on beer and popcorn," suggested Scott Reid, Martin's director of communications, during a televised panel discussion. "Give them child care spaces that work."

In fact, there is now significant evidence that giving money to families is a good way to improve child welfare—and that the money is ultimately well spent by the parents who receive it. "They are purchasing more basic necessities, and as their resources increase, they are directing increasingly more of the money towards those items that directly affect learning, such as educational tools," Lauren Jones, Kevin Milligan, and Mark Stabile reported in a 2015 study of existing federal child benefits. "Interestingly, they significantly cut back spending on alcohol and tobacco."

So the Liberal Party was returned to power on a promise of giving parents even more money. Once in office, the Liberals also put new funding into other transfers and benefits, including the Guaranteed Income Supplement and the Working Income Tax Benefit (rebranded as the Canada Workers Benefit), both of which were made automatic for eligible individuals who file a tax return. The age of eligibility for Old Age Security was reset to sixty-five. Student grants were increased for low- and middle-income families. Subsequent budgets put an emphasis on training for workers and helping young people buy their first homes.

In June 2016, with a modicum of fuss, Bill Morneau negotiated the most significant expansion of the Canada Pension Plan (CPP) since the program was established in 1965, accomplishing what former Conservative finance minister Jim Flaherty had backed away from six years earlier. Amid a general decline in corporate pensions, Finance Canada had projected that as many as 1.1 million families might not have enough saved to maintain their standard of living once retired. Under Morneau's plan, a gradual increase in contributions will pay for a second tier of CPP that provides increased retirement benefits to middle-income earners.

Flaherty had seen the same problem and proposed a similar solution in a letter to his provincial counterparts in June 2010. "If we choose to do nothing about that, then it's likely that a group of Canadians—a minority—will reach retirement age and not have sufficient savings to take care of themselves in their retirement," he said at the time. But the Progressive Conservative government in Alberta balked and the Canadian Federation of Independent Business complained. Flaherty backed off, insisting the economy was too fragile to proceed.

By 2016, Ontario was ready to go it alone, and that gave Morneau an opening to push for broader agreement. Andrew Scheer's Conservatives nonetheless condemned the move as a "payroll tax."

At times, the middle-class agenda could still look and sound like an inequality agenda. The Liberals committed billions to affordable housing, for instance, and Duclos tabled legislation to establish an official measure of poverty and a series of targets for reducing the number of Canadians who live below the threshold. But the Liberals never stopped talking about the middle class.

Miles Corak, one of the more high-profile Canadian voices in the discussion about inequality and an advisor to Duclos on the Liberal poverty strategy, says he has grown to like the Liberal mantra. The Liberals, he says, have been "trying to get legitimacy for an inequality agenda up into the income distribution."

"Making the middle class a core part of the agenda raises the chances that they see themselves in the policy thrusts that also help those further down in the ladder. This leads to public policy that is more politically sustainable in the long run, and does not stigmatize those on the lowest rungs of the ladder. It also speaks to a need that the middle class have that is not captured in the statistics on income distribution: the need for more security in their incomes," Corak argues.

"There is a long-standing issue in policy design for the poor that has to do with how targeted programs should be. A very tightly targeted program focused just on those most in need might be able to more tightly focus available resources on the poor, but the trade-off is that the program engenders an 'us versus them' mentality, stigmatizing the poor and over time likely becoming less generous because distinctions come to be made between the 'deserving' and 'undeserving.' The majority not benefiting from the program will be less likely to support them."

A universal benefit, on the other hand, risks distributing resources too thinly and providing a benefit to those who don't need it. "The point is to find the middle ground, and that is what I think the CCB and other programs under the middle-class agenda have done," Corak says. The Liberals had derided Harper's Universal Child Care Benefit for the fact that it could be claimed by wealthy households—sending "cheques to millionaires" was how Liberals described it—and a handful of other measures were eliminated once the Liberals were in office: the Public Transit Tax Credit, the Children's Fitness Tax Credit, the Children's Arts Tax Credit, the Textbook Tax Credit. Such micro-targeted and easily marketed tax breaks were a hallmark of the Harper era, even as economists derided such measures as inefficient policies that generally rewarded people for behaviour that would have happened anyway.

The right-wing Fraser Institute complained that, on a strict tally of all tax changes, the middle class was actually left worse off: that the tax cut had been washed away by those other changes. In September 2018, the Finance Department countered with a report on "Real Progress for Canada's Middle Class." The federal analysis suggested that 90 percent of households were better off after the government's changes to both taxes and direct transfers were taken into account. Notably, it was actually the lowest earners—the bottom third of the income scale—who had seen the biggest proportional improvements.

But the Fraser Institute also disliked those transfers. Two of its analysts had previously described the Canada Child Benefit as "a transfer program that fosters dependence on government" and "a disincentive to hard work and independence."

The middle-class tax cut was also challenged from the left: an analysis conducted in 2015 by David Macdonald, an economist with the Canadian Centre for Policy Alternatives, showed that wealthier households saved the most from the change in rates. In time, a broader progressive critique took shape. The Liberals were not doing enough, it was said, to eliminate tax breaks for the richest. They were not moving fast enough or boldly enough to spend on social goods like affordable housing and subsidized child care space (though Duclos did agree with the provinces to spend $7.5 billion over eleven years on early learning and child care). A new housing benefit, which would subsidize the rent of low-income earners, wouldn't take effect until 2020. Steps toward a national pharmacare program were being taken gradually.

Such criticism found a home in a newly emboldened NDP. In 2015, Thomas Mulcair's NDP actively opposed raising taxes on the highest earners and insisted on balancing the federal budget. But, by the spring of 2019, Jagmeet Singh's New Democrats seemed set to run on a more aggressive version of the Liberal's 2015 platform: even higher taxes for the rich and even more spending to benefit the rest.

If nothing else, the Canadian left might at least credit Trudeau for expanding the NDP's imagination of what is possible.

Ultimately, though, your view of Liberal tax policy in the Trudeau era depends on where you stand. When Stephen Harper's government left office, federal tax revenues as a share of GDP stood at 11.5 percent, a historic low and well below the pre-Harper average of 13.3 percent. Under Trudeau, tax revenues were set to settle at 12.4 percent, exactly halfway between two different ideas of how much a federal government should properly need.

———

IN 2017, THE NATIONAL poverty rate dropped to 9.5 percent, a full percentage point drop from the year before. What's more, Statistics Canada reported that 278,000 fewer children were living in poverty as compared to 2015. The Liberal child benefit was credited with contributing to that change.

The CCB had already received plaudits from the governor of the Bank of Canada, but for reasons that were not part of the original promotion. In the summer of 2017, Stephen Poloz credited it with being "highly stimulative" for the economy.

Stimulating the economy had been the other part of the Trudeau agenda. In addition to helping the middle class and low-income earners, the Liberals were also going to spend into a deficit to boost a sluggish economy. But that stimulation was to be derived from putting billions toward new infrastructure—Trudeau's pivotal announcement during the 2015 campaign had come in front of a backdrop of construction equipment and people in hard hats.

Once in government, the Liberals struggled mightily to move that infrastructure funding fast enough. A study by the parliamentary budget officer found just $7.2 billion had moved in the first two years, half of what was originally projected. The impact on real GDP was about 0.1 percent. This was either a failure to execute or a failure to manage expectations around the multi-level negotiations that are required for infrastructure projects.

The Canada Infrastructure Bank, an initiative meant to capitalize on private investment to fund some public projects, was similarly slow to get up and running—it didn't have a CEO in place until May 2018. A new minister, François-Philippe Champagne, was brought in with a mandate to ensure infrastructure funds did not lapse. By the spring of 2019, with an election looming, the Trudeau government moved to fast-track $2.2 billion directly to municipalities to get around four conservative provincial governments—Ontario, Saskatchewan, Manitoba and New Brunswick, the four charter members of the anti-carbon-tax club—that were apparently moving too slowly for the Liberals' liking.

That the economy continued to grow at a decent rate was eventually credited, in part, to something else entirely: immigration.

In October 2016, an economic advisory council appointed by Morneau came back with a rather ambitious suggestion. The council—chaired by Dominic Barton, the highly regarded McKinsey consultant—recommended that the federal government aim to increase immigration to

450,000 new residents annually. The council suggested Canada could get to that number by 2023. The country's annual intake had hovered between 221,000 and 280,000 between 2000 and 2014. In that last full year of the Harper government, Canada accepted 260,000 people.

The council's recommendation was not borne out of mere open-mindedness or virtue. The suggestion was that the Trudeau government focus on business talent and international students. The resulting influx would address existing skills shortages, stimulate economic activity and compensate for an aging population. "Without making significant changes to counteract current demographic trends in Canada, the number of working-age Canadians for every senior is expected to drop from 4.2 in 2015 to 2.7 in 2030, adding significant fiscal strain to the system and threatening the health of the Canadian economy and social safety net for Canadians," the council wrote.

John McCallum, the immigration minister at the time, described the council's number as "huge." "There was complete consensus that immigration should go up. The question was by how much," says McCallum of the discussion among cabinet ministers. "We all agreed that for demographic reasons, for economic growth reasons, more immigration was a good idea. But how fast could we increase immigration was the issue."

The concern was integration: how quickly new Canadians would find work, and how well settlement services could help them get established in their new communities.

For 2017, the government settled on a target of 300,000. But then the Liberals started nudging that number upward. For 2018, the target was 310,000. For 2021, under a new system of three-year projections, the target is 370,000. McCallum acknowledges that he might have wanted to move faster.

The actual numbers moved more slowly: 296,346 in 2016 and 286,480 in 2017. But that much was still hailed as "human stimulus." From 2010 to 2017, Bloomberg reported, Canada's population grew at a higher rate than that of any other G7 country. As the Liberals moved to expedite the arrival of individuals with certain skills, reports flourished of tech talent that was passing over Donald Trump's America to settle in Canada. Similar reports pointed to an influx of international students to Canadian universities. In 2018, immigration hit 321,065.

Whatever the economic imperative, it was a conspicuous thing to be welcoming more people from abroad at a moment when populist nationalism seemed to be on the rise globally. And even within the peaceable kingdom there were hints of misgivings. In February 2018, 60 percent of respondents to an Environics survey disagreed with the statement that "immigration levels are too high." But a few months later, 49 percent of respondents to an Angus Reid Institute poll said Canada should reduce its target of 310,000 immigrants. A subsequent poll by Ipsos found 40 percent strongly or somewhat agreed "that immigration has made it more difficult for Canadian people to get jobs." Forty percent is not a majority, of course. But it suggests a significant minority are not inclined to believe that immigration is a net benefit to Canada's economy.

Ideally, a government might hope to maintain a virtuous cycle: economic growth and middle-class security making it easier to pursue increased immigration, which helps maintain economic growth, which reduces middle-class anxiety. But global politics in 2018 seemed to suggest that calculation was fragile, and subject to forces that extended well beyond economics.

By year's end Trudeau was already facing a direct domestic challenge: Premier François Legault and his new Coalition Avenir Québec government were demanding that their province's annual share of Canada's immigration be reduced from 50,000 newcomers to 40,000. Legault also wanted more money from the federal government to cover the expense of sheltering and supporting the thousands of asylum seekers who had walked across Quebec's southern border.

———

ON A MID-JULY MORNING in 2018, Trudeau wanted to talk about the Canada Child Benefit. He was to spend the day marking the fact that the benefit was now going to be indexed to inflation.

"At the heart of everything is why I am doing this, right?" he says, asking himself a question so that he can answer it. "The CCB is I think at the heart of everything that we promised to do, that I promised to do in my launch speech in Papineau for my leadership . . . figuring out how to do work for the middle class and those working hard to join it and how to make a real difference."

He is chided for the talking point, but continues with his story. He fondly recalls how much time he and his team spent fiddling with the curve on a line graph as they debated how the benefit would phase out along an income scale. He remembers going to the house of a family in the riding of Greg Fergus, the Liberal MP for Hull–Aylmer, to shoot a promotional photo. He played Lego with the kids and he asked their mother what the family's income was. She said the child benefit wasn't really for a family like hers, but he persisted and they figured out she'd receive about $350 per month. She was surprised and delighted.

"This idea that the middle class have often not been recipients of real policy tools directed at them because, to a certain extent, it's easy to do something for the most marginalized, there's lots we can do for that; there's lots we can do for the wealthiest in terms of complicated tax cuts and things like that. But the mass of Canadians in the middle who if you want to do anything for them it ends up hugely expensive is really what we were trying to get at. And what it has resulted in, in terms of economic benefits and confidence of Canadians and the conversations I have with people, totally unscientific one-off conversations— you really, really feel it. And that—making a tangible difference both in people's lives and their day-to-day, but also in how they see their institutions, their government and their future, as being invested in their success and part of their success—is at the centre of what I think we are trying to do in this whole thing."

There is a hint here of something Wilfrid Laurier once said. "We are a free and happy people, and we are so owing to the liberal institutions by which we are governed, institutions which we owe to the exertions of our forefathers and the wisdom of the mother country," he said in a speech in 1877. "The policy of the Liberal party is to protect these institutions, to defend and extend them, and, under their sway, to develop the latent resources of our country. That is the policy of the Liberal party: it has no other."

Butts says one of Trudeau's motivations is "the fundamental belief that the government, the public sector, can be an agent for people coming together to do things for each other that they can't do for themselves . . . the fact that the federal government can tangibly prove itself to be a potential source of benefit and relief in the lives of everyday people is a good fringe benefit."

That a large, means-tested benefit aimed at low- and middle-income families could improve the way people see their institutions and their governments is not far-fetched. Consider the case of 2,000 unemployed Finns.

In 2017, the Finnish government began an experiment with a policy known as "basic income." A random sample of 2,000 unemployed citizens was selected and each was given a monthly, tax-free benefit of 560 euros. The experiment ran for two years and recipients were surveyed at the end of the second year.

As compared to a control group of unemployed citizens who did not receive the basic income, those who received the monthly benefit reported a higher degree of trust in other people, the legal system and politicians.

For Trudeau's Liberals, the CCB is also the most tangible of their policy changes—a straightforward initiative amid a litany of high-minded pursuits. And they have expended great effort reminding Canadians that it exists and that they did it (though without the splashy TV ads that the Conservatives used to promote the "Economic Action Plan" from 2009 to 2015). The output is easy enough to measure in dollars and recipients. Whether it, and the rest of the Liberal agenda, has left the middle class feeling any better is more difficult to ascertain.

EKOS Research has continued to poll public opinion around the middle class, and there have been hints of a possible improvement. But only hints. In the fall of 2018, 50 percent of respondents to an EKOS survey identified themselves as "middle class," up seven points from a low of 43 percent in October 2017. Thirty-seven percent said they were better off than the previous generation was twenty-five years earlier, up four points from a low of 33 percent. The same share, 37 percent, said they expected their personal financial situation to be better in five years, the highest percentage EKOS had recorded on that question since May 2013.

Nonetheless, to the majority, the future still looked grim: 56 percent said the next generation will be worse off in twenty-five years. Granted, anyone with even a vague awareness of the science and reality of climate change would be hard-pressed to say otherwise.

The anxiety that the Liberals had focused on and aimed to address was still present. Proof of that was the fact Conservatives started talking about the same thing. Canadians were getting by, the Conservative Party began to argue in 2018, but they weren't getting ahead. Life kept getting more expensive, in part because of Liberal policies like the federal carbon price. One of Andrew Scheer's first promises was to eliminate the GST on home heating.

The Conservatives were still not talking about the "middle class" as much as the Liberals, but they were now aiming at approximately the same problem. The Liberals, if they could not match the Conservative tax cuts, would have to convince Canadians that the Trudeau government still had a better idea of what the future should look like.

CHAPTER 4

HIGH-CLASS PROBLEMS

"Here's the real problem," said Andrew Scheer, speaking to a Conservative Party convention in August 2018.

The Conservative leader had just told the story of a struggling small business owner he'd met in Fredericton. She voted Liberal in 2015, but apparently now regretted it (if she hadn't regretted it, of course, Scheer probably wouldn't have mentioned her).

"Justin Trudeau has no idea what she or any middle-class Canadian family is going through because of him," Scheer continued. "He has no concept about how to stretch a dollar. How to make it to the next payday. How to stick to a monthly budget. I'm not sure he's even seen a monthly budget. He just doesn't get it. He doesn't understand the problems Canadians face. And he can't be trusted to fix them."

Justin Trudeau, you see, had been born into privilege. This was indisputable. And that fact could be used to explain just about everything Scheer could think to criticize about Trudeau and the Liberal government—from tax policy to the budget deficit to ethics controversies. More implicitly, it was an attack on the empathy, openness and connectedness Trudeau had tried to demonstrate as a politician and prime minister. It was a suggestion that Trudeau was not a guy like you.

This was not the first time a rival of Trudeau's had tried this argument. In February 2013, during a Liberal leadership debate, Martha

Hall Findlay stood beside Trudeau and challenged him directly. "You keep referring to the middle class but you yourself have admitted you don't belong to the middle class," she told him. "I find it a little challenging to understand how you would understand the challenges facing real Canadians."

Trudeau's relative wealth was not a secret. But, days earlier, he and his team had laid out details to the *Ottawa Citizen*. His personal inheritance was worth $1.2 million at the time, and he'd done well on the public-speaking circuit, earning as much as $450,000 in one year.

So Hall Findlay took a shot. Some of the Liberals in attendance jeered. Marc Garneau, another candidate, said "financial resources" should not be reason to look down on anyone. "Let's not be petty, Canada," he said. The next day, Hall Findlay apologized.

Trudeau's subsequent policy choices—raising taxes on the top one percent of earners, replacing a universal child credit with a means-tested benefit—largely insulated him from this line of attack during the 2015 election. But Hall Findlay was really just ahead of her time. And her Conservative successors would be unapologetic.

For Scheer, it wasn't just that Trudeau had grown up with an above-average amount of wealth. It was also that Scheer hadn't. Andrew Scheer was never going to be as interesting or as compelling as the man he was seeking to displace as prime minister. But he could at least claim to be everything Trudeau was not. The Conservative leader was, for instance, fond of telling people that his family hadn't owned a car when he was growing up.

Left out of Scheer's public narrative is that he himself has done pretty well as an MP, Speaker of the House of Commons and leader of the Opposition (at the age of twenty-five, when he was first elected as an MP, his salary was $141,000). But Trudeau's greater wealth became a handy cudgel.

"Millionaire Liberals like the prime minister might not mind paying higher gas prices, but hard-working Canadian families do," Scheer told the House of Commons one day in June 2018.

"Mr. Speaker, it is funny to listen to a trust fund baby lecturing

Canadians about being too rich," Pierre Poilievre, the Conservative finance critic, remarked in February 2019. "We have a millionaire prime minister and a gazillionaire finance minister," said Poilievre, who showed a particular zeal for this line of attack.

Unfortunately for Trudeau, he and his team had helped lay the groundwork for such attacks.

———

SHORTLY AFTER CHRISTMAS IN 1977, Pierre Trudeau and his sons travelled to Jamaica for a family vacation. They took an Air Canada flight—in those days, the prime minister flew commercial—to Montego Bay and then stayed at a private beach house in the town of Ocho Rios. R.H. "Hap" MacDonald, the former RCMP inspector who was in charge of Pierre Trudeau's security at the time, later recalled that it was a "quiet, restful" holiday. But then, a day before they were scheduled to fly back, Justin came down with the chicken pox.

This presented a problem beyond a young boy's discomfort: Air Canada would not transport anyone with a contagious disease. "How will we get home?" the prime minister wondered. MacDonald informed him there was only one option: a government jet could be sent down to Jamaica to pick them up.

According to MacDonald, Trudeau hesitated, then wondered aloud what "people would think." MacDonald suggested that, given the circumstances, such complaints would reflect poorly on the complainers. But Trudeau took an hour to think it over. When he came back to MacDonald, he told him to go ahead and make the arrangements.

The Trudeaus returned to Canada without incident, and the use of the plane was not reported on. But the important point is that Pierre Trudeau paused and asked himself the question that every politician should ask themselves before doing pretty much anything: What will people think?

If that question occurred to Justin Trudeau before he and his family flew to a private island in the Bahamas just after Christmas in 2016, it was unfortunately dismissed.

From December 26, 2016, to January 4, 2017, the Trudeau family stayed as guests of the Aga Khan on Bell Island, a private island owned by the spiritual leader of the world's Ismali Muslims. The Aga Khan— Prince Shah Karim Al Hussaini—was an old friend of Pierre Trudeau and an honorary pallbearer at his funeral in 2000. Justin Trudeau and the Aga Khan reconnected after Trudeau became leader of the Liberal Party in 2013, and a standing invitation had been extended for Trudeau and his family to stay at the Aga Khan's estate on Bell Island (it would later emerge that Sophie Grégoire Trudeau and the three Trudeau children had visited the island in March 2016).

Where the prime minister was holidaying was not immediately disclosed to the public. Though Trudeau's office had adopted the practice of sending out a daily itinerary, days off were simply listed as "personal." In response to initial inquiries from reporters, his office acknowledged that the family had flown to Nassau. But then, two days after the Trudeaus returned to Canada, the *National Post* revealed they had been on the Aga Khan's private island.

That report noted both the opulence of the situation—the Aga Khan had a net worth in excess of $1 billion and had purchased the island for $100 million—and the potential conflict of interest. The Aga Khan's development network had received Canadian foreign aid, and the Aga Khan's foundation was registered to lobby the federal government. Shortly thereafter, it was also disclosed that, after flying on a government plane to Nassau, Trudeau and his family had used the Aga Khan's private helicopter to reach the island.

That helicopter ride was the clearest evidence, at least initially, that an actual wrong had been committed: the Conflict of Interest Act prohibits public office holders from travelling on "non-commercial chartered or private aircraft for any purpose unless required in his or her capacity as a public office holder or in exceptional circumstances or with the prior approval of the commissioner." A vacation probably did not meet the standard of an exceptional circumstance. And the ethics commissioner had not been informed.

"We know the prime minister violated the act in this context,"

Conservative leader Rona Ambrose charged when the House reconvened in January. "My question is simple: Why does the prime minister think that the rules do not apply to people like him?"

"People like him" was likely not an accidental turn of phrase. The point was that Justin Trudeau is not a person like you. Only later would it emerge that Rona Ambrose and her partner had spent eleven days that January on the yacht of billionaire oil financier Murray Edwards near St. Barts and St. Martin.

For Trudeau, the furor dragged on for twelve months. Each new disclosure of a cost associated with the trip prompted another round of snide references. Opposition MPs took to referring to "billionaire island" as a shorthand for the controversy.

Finally, in December 2017, the ethics commissioner came back with a ruling: Trudeau, she found, had violated three sections of the Conflict of Interest Act. He had accepted an inappropriate gift, failed to recuse himself from discussions that involved government business related to the Aga Khan and improperly used a private aircraft. The Conflict of Interest Act provides an exception that allows office holders to accept gifts from a "friend," but, in a final twist, the commissioner ruled that the relationship between the Aga Khan and Trudeau did not meet that standard.

At the news conference to respond to the commissioner's report, the prime minister noticeably struggled when a reporter wondered aloud how it hadn't occurred to him that the trip was a bad idea.

There was no suggestion the Aga Khan had received anything in exchange for his hospitality—there was no actual corruption to speak of. But that was never really the issue. The problem was that it was against the rules and, worse, it was fancy.

It was also just one of a series of affairs for the Liberals that concerned money and privilege.

Two weeks after the new government was sworn in, for instance, it emerged that Trudeau's official household staff would include two nannies. The publicly funded household budget was to remain the same, and both Brian Mulroney and Pierre Trudeau had employed nannies. But Justin Trudeau had just finished campaigning against the Conservative government's universal child care benefit on the basis that wealthy families like his didn't need the assistance.

A year later it was reported that Gerry Butts and Katie Telford had charged the government more than $200,000 in moving expenses when they and their respective families moved from Toronto to Ottawa. Both insisted they had only followed the existing procedures for such relocations, but they ultimately agreed to pay back a total of $65,000. "While the rules were clear and we followed them, we both know that's not always enough," they explained.

The Conservative opposition happily seized on those and all other hints of excess. Environment Minister Catherine McKenna spent more than $6,000 for a photographer at the Paris climate conference. Trudeau brought his in-laws to a state dinner in Washington.

Trudeau was also not shy about meeting in an official capacity with CEOs and investors to discuss how Canada might be a destination for the money they controlled. In July 2016, he went to the Sun Valley Conference in Idaho, a gathering once labelled as "summer camp for billionaires." Such an effort to woo foreign investment was likely justifiable, but the Conservatives were nonetheless happy to portray it as rarefied frivolity.

Other gatherings were less defensible. A month before Trudeau left for the Bahamas, the *Globe and Mail* broke news that the prime minister had mingled with "several Chinese billionaires" during a private fundraising event held in "the mansion of a wealthy Chinese-Canadian business executive." Attendees paid $1,500—the maximum allowable donation under federal law—to dine with Trudeau. Pictures emerged of the grinning prime minister hoisting a beverage with his hosts.

That was one of a set of stories about the participation of Liberal cabinet ministers in so-called cash-for-access events. Jody Wilson-Raybould attended a $500-per-person fundraiser that was hosted by a prominent law firm in Toronto. A handful of business executives in Halifax paid $1,500 each to be in the company of Bill Morneau.

Such events weren't illegal, but the practice was, in the words of the ethics commissioner, "not very savoury." "One asks questions about it," Mary Dawson told reporters, while explaining that party fundraising was beyond her purview. "One wonders whether indeed people are getting unfair access." It was at least difficult to square the practice with the guidelines Trudeau himself had issued to his ministers in November 2015: "There should be no preferential access to government, or appearance of preferential access, accorded to individuals or organizations because they have made financial contributions to politicians and political parties."

Finally, in the midst of questions about Trudeau's trip to Bell Island, the Liberals announced they would change their own practices and introduce new laws to regulate partisan fundraisers.

———

ASKED TO EXPLAIN HIS trip to the Aga Khan's island, Trudeau refers back to the trip he and his family took the year before.

Shortly after Christmas in 2015, the Trudeaus went to Nevis, an island in the Caribbean. TMZ, the American gossip outlet, took notice. "Canadian Prime Minister—Ballin' Out In The Caribbean," read the headline over an item that reported Trudeau had "dropped at least $2,500 a night to stay in a 3,400 square foot villa." It was eventually disclosed that the federal government spent $64,000 on accommodations for the RCMP officers who travelled with the family. The *Globe and Mail* later dispatched a travel correspondent to review the resort.

Trudeau says he thought a trip to the Aga Khan's island would be less expensive. But it also provided "actual privacy." And he'd be "staying at a friend's place."

That reference to privacy is perhaps revealing. "The perspective I see it from is knowing that he doesn't care much about luxury," says Marc Miller, the Liberal MP and close friend of Trudeau. "That's not why he goes. He goes to get away and chill and not be judged when he's chilling. That is extremely valuable and it's extremely hard to find. He finds that at Harrington Lake, he finds that with his buddies and he finds that at home. Other than that it's hard to find. You find it on an island where you have a friend who happens to be exceedingly rich."

That friendship with the Aga Khan is something Trudeau is adamant about. "I totally accept that the standards for who is considered, in a legal or objective sense, a family friend, is different," he says. "I fully accept the ethics commissioner's findings on that, but she doesn't get to tell me who my friends are. I know that the Aga Khan is a friend, a family friend."

In private, Trudeau has been known to refer to the Aga Khan as "Uncle K." But friendship only gets you so far. Even if the ethics commissioner had found a certifiable kinship, there was still the basic idea of Trudeau vacationing on the private island of a billionaire.

"It was certainly a bit of a surprise that that ended up being what it was because we're not . . . We're not fancy people," he says. Yes, he says, he grew up with a life that included meeting the Queen and flying around the world, but his father raised him to be comfortable in both a black tie and flip-flops. Sophie, he says, is more comfortable walking around the woods in jeans than wearing designer clothes.

He suggests he's had advisors warn him when something wouldn't look right. "I'm like, 'That's frustrating because that's not who I am,'" he says. "But it's about not leaving openings for people with intent to create a counter-narrative."

There would be more openings for that counter-narrative.

———

In March 2017, Bill Morneau tabled his second budget. At page 199, under the heading "A Tax System That's Fair for Middle Class Canadians," was a section on "tax planning using corporations."

"The review of federal tax expenditures highlighted a number of issues regarding tax planning strategies using private corporations, which can result in high-income individuals gaining unfair tax advantages," it was explained. These issues included "income sprinkling" among family members to lower the applied rate of income tax, the use of corporate income to make and hold investments and the conversion of corporate income into capital gains.

This was not the most riveting stuff. But here were the makings of a great drama.

From the left, Trudeau has been criticized for not going far enough to correct inequality at the top, for not doing more to reduce tax advantages that disproportionately benefit the wealthiest Canadians. The Liberals had walked away, for instance, from a campaign promise to fully tax stock-option compensation, bowing to arguments from the tech sector that going ahead would remove a measure that helped small and growing enterprises attract and retain talent.

But when the Trudeau government did go ahead with a commitment to deal with private corporations, it ably demonstrated how badly such things can go.

That section of the 2017 budget harkened back to a minor tempest from the 2015 campaign. Trudeau, asked by an interviewer in September 2015 whether the Liberals would reduce the small business tax rate, commented that "a large percentage of small businesses are actually just ways for wealthier Canadians to save on their taxes." The Conservatives, New Democrats and the Canadian Federation of Independent Business (CFIB) wailed at the aspersion cast against the proprietors of the nation's noble small businesses.

Trudeau had arguably overstated the extent of the problem. But there was a basis for what he was getting at.

"Piercing the Veil: Private Corporations and the Income of the Affluent," a study of income-tax returns led by Michael Wolfson, a former statistician with Statistics Canada, had been circulating for more than a year by then. Wolfson and his co-authors explained that, because the corporate tax rate in Canada was significantly lower than the highest personal rate, there were significant advantages to earning and holding income within a private corporation. Looking at tax returns, they found that more than half of those in the top one percent of earners were using private corporations. And when the income from those private corporations was included in personal income figures, the extent of income inequality in Canada deepened.

When the Liberal government came back to the issue in March 2017, there was little outcry. "When we put that in the budget, we thought that would make some noise," says a Liberal. "Nothing. Nobody even noticed it was there."

Four months later, Morneau summoned reporters to the National Press Theatre and announced he was releasing a discussion paper with a set of proposals to address the "loopholes" in the tax code. The "consultation document" was sixty-three pages long, with both "proposed solutions" and "possible approaches" laid out for consideration. Anyone with something to say was directed toward a government email address.

"We look forward to hearing from Canadians on these issues," said Morneau.

Once again, he was not immediately denounced. But as that summer went on, a great grumbling grew.

At the end of August, the CFIB announced that thirty-five organizations—from the Canadian Cattlemen's Association to the Ontario Association of Radiologists—had come together to form the Coalition for Small Business Tax Fairness in protest of Morneau's proposals. A group called Concerned Ontario Doctors claimed that a mass exodus of doctors would take place if the proposals were implemented. Perrin Beatty, the former Progressive Conservative minister now leading the Canadian Chamber of Commerce, claimed he'd never seen the chamber's members so worried.

"On behalf of our 109,000 members, CFIB sprang into action. We fielded hundreds of calls, surveyed our members, launched alerts and petitions, and helped share information through web posts, social media campaigns, webinars and hundreds of media interviews," Dan Kelly, president of the CFIB, later crowed. "My 400 staff at CFIB lived and breathed the file for months."

The Conservatives happily joined the parade. For the Official Opposition, the changes were not a move against the one percent, but rather an attack on neighbourhood mechanics and pizza-shop owners. Poilievre gleefully needled Morneau each afternoon in the House of Commons and later filmed himself at a restaurant in his riding, using a pizza cutter to demonstrate just how much of the pie the Trudeau government was allegedly plotting to consume.

Liberal MPs heard about it in their ridings and the caucus got antsy. When the Conservatives put forward a motion on the tax changes, one Liberal backbencher—Wayne Long, the MP for Saint John–Rothesay— defied the whip and voted against the government.

An internal review by the Finance Department, unearthed by the Canadian Press, later concluded that the consultations "provided lessons learned for the Department." Chief among these was "the need to more rapidly adjust communications strategies and messaging to effectively address misconceptions, especially those that are widely and actively diffused through well-funded public relations campaigns." In the midst of the summer recess, "misinformation was propagated, causing dissent to grow in a vacuum and balloon in late summer."

To critics, the decision to release a discussion paper in July was evidence the Liberals hoped to sneak this through. But from the department's perspective, the timing hindered the government's ability to manage the debate.

"The consultations would have benefited from additional planning for contingency scenarios," officials concluded. "Although communications plans developed in advance of the launch explicitly anticipated these developments, there was a lag in effectively responding to them. The lag may be attributed to the summer timing of the launch and corresponding availability of Government members to immediately address misconceptions and reinforce messaging."

Providing an email address for responses was apparently not enough. Morneau eventually set off on a "listening tour" in September, but by then it was too late.

The last half century of Canadian political history is strewn with tales of finance ministers who proposed tax changes and the yelling that ensued: Edgar Benson and his white paper in 1969, Allan MacEachen and the 1981 budget, Jim Flaherty's decision to tax income trusts in 2008. But the Liberals seemed unprepared for the fight, or slow to realize they were in a fight. And as the shouting got louder, they seemed incapable of countering what was being hurled at them.

There were other issues. For one thing, there was no spoonful of sugar to help the medicine go down. "There have to be winners from tax reform and Morneau has failed to show who benefits," Scott Clark, a former deputy minister at Finance, observed at the time. Flaherty's move on income trusts—a change that was also presented under the heading of "tax fairness"—is instructive. In that case, the imposition of a new tax was wrapped in a package that included three different tax breaks.

In the case of private corporations, the Liberals eventually committed to implement a previously deferred cut to the small business rate. But by then, in mid-October, it looked like the desperate gesture of a scrambling government.

At that announcement, held at a family-owned Italian restaurant in Markham, Trudeau awkwardly declined to let the finance minister step forward when a reporter attempted to ask a question of Morneau. Poilievre was delighted with the optics. "Trudeau bans Morneau from answering questions at today's Finance press conference," he tweeted. "Good move."

Bill Morneau seems like a nice man, but a natural public performer he is not. He came to politics with an indisputable record of achievement in the private sector. He helped turn his father's benefit-consulting firm, Morneau & Associates, into Morneau Shepell, a billion-dollar company with more than 4,000 employees. He is said to be a formidable figure behind closed doors, and his first three years as finance minister were highlighted by a set of significant negotiations and deals: an agreement with the provinces to expand the Canada Pension Plan, the renewal of federal-provincial health care accords and the purchase of the Trans Mountain pipeline.

"He's a tough negotiator. He knows his stuff. It was impressive watching him in action," says one provincial source who saw Morneau during the Canada Pension Plan talks. The finance minister for Saskatchewan, a province that had been reluctant to go along with the CPP expansion, later praised Morneau for doing a "a masterful job" of creating consensus.

But he is unlikely to ever win you the day in Question Period. And little victories can persuade both onlookers and your own side that it's not going so badly, particularly in times of trouble.

"He didn't get here because he's a talented politician. He brought a really good record and a list of things he wanted to do," says one Liberal official. "There was probably a period of time in the first two years where the conventions of politics kind of grated on him and he sort of thought of those as the unimportant things and theatre. And that the important things happened when he was in the boardroom with people or making decisions. And what he came away from that with was, I've got to get better at the political stuff if I'm going to be allowed to keep doing the important things I came here to do. They're both important."

The last person to become finance minister without previously holding political office was Walter Gordon in 1963. And the past thirty years at Finance have been dominated by ministers who were significant political forces: Jim Flaherty, Paul Martin and Michael Wilson. Morneau has not fit that profile, at least not outwardly. Nor did the private-corporation saga convert him into a lion of the political arena. But he might at least be slightly better prepared for the next tempest.

"I learned that—while I may have come into this life with the idea that you can get big things done in public life and bring your previous experience and hopefully your talents to make a big difference—you do need to focus on the politics of the situation and understand them and to the best of your ability respond to and manage them," Morneau says.

He says he likes dealing with constituents and enjoys giving speeches and trying to convince people that what the government is doing is wise and beneficial. He's less keen on Question Period and parliamentary hearings, with the gamesmanship and point scoring. "So you feel frustrated because you realize we all have a limited amount of time on this planet and we have only a limited amount of time in our job," he says. "But it is part of the process, so you do have to go through that. You do have to realize that's also important for people to understand what you're trying to achieve. And the fact that it's in an adversarial environment—sometimes that does bring out the stark contrasts for people to understand. So it's not all negative."

The other thing about Bill Morneau is that he's rich. He is a member of the one percent. His public earnestness seems almost to underline that fact. And as the fight over tax fairness carried on, people started poking around into Morneau's substantial wealth. And they found things.

He had disclosed to the ethics commissioner that he owned a villa in France. But he had failed, it turned out, to disclose the numbered company he'd set up to hold the ownership of that villa. The actual harm to the nation of that oversight was relatively minor. But, at that particular moment, it didn't help to remind people that the finance minister owned a villa in France.

Then it emerged he had not put his personal investments, including shares he owned in Morneau Shepell, into a blind trust. The assets were instead held by a numbered company registered in Alberta. Morneau and his office pleaded that they had consulted with the ethics commissioner and she had said it wasn't necessary in his case to establish a blind trust. But the commissioner was offering him legal advice, not political counsel. The Opposition pounced on the arrangement and then howled when they realized that Morneau had been holding those shares when he tabled legislation to reform private-sector pensions in 2016—Morneau Shepell is primarily a human resources provider, but it does offer some pension services.

Four days after the blind trust story broke, Morneau announced he would sell his shares in the family business and put the rest of his assets in a blind trust. A week later, he committed that the proceeds from the sale would be donated to charity. Undaunted, Scheer later made a great show of demanding Morneau's resignation.

In the end, the ethics commissioner ruled that Morneau's only violation of the rules for public office holders was his failure to disclose the company that owned the villa. He was duly fined the sum of $200. On the pension bill, he was cleared of a conflict of interest, though the government had effectively abandoned the legislation anyway.

A revised set of proposals to implement tax reform were eventually put forward and passed. The CFIB called the changes "less bad." Morneau said the "crowdsourcing" had worked. The government estimated that the new measures would add approximately $925 million in additional annual revenue. One might debate whether it was worth the trouble.

"I think maybe one prediction we can make, perhaps with some sort of certainty, is that he won't be the minister of finance going into the next federal election," one pollster predicted of Morneau in November 2017. "It's a no-win situation—just because of his personal financial situation—for him to be the key advocate for the middle class."

As of this writing Morneau is still the finance minister. But then perhaps the prime minister is not inclined to agree that personal wealth should be a disqualifying characteristic.

———

MORNEAU'S FOLLOW-UP TO THE private-corporation fight was unconventional: a budget built around the goal of gender equality.

There was a clear economic justification. Women's participation in the workforce had plateaued over the previous decade, and bringing women closer to parity with men would add that much more activity to the national economy. "RBC Economics estimates that if Canada had a completely equal representation of women and men in our workforce, we could have increased the size of the economy by 4 percent last year," Morneau explained.

But this was rather less stuffy than the usual budget. And in tabling it Morneau had noticeably sidestepped the corporate sector's latest demands.

In December 2017, the Trump administration and Republicans in Congress had worked together to pass a sweeping set of tax breaks for American businesses, including a cut in the corporate rate from 35 percent to 21 percent. Those cuts seemed wildly irresponsible and likely unsustainable. But Canadian business groups commenced worrying aloud about the competitiveness of the Canadian tax code and clamoured for Morneau to respond. In late February, when he tabled his budget, the finance minister was still considering his options. "It's not news to me that business is asking for lower tax rates," Morneau told reporters. "I was in business; that's a pretty common refrain."

This was about as sassy as Morneau was ever going to be. But this was also perhaps symbolic of a certain distance between the Trudeau government and the nation's C-suite residents—for as much as some on the left might find this government too friendly with business, executives might say they are underappreciated.

"Generally I'd say the business community doesn't feel any love from this government," says John Manley, the former Liberal cabinet minister who was president of the Business Council of Canada until October 2018. "They don't see themselves in the government's narrative around growth: you know, being built on the private sector. And they certainly didn't feel that the government was quick to respond to some of the challenges that got thrown at Canadian business because of the Trump tax cuts."

There is, of course, a great irony here: the Trudeau government's greatest crisis would later emerge around a question of whether it had gone too far in trying to protect a private company.

When Morneau did move to address the corporate sector's grievances, with a series of measures in the fall of 2018, he simultaneously exacerbated another potential weakness. Businesses would have access to new tax breaks, but the foregone revenue would contribute to a larger-than-projected deficit. "We could have ignored the concerns of business leaders . . . and we would have had a lower deficit as a result," Morneau said. "To do so would be neither a rational response nor a responsible one."

On the campaign trail in the summer of 2015, the responsible plan was to run three years of budget deficits—$9.9 billion, $9.5 billion and $5.7 billion—before returning to balance in 2019–20. Just two weeks after he was sworn in as Canada's thirty-ninth finance minister, Morneau announced that those numbers would have to be amended. Slower economic growth and lower oil prices had already pushed the budget into deficit, even before new spending was accounted for.

But what followed could not be entirely put down to changed circumstances. Rather, according to an analysis conducted by the Institute of Fiscal Studies and Democracy, it was the government's choices to spend on its priorities that were most responsible for the deficits that Morneau proceeded to run in successive budgets: $17.8 billion in 2016–17, $19 billion in 2017–18, $14.9 billion in 2018–19 and a projected $19.8 billion in 2019–20.

The deficit is projected to decline in subsequent years, and the Liberals can point to a declining ratio of debt-to-GDP as an indication that federal finances are ultimately sustainable. But the budget is now not expected to be balanced again until sometime after 2024.

This necessarily complicates Morneau's image as finance minister. He has presided over a growing economy: annual GDP growth was 1.4 percent, 3.0 percent and 1.8 percent in his first three years. The unemployment rate reached its lowest mark in over forty years. But going back to Paul Martin in 1995, Morneau's immediate predecessors have preached that a balanced budget is the hallmark of responsible administration. Indeed, balancing the budget in a moment of real fiscal crisis was perhaps the signature achievement of the Liberal government that held power from 1993 to 2006.

"His fundamental problem as finance minister is that people need to know that he's saying no to stuff, and it's not obvious now," says one Liberal.

Manley was given the job rather unexpectedly in the summer of 2002, when Jean Chrétien dramatically fired Martin, the deficit-slaying finance minister who was agitating for Chrétien's office. The next day, Manley was dispatched to Montreal to speak to a meeting of global bankers; afterwards, he was scrummed by an excited crowd of reporters. "It was all about, you know, Paul Martin walks on water and you don't even know how to swim—the kind of questions only you and your colleagues could ever do. And I said, 'Look, I know how to say no,'" Manley recalls. "The fundamental difficulty of being finance minister is you have to say no to your colleagues, including your boss. And we don't know what goes on behind closed doors in cabinet, but the impression that is out there is that this minister of finance has not been able to marshal the fiscal discipline that many in the business community think is necessary in good times."

Those who do know what goes on behind closed doors insist Morneau says no more often than he is given credit for. In one telling, he simply doesn't seek credit for it. "It's just he doesn't have a need to tell that story externally," says one senior Liberal. "Or to quietly seed those stories through the Hill, because he has no ambition of having the prime minister's job. And I think the city is more used to a situation where the finance minister was after the prime minister's job."

That Morneau's mind might not be finely attuned to such politics is entirely plausible.

"I say no on a very regular basis," Morneau says. "If the image is that I'm not, then that's great because that means what I'm able to do is to manage people's expectations and the outcome in a way that allows them to say, 'That got done without Bill necessarily saying no directly.'"

When Trudeau announced that he was willing to run a deficit, a stagnant economy seemed in need of a boost. On a visit to Ottawa in September 2016, Christine Lagarde, the managing director of the International Monetary Fund and a former minister of finance in France, praised the Trudeau government's commitments to infrastructure funding and gender equality and said she hoped the new Canadian approach would go "viral." "There are countries which do not have fiscal space, they should not go there," she said. "Canada does have the fiscal space."

As a matter of fiscal policy, the deficits that followed were not the end of the world. The restraint that dominated between 1995 and 2015 left the federal government in a healthy fiscal position, and successive reports by the parliamentary budget officer stated that federal finances were still sustainable. In the mid-nineties, by comparison, the federal debt-to-GDP ratio reached 67 percent. That was a crisis. By 2015— and even after a round of stimulus spending and deficits in response to the Great Recession—the ratio was 31 percent. Under Morneau's fiscal plans, it is set to decline to 28.6 percent in 2023–24.

But by 2018, it was perhaps less obvious the Liberals were pursuing a wise course. The Organisation for Economic Co-operation and Development, for instance, mused that "reducing the structural budget deficit would ease the burden on monetary policy and create more room to support the economy in the event of an unexpected downturn." The risks of a downturn were not insignificant—the American economy was perhaps running too hot for its own good, Trump's tariffs were weighing down global markets, China's economy seemed to be slowing down and the real estate markets in Toronto and Vancouver were still arguably overdue for a correction.

Even in the event of an economic shock, the federal government could afford to spend deeper into deficit without necessarily creating a real crisis. But a deficit had the potential to become a political liability sometime before then.

While choosing to forget the six annual deficits—totalling $139 billion—that the Harper Conservatives ran during and after the Great Recession, Scheer's Conservatives loudly worried about the debt that Trudeau would leave behind for future generations. In one Conservative video, a fidgety young child carrying a backpack was shown standing on the sidewalk, apparently ready for his first day of kindergarten. His name was given as Tyler. The narrator ominously lamented how much public debt was now hanging over each of Canada's five-year-olds. Tyler was said to already owe more than $17,000.

Curiously, the narrator made no mention of climate change—a far graver threat to Tyler's future than government debt. The Conservative script also didn't mention how much Tyler's parents were receiving from the Canada Child Benefit, or whether they'd be willing to return it to the receiver general to help pay off their son's share of the federal debt.

For that matter, any debate about intergenerational debt requires consideration of what the money has been spent on. Tyler might, for instance, stand to benefit if the result is a more prosperous economy or a more equal society.

But the simpler argument is recklessness. Scheer had guffawed about this in Halifax: Trudeau's probably never even seen a household budget. And now he and another rich guy, Bill Morneau, were throwing around your money with careless abandon.

However trite that narrative—a household budget and a government budget are fundamentally unalike—it had some potential to resonate. Not just because the Trudeau Liberals are running deficits, but also because they have not been unambitious in what they've put that money toward: $950 million for the formation of five "innovation superclusters" across the country, $35 billion for that new infrastructure bank.

There were no great boondoggles discovered in the first four years, but a bad investment or two could turn up in time. At which point, it would be that much easier to advance the argument that Trudeau could not be trusted with the chequebook.

A deficit, if left behind, would also be a handy excuse for some future Conservative government to make cuts, to roll back or outright eliminate initiatives that the Trudeau Liberals might have liked to see preserved. Consider that within six months of taking office in Ontario in 2018, Doug Ford's Progressive Conservative government eliminated the office of the environment commissioner, scrapped plans for a francophone university and cut funding for Indigenous education and arts programs.

Morneau says he doesn't think observers will conclude the government lacked discipline, that the conclusions instead will be that the economy did well, that the government found a way to reduce the sort of middle-class anxiety that feeds populism, and that it did so in a responsible way.

"I need to go up another level and say, Did we get the balance right for the long-term health of our country? Did we give people confidence in that long-term health? Did we create the kind of growth that we expected? Did we find a way to make people more optimistic about the outcomes for their children? And did we do it in a way that managed our balance sheet appropriately?" he says.

"I am of the view that we are going to be able to continue to manage down the debt as a function of the economy. All that you're debating is whether we should do it more aggressively, more rapidly. The response that I would have is that in the light of what we're trying to achieve, that that would actually be an irresponsible approach."

That a deficit can be responsibly run is perhaps still an open question. But oddly enough, as it pertained to the federal budget, Scheer's Conservatives would end up moving closer to the Liberal position. In 2017, when he was seeking the Conservative leadership, Scheer had said he would have the budget balanced in two years after taking office. By the spring of 2019, with a general election in sight, he decided to moderate that position. Now the Conservatives promised to balance the budget in five years.

Scheer tried to claim this had something to do with the way the Liberals had managed federal finances, but the more plausible explanation was simple politics. It is easy (and fun) to say the budget should be balanced. It is harder to say what exactly you would cut to achieve that. And so Scheer's Conservatives had decided to try to reduce the degree to which they would have to cut. Poor "Tyler" was apparently not in so much distress that the budget needed to be balanced right away.

It was, in a way, a victory for Trudeau. In 2015, his willingness to run a deficit was considered a bold and risky position. Four years later, the debate had nearly reversed and now his Conservative opponent saw risk in promising a balanced budget.

Even still, the basic debate over spending would likely persist. In 2019, the Liberals would have to again justify their willingness to spend more—this time with visions of the Aga Khan's island and a villa in France hanging over them.

———

TRUDEAU'S INHERITED WEALTH GOES back to his grandfather, Charles-Émile Trudeau. Charles-Émile was a lawyer and a successful entrepreneur who owned a number of gas stations and an automobile servicing program. In 1932, he sold that business to a subsidiary of Imperial Oil for a million dollars. Pierre Trudeau grew up with the resulting advantages—a chauffeur often drove him to school—and questions about his privilege and upbringing followed him into politics.

"I don't judge a man's idea or his performance by the size of his pocketbook. I look at what he does, what he produces," he told an interviewer who asked about it in 1972. "And I ask that we judge our political leaders by that."

Four years later, with inflation rising and Trudeau implementing wage and price controls, he was again confronted about his wealth. "A lot of Canadians don't think you understand them because you are privileged yourself, you are secure yourself," the CBC's Barbara Frum told him during an interview. "That's a very isolating thing for a hard time." Trudeau responded that all prime ministers were secure in some sense. "But what you call isolated," he continued, "do you know any prime minister who has travelled more than I in the country, and met more groups more often?"

Afterwards, off camera, Trudeau incredulously asked Frum why she had pursued this line of inquiry. Around the time of that interview, coincidentally, there was some grumbling about the fact Pierre Trudeau had been vacationing on the Aga Khan's yacht.

Intellectually, it must be understood that Pierre Trudeau had a valid point: a political leader should be judged on his policies, not his pocketbook. But then Pierre Trudeau also surely understood the power of narrative, image and simple explanations.

For Justin Trudeau, the challenge is even greater. There is no getting away from the facts of his life because nearly all of it has been lived in public. And the facts are that he has led a unique and privileged life. That lifelong celebrity is inherent to his political career. His upbringing and his story were some of his greatest advantages in entering politics. But those same things also serve to remind that he is not like most people. So he can wade into crowds and take questions in community centres and university gymnasiums, he can talk about the middle class and pursue an agenda that focuses on inequality, but he is also still Justin Trudeau.

The worst thing a politician can be is "out of touch." And proving you aren't becomes harder the longer you are in power. Maybe no other prime minister has ever had quite the relationship with the public that

Justin Trudeau has had. And maybe few have ever been more front and centre with the public on a day-to-day basis. But rarely, if ever, has it been easier to frame a prime minister as someone who stands apart from the average voter.

That is a counter-narrative with which Trudeau is still contending.

CHAPTER 5

DONALD TRUMP MOVES IN NEXT DOOR

In late August 2016, David MacNaughton, Trudeau's ambassador to Washington, travelled to Sudbury to brief the cabinet during a two-day retreat ahead of the fall sitting of Parliament.

Entering that third week of August, Hillary Clinton had a six-point lead over Donald Trump in national polls. One projection gave her an 84.7 percent chance of winning the election. Odds were that Hillary Clinton was going to become the forty-fifth president of the United States. But those odds still meant Trump had a one-in-six chance.

"All of the smart people in Washington were saying the Democrats were going to win the House, the Republicans would retain the Senate and Hillary Clinton would win the election," MacNaughton recalls telling cabinet. "And I qualified it by saying, all of the smart people in Washington have been consistently wrong for eighteen months, so don't count on it. And that we need to be prepared for any eventuality."

MacNaughton had only just become ambassador in March, and Conservatives had harrumphed at his appointment. Stephen Harper's ambassador was Gary Doer, a former NDP premier in Manitoba. MacNaughton was a long-time Liberal insider and advisor. He was a friend and mentor to Trudeau's top two advisors: Gerry Butts had worked for MacNaughton in Dalton McGuinty's office, and MacNaughton was chairman of Strate-gyCorp when the prominent Toronto consulting firm hired Katie Telford in 2009. MacNaughton had also co-chaired the federal Liberal campaign in Ontario in 2015.

His assignment to Washington was thus criticized by the Opposition as a "reward" for a friend. One Conservative MP said it was as if Trudeau was "appointing a family member." But that was also the best argument for sending MacNaughton: American officials would know that when they spoke to MacNaughton they were speaking to someone who was connected to Trudeau's inner circle.

Any notion that "Canadian ambassador to Washington" was much of a reward would also soon be erased.

Chrystia Freeland, minister of international trade at the time, was prompted by MacNaughton's warnings to ask her department's trade officials to prepare a briefing note that covered the various scenarios for NAFTA, keeping in mind that Trump was talking about withdrawing completely from the deal. She had that note in hand, several months later, when Trudeau convened a cabinet meeting to discuss the U.S. election result.

No matter who became president, the Trudeau government was likely going to have to worry about NAFTA, the twenty-four-year-old deal that governed the movement of goods between Canada, the United States and Mexico. Free trade between Canada and the United States goes back even further, to the bilateral agreement signed by Brian Mulroney and George H.W. Bush in 1988. But trade had become a convenient scapegoat, particularly when American political leaders needed something to blame for the loss of manufacturing jobs across a swath of politically important states. There was, says MacNaughton, an "underlying attitude of protectionism that was coming up in American politics, not just from Republicans, but also Democrats."

Though Clinton did not match Trump's blustery denunciations, she had also pledged to renegotiate NAFTA, a deal her husband signed as president. In fact, her position on that was long-standing: she'd first called for it to be renegotiated when she ran for president in 2008.

Clinton had also recently decided to oppose the Trans-Pacific Partnership, after supporting it when she was Barack Obama's secretary of state.

"It's true that too often, past trade deals have been sold to the American people with rosy scenarios that did not pan out," Clinton said during a speech delivered a week and a half before MacNaughton briefed the Trudeau cabinet. "But the answer is not to rant and rave—or cut ourselves off from the world. That would end up killing even more jobs. The answer is to finally make trade work for us, not against us."

Had Clinton become president, there likely would have been less ranting. But there still might have been some kind of renegotiation.

In October, MacNaughton had dinner with a group of American labour leaders. They told MacNaughton they were all supporting Clinton, but their members were leaning toward Trump. This was a hint of what was about to unfold.

On November 8, Election Day, Clinton remained the heavy favourite, though perhaps not quite as heavily as she had been in August. Sources in the Democratic Party had given Trudeau's team reason to believe Clinton would win. Butts recalls reviewing drafts of the official statements that would be released in the event of a Clinton or Trump victory and thinking to himself that the latter would be a remarkable artifact of alternate history. But there was still some sense that a Trump victory was not entirely implausible.

"I'm not going to pretend that we fully expected and predicted Donald Trump would win. I don't think anybody really did. But we were not surprised by it, at the same time," says Brian Clow, who would move to the Prime Minister's Office to lead a small team dedicated to overseeing Canada-U.S. affairs. Within Clow's sparsely decorated office would hang an illustration of the globe that depicted just the United States, as if all other countries had disappeared.

That night, Trudeau and several of his senior advisors watched coverage of the results on the projection television in the basement of Rideau Cottage, the nineteenth-century brick house located on the grounds of Rideau Hall that the Trudeau family had moved into after the 2015 election. They sat around, ate chips and watched the world change.

The *New York Times* had created a live probability dial that was updating constantly as votes were counted across the United States, and Trudeau watched as the needle moved in Trump's favour. Trump's chances hit 80 percent, then 90 percent. If it was going to swing back, Trudeau thought, it would have to do so soon. Sometime after 9 p.m., the vote in Florida started to solidify for Trump. Butts remembers that for a few minutes no one spoke. Then someone called it: "This thing is over."

The prime minister called it a night shortly thereafter. He awoke at 2 a.m. and checked his phone. The result was the same. "It was like, 'Okay, this is going to be an interesting challenge,'" Trudeau says.

About an hour later, Trump walked onto a stage in New York to accept his victory. "I want to tell the world community that while we will always put America's interests first, we will deal fairly with everyone—all people and all other nations," he said. "We will seek common ground, not hostility; partnership, not conflict."

Did Trudeau and his team realize then how much was about to change? "I don't think any person could have realized quite how much everything was going to change and is changing, in terms of global ramifications," says Telford. "Having said that, there was no doubt that this was going to be an entirely different experience than we had had with Obama and predecessors."

The next day, Trudeau was scheduled to appear at WE Day, a travelling pep rally for social change that packs thousands of do-gooding teenagers into an arena for a day of inspirational speeches and performances by famous and impressive people. Trudeau bounded onstage to the sound of Justin Timberlake's "Can't Stop the Feeling!" There were delighted screams from the audience. He encouraged the young people in attendance to think of themselves as the leaders of today, and he told them that what they did mattered.

Then he awkwardly segued to the issue that was now hanging over everything.

"I know that a number of you probably stayed up a little later last night to watch some of the election returns with your families," he said. There was a murmur in the crowd, some laughter and a smattering of boos.

"And I know that some of you might have questions for your parents this morning. So I want to take a minute to chat with you a bit about that."

It was as if Trudeau wanted to talk to everyone about a scary movie they'd all just watched.

"First of all, the relationship between Canada and the United States is based on shared values and shared hopes and dreams, and we will always work well together," he said. "We are strong because we listen to each other and we respect each other."

This was perhaps as close as he could get to telling everyone it was going to be okay.

"And the fact is we've heard clearly from Canadians and from Americans that people want a fair shot at success," Trudeau continued, apparently trying to draw a link between his election and Trump's. "People want to succeed. People want to know that themselves, that their families, that their kids, that their grandkids will be able to succeed. And we need to work together to get that. We share a purpose, our two countries, where we want to build places where the middle class and those working hard to join it have a chance . . . We're going to keep working with people right around the world. We're going to work with our neighbours. And I'm going to work with president-elect Trump's administration as we move forward in a positive way, not just for Canadians and Americans, but the whole world."

This would be the basic tone for Trudeau and his government: diplomatic, positive and focused on economic imperatives. It followed from an approach the Liberals had adopted during the presidential campaign.

At regular intervals over the preceding months, Trudeau had been asked to comment on whatever the Republican candidate had most recently said or done, and on the prospect of dealing with Trump as president. Six weeks after he was sworn in as prime minister, Trudeau responded fairly aggressively when asked at a forum organized by *Maclean's* whether he would condemn Trump's "hateful rhetoric"—"I don't think it comes as a surprise to anyone that I stand firmly against the politics of division, the politics of fear, the politics of intolerance or hateful rhetoric," he said—but otherwise Trudeau was restrained. And even when he did have something pointed to say—about, say, the treatment of women or religious minorities—he typically did so without directly criticizing Trump. "There was a discipline that I imposed on myself early," Trudeau says.

"Ambassador MacNaughton was very big on spreading the message internally," says Clow. "We were not going to get involved, we were not going to opine and we were going to work constructively with whoever was elected."

"We shut down any criticism of him during the campaign and subsequently," MacNaughton says. "Ministers were under pretty strict orders. There was nothing wrong with having policy differences. But it couldn't get personal. Because if it got personal, you knew what the reaction was going to be."

It was decided that MacNaughton would be the primary spokesman in the first twenty-four hours after the U.S. election result, and in those initial media appearances the ambassador made clear that Canada was willing to renegotiate NAFTA. Later, this would be criticized by Conservatives as an unnecessary invitation, as if Trump might've forgotten to bother with Canada if MacNaughton hadn't put his hand up. MacNaughton says he thought there was no point denying reality and that he hoped to get ahead of any move Trump might make to unilaterally pull out of the agreement. "The notion that somehow or other the status quo was going to continue to exist and that if we just ragged the puck that somehow or other we'd end up with a better result—I was just never convinced of it," he says.

The prime minister and the president-elect spoke for the first time, by phone, on the evening of November 9. "My initial strategy was to ensure that we had a genuine, human interaction," Trudeau says. "That there was a person-to-person relationship."

Trudeau and Trump have come to represent diametrically opposing views of the world and the future. But Trudeau looked for things they had in common. "The big hook for me was growth for the middle class and Make America Great Again both had an underpinning similarity in the goal of saying, look, let's create economic growth that actually works for people who don't feel it's worked for them recently," he says, though he stresses that their answers to that problem were very different.

In their early conversations, Trump was enthusiastic about his success in the presidential election. Trudeau could remember the rush that followed his win in 2015 and talked about how he too had been discounted and come from behind to win and how the media was "challenging" for him too. "I looked for commonalities in conversations that weren't disingenuous, that were actually genuine," Trudeau says, "and it allowed for finding of common ground with someone with whom, obviously, there are a lot of things I disagree on in pretty important ways."

In theory, Trudeau says, such relationship-building means things won't turn personal when there are inevitable disagreements. "One of the easy ones is to say, 'Look Donald'—and I'll say this with any number of leaders—'you have that position. My job is to look out for my folks and therefore I have this position.' I'm going to state firmly my position, but there's an understanding; if you have a personal relationship it becomes harder to then make it personal in a negative way . . . That human interaction does count for something."

Trudeau says this during a conversation in late September 2018, three months removed from Charlevoix and the tweets. But Trudeau says he and Trump just recently had a cordial conversation. They talked about their wives possibly getting together, and about Trudeau's mother, who Trump had once seen, years ago, at Studio 54.

But on November 9, 2016, Trudeau and his advisors were largely bereft of acquaintances in what was to become the Trump administration; perhaps unsurprisingly, the two teams did not travel in the same social circles. Efforts to connect began in earnest.

Freeland had friends in New York who were friends with Jared Kushner, the husband of Ivanka Trump. Kushner, previously known for managing the New York real estate company his father founded and owning the *New York Observer*, had assisted the Trump campaign during the presidential election and would soon join the White House as a senior advisor. Through her friends, Freeland connected with Kushner and set up a meeting.

On December 7, Freeland and Telford sat down with Kushner at 666 Fifth Avenue, the office tower in midtown Manhattan that the Kushner family had purchased in 2007 for $1.8 billion. It apparently went well: during the meeting, Kushner called Wilbur Ross, the future secretary of commerce, and enthused, "You've got to meet these guys; you're going to love these guys." Freeland, coincidentally, also knew Ross, having interviewed him several times when she was a journalist in New York.

Freeland and Telford went back to New York on December 13 to meet with Peter Navarro—future director of the Office of Trade and Manufacturing Policy and an economist known for his concerns about China—as well as another Trump advisor, Jason Greenblatt. On December 22, they met with Navarro, Greenblatt and Ross. Around Christmas, Telford and Kushner were on the phone when Telford mentioned she had an idea about doing something on the theme of women in business for Trudeau's first visit to the White House and wanted to talk to Ivanka about it. Kushner put the call on speakerphone so "Iva" and Telford could chat. Then it was back to New York on January 3, this time so Freeland, Telford and Butts could meet with Kushner and Steve Bannon, the populist impresario who guided Trump's campaign after nurturing a far-right audience at Breitbart, a conservative media site.

As the members of Trudeau's team sought to pair up with their counterparts in the Trump administration, Butts and Bannon became the most curious pairing: possibly more dissimilar than even Trudeau and Trump, in any other situation they likely would have been dedicated to crushing the other's agenda. "We give Gerry a hard time about his relationship with Bannon," MacNaughton jokes.

In August 2017, a report in the *New Yorker* suggested that Bannon and Butts had become "friends," and that Bannon, with Trudeau's example in mind, was pushing Trump to raise taxes on the wealthiest Americans. NDP leader Tom Mulcair, having previously described Donald Trump as a "fascist," promptly declared that Trudeau's "closest friend and advisor must immediately disavow any friendship he has with Steve Bannon." That there was ever a "friendship" is debatable, but the question was also soon moot. Three days after the *New Yorker* story, Bannon was out of the White House.

The Telford-Kushner relationship, however, became one of the most enduring and crucial points of contact between the Trudeau government and the Trump administration—not least because everyone else kept changing. "We have this joke around here," MacNaughton says. "I had dinner with Rex Tillerson before Christmas last year. And then he got fired. Then we had H.R. McMaster and his wife over for dinner. And then he gets fired. And so everybody's suggesting to me I should have Peter Navarro over for dinner."

But Kushner was family. So he stuck around and he and Telford developed a rapport and a comfort in challenging each other. Their conversations have gone beyond NAFTA to include topics like the Middle East and the opioid epidemic. They worked together on the successful joint bid by Canada, the United States and Mexico to host the FIFA World Cup in 2026.

The Trudeau government's much-celebrated campaign to reach out beyond the White House, to get in front of every member of Congress and governor who would take a meeting, began to come together over the holiday break in 2016. "We essentially need to become lobbyists in the United States," Clow says, recalling the basic premise. "Knocking on peoples' doors, promoting Canada's interests, correcting facts, finding allies."

Canada had been appealing to Americans as a friend, neighbour and partner, MacNaughton says, but that message had to sharpen. "It was kind of 'Aren't we nice people and don't you think you should be nice to us?' While it created a general sense of goodwill, it wasn't worth anything when we really got to the crunch. The Obama administration was really friendly to us, but at the end of the day they didn't do anything for us on softwood lumber," he says. "What we really needed to do, if we were going to get through all of the stuff that was coming, regardless of who won, was to do a better job of making sure that the

Americans—not just politicians in Washington, but people across the country, business, labour leaders, everything else—understood the degree to which their prosperity depended, at least in part, on trading with Canada. That we were their biggest customer and all this kind of stuff. And what I realized was, there really weren't many people who understood that."

In the meantime, Trudeau made the first significant shuffle of his cabinet.

Stéphane Dion had been his initial pick for Foreign Affairs. A case could have been made for Freeland, but Trudeau didn't think her French was strong enough. And anyway, he wanted Dion for the job. It was a remarkable turnaround for Dion, from the ignominy of defeat in 2008 to foreign affairs minister in the government that finally replaced Stephen Harper. But it was not always the most elegant fit. Dion struggled to explain why the federal government was going ahead with a previously agreed-to contract to sell light armoured vehicles to Saudi Arabia. He quoted Max Weber, the nineteenth-century German philosopher, and championed a foreign affairs vision he called "responsible conviction." One of Dion's advisors, Jocelyn Coulon, would later write a book that ripped into Trudeau's treatment of Dion and the prime minister's handling of foreign affairs.

In 2015, Dion had been an inspired pick. In 2016, the Trudeau government was faced with Donald Trump. And waiting in the wings was Freeland. She had worked for several years in New York, was well known in American media circles and had made a name for herself as a chronicler of the rich and powerful. She already chaired the cabinet's internal committee on Canada-U.S. relations and, as trade minister, she had pushed the Canada-Europe agreement to completion. She had also spent the last year working on her French.

She was already a prominent symbol of the Trudeau era. A cosmopolitan journalist and author, born in rural Alberta to a Ukrainian immigrant and now residing in downtown Toronto, she spoke five languages and was fascinated with the issue of income inequality. She was the first star candidate that Trudeau, Butts and Telford had successfully recruited—the first evidence that smart and talented people with any number of other career options were willing to work with and for Trudeau. She was ambitious and successful and a woman. She even wore red a lot.

Setting aside the notable examples of ministers who deserted him, Trudeau tended to stick with his ministers. Of the thirty ministers he chose in November 2015, twenty-four were still in cabinet at the start of 2019, thirteen of them in the same job. But Dion would not be among them. Nine days before Trump was inaugurated, Freeland was made foreign affairs minister with responsibility for Canada-U.S. trade. Dion was awkwardly shuffled to a diplomatic posting in Europe.

"Quite frankly there probably isn't a day that goes by where I don't thank my lucky stars for having been able to convince her to leave her great job in New York to run in an uncertain by-election where I couldn't even guarantee she was going to win the nomination, and then come to sit with the third party in the House," Trudeau says now. "Because she was the kind of person I knew Canada needed serving within Parliament and hopefully serving within government, if we were able to form that. She is exactly the right person to do what she's doing."

There were close to ten meetings between Canadian and American officials through the middle of January 2017, but all such interactions were announced only after the fact, part of a plan to keep things low-key at the outset of the budding relationship. There was, at one point, a suggestion from the Americans that perhaps a new agreement on NAFTA could be settled within two weeks of Trump's inauguration. That turned out to not be feasible. It also would have required the Canadians to accept a number of undesirable demands.

Stephen Schwarzman, the billionaire chairman and CEO of Blackstone Group and a friend of Trump's, was invited to Calgary to speak with the Trudeau cabinet in late January. "There may be some modifications, but, basically, things should go well for Canada in terms of any discussions with the United States," Schwarzman told reporters.

That prediction wasn't entirely wrong, even if it vastly understated the breadth and depth of the drama that would play out over the next twenty-one months.

On the morning of February 13, 2017, Trudeau and his top advisors flew to Washington for a highly anticipated state visit. Upon arrival, the Canadians noticed the White House looked different than the last time they'd been there: there were televisions everywhere, all turned on and tuned to cable news. The images often distracted whomever they were trying to talk to.

In meeting the new family next door, the Canadian delegation displayed a remarkable attention to detail.

During their first phone conversation in November, Trump had told Trudeau about meeting his father at a dinner in 1981. Trudeau was unaware of any such meeting, but his office tracked down a black-and-white photo from the event: Pierre Trudeau, in a tuxedo and bow tie, seated as Trump speaks to a ballroom crowd at New York's Waldorf Astoria. A copy of that picture was put in a silver frame and presented to Trump upon Trudeau's arrival at the White House. Trudeau signed the White House guest book with a quote from Ronald Reagan, the fabled Republican who first promised to make America great again; he then invoked Winston Churchill, one of Trump's favourite historical figures, in his prepared remarks to reporters. Trump and Trudeau also sat down to inaugurate the Canada–United States Council for Advancement of Women Entrepreneurs and Business Leaders—the ultimate result of that conversation between Telford and Ivanka two months earlier.

During the news conference, Trudeau seemed to score a small victory when Trump publicly stated that the U.S. trade arrangement with Canada needed only "tweaking." "It's a much less severe situation than what's taking place on the southern border," Trump said. Trudeau also managed to sidestep the inevitable question about how he and the president differed, in this case about resettling refugees from Syria. "The last thing Canadians expect is for me to come down and lecture another country on how they choose to govern themselves," Trudeau said. "My role and our responsibility is to continue to govern in such a way that reflects Canadians' approach and be a positive example in the world."

Possibly none of this mattered as much as the handshake.

Trump had displayed a habit of yanking his acquaintances forward when shaking their hands, an act of physical dominance that made the other man look weaker. A week before Trudeau visited, Trump had rag-dolled Japanese prime minister Shinzō Abe's arm and patted his hand during an unnecessarily long grip-and-grin for cameras in the Oval Office. These handshakes had become a point of media fascination. And so the customary greeting of two world leaders could not go unaccounted for as Trudeau and his team prepared for the visit.

"Gerry's line to me was, think of the physicality of it," Trudeau says. The basic idea was to stay on balance. It was a topic of discussion on the flight to Washington, Trudeau recalls. "It's sort of silly that we do that but . . ."

But, of course, it mattered. If Trump had yanked Trudeau around, the image of the prime minister being physically dominated would have played on an endless loop of news clips, Facebook videos and Conservative attack ads. As it was, CBC's *The National* still devoted a segment that night to Trudeau's successful completion of two handshakes with Trump—in the first, Trudeau braced himself with his left hand on Trump's right shoulder—while international media scrutinized the prime minister's technique. "This is a great moment for the prime minister. He meets Trump, facing him directly. He is facing his bellybutton directly toward the president," a body language expert later told the *New York Times*. "He gives the perception he is ready and an equal to Trump."

"There wasn't a huge strategy around it," Trudeau says. "It was just, okay, this might be a thing, so let's make sure it's not a thing."

Even if it wasn't a thing, it was something. In terms of public perception, Dan Arnold, the director of research, singles it out as one of the most important moments of the first few years. "When Trump was first elected we heard a lot in focus groups of attitudes along the lines of, 'I like Justin, he's a good guy, but Trump is going to walk over him. Trump's like this tough negotiator, he's just going to bully Trudeau into taking a bad deal, or it's not going to work out very well for us,'" Arnold says.

Kevin O'Leary, the television pitchman who briefly showed interest in being the next leader of the Conservative Party, liked to say that Trudeau going up against Trump was like Bambi versus Godzilla.

But Arnold says there was a noticeable change after the trip. "There was this one woman in the Winnipeg groups we were doing right afterwards, when the moderator brought up Canada-U.S. relations, she got all excited and said, 'Oh yeah, the prime minister went down to D.C. and he shook Trump's hand and Trump tried to pull his hand in, but he held his ground and he looked Trump in the eye and said, you're not going to pull Canada around.' She had read this from his facial expression and clenched jaw, I guess. Since then, whenever you've asked how the PM is handling Trump and dealing with Canada-U.S. relations, it was always his strongest attribute, across the board."

As the prime minister's plane flew back to Ottawa, the most remarkable aspect of the day was how relatively unremarkable it had been. Nothing particularly crazy had happened. In the Trump era, this was unusual.

———

EVEN STILL, the chaos was not far away. During lunch at the White House, the Canadians watched Steve Bannon walk over to where Michael Flynn, Trump's national security advisor, was sitting. The two walked out of the room together, but only Bannon returned. That night, after Trudeau had departed, the White House announced Flynn's resignation, a result of providing "incomplete information" to the White House about his interactions with the Russian ambassador. Nine months later, Flynn pleaded guilty to lying to the FBI and agreed to co-operate with the special prosecutor's investigation of Russian interference in the 2016 presidential campaign.

A month after the White House visit, Trudeau went to New York and Ivanka Trump was Canada's guest at a special performance of *Come from Away*, the Canadian musical that celebrated how the people of Newfoundland had taken in stranded Americans after the terrorist attacks of September 11, 2001. As with the women's business council, it was hard to tell whether the Canadians were being smartly charming, overly nice or quietly subversive. The *New York Times* led with the irony: "Prime Minister Justin Trudeau of Canada, whose emphasis on welcoming refugees has been at odds with the harsher stance of the Trump administration, on Wednesday night brought Ivanka Trump to a Broadway show that celebrates generosity toward foreigners in need."

Trump, a man accused by multiple women of committing sexual misconduct, was also able to boast of establishing the women's council when he spoke to a joint session of Congress in February. But the work of the council was also referenced extensively in the budget that the Trudeau government tabled two years later. "It was a tangible thing that did well," Trudeau says.

Of the possibility of "normalizing" Trump—the underlying threat that his presidency would distort the standards of acceptable behaviour—Trudeau says he thinks he struck a justifiable balance. The citizens of the United States elected Donald Trump as their president. As prime minister of Canada, it is Trudeau's responsibility to work with whoever is president to protect the economic well-being and security of Canadians. At the same time, he says, he has publicly expressed his "concerns around populism, around the politics of fear, the politics of anger." "I haven't made it personal, right?" he says. "But I have said there are trendlines that I think we can all see that are worrisome in democracy."

He thinks the path he chose is justified, but he concedes that other leaders might be able to justify a different approach. He thinks Canadians understand that it's a balancing act. He also believes it might have been even harder for his predecessor. "In a certain sense, there was a context that I was aware of where Mr. Harper or a right-wing conservative prime minister might have to be careful about distancing themselves from a Donald Trump," Trudeau suggests. "I don't think anyone suspected that the fact that I was able to have a constructive relationship with Donald Trump meant that I was suddenly going to weaken on a whole bunch of my progressive ideals."

Ideally, the Trudeau government might have also succeeded in moving Trump toward some of those progressive ideals, if even just a little bit. Some effort, for instance, was apparently expended trying to convince the Trump administration that the United States should remain in the Paris Agreement on climate change. Subsequent reporting suggested Kushner and Ivanka were also pushing Trump to stay in. But, in the end, Trump announced that the United States would withdraw. Trudeau allowed himself to say that he was "deeply disappointed" with the decision, and pledge to work with state governors who were committed to combating climate change.

=====

BEGINNING IN MARCH 2017, the United States experienced an invasion across its northern border unlike anything since 1812. The foreign agents came bearing colourful pamphlets featuring trade statistics. "Canada & the U.S. trade an average of $1.3 million in bilateral goods & services every minute of every day," the Americans were informed. The attention of officials in Indiana was drawn to the fact that businesses in that state purchased $418 million worth of engines and turbines from Canada. The people of Wisconsin were reminded that Canadians buy $402 million of their plastic products.

This was the campaign to reach out beyond Trump and beyond Washington to make the case for continued free trade between Canada and the United States.

In the initial stage, eleven states were targeted, selected for their economic and political significance: Wisconsin, Michigan, Ohio, Pennsylvania, Indiana, Kentucky, Iowa, New York, Texas, California and Florida. At least one minister was assigned to each, some for particular reasons. Marc Garneau, the former astronaut, was sent to Florida. François-Philippe Champagne had studied law at Case Western Reserve University in Cleveland, so he was dispatched to Ohio.

Meanwhile, cabinet ministers also reached out to their counterparts and MacNaughton set about chatting up senators, members of Congress and governors. "I can tell you that the fact that I follow college football and pro football and every sport imaginable and fish and hunt makes a difference with them," the ambassador says. "Because they love to talk about it and it's a great icebreaker."

Catherine McKenna spent a lot of time talking about baseball, but got nowhere with Scott Pruitt, Trump's choice to lead the Environmental Protection Agency. Other ministers were more successful building relationships: Finance Minister Bill Morneau with Treasury Secretary Steve Mnuchin, Defence Minister Harjit Sajjan with Defense Secretary Jim Mattis, Agriculture Minister Lawrence MacAulay with Agriculture Secretary Sonny Perdue.

Labour Minister Patty Hajdu got on with Labor Secretary Alexander Acosta after finding her own way to break the ice. "It was the very first time we met. I actually kind of pushed him a little and I think he liked it," she recounts. "He was telling me that the ultimate thing that Americans value is freedom, because I was talking about equity and he was talking about freedom. And I said, 'Well, I get it. But do you think that everyone has the same access to freedom in your country or in mine?' He stopped and he thought about it and he just started laughing. And from that moment on we had a really good relationship where he would be super-honest with me about things and I would be able to push him a little."

"People referred to it as a charm offensive, and I always thought that was a bit of a misnomer," MacNaughton says. "I mean, there's no question that we did try to make sure that there were relationships with the new administration, right from the outset, but the real focus of it was to try to make sure that they understand that at least a portion of their prosperity depended on having a good trading relationship with us."

Consider, for instance, the pitch that Ralph Goodale, the minister of public safety, made to the Kentucky chamber of commerce during a trip to the state in January 2018.

Goodale talked a fair bit about basketball. His mother's family was from Bushnell, Illinois, and Goodale recalled that his cousins were basketball fanatics. In his youth, Goodale had delighted in reminding them that the inventor of basketball was from Canada. The people of Kentucky also liked their basketball, Goodale noted, and the new American ambassador to Canada, Kelly Craft, was a big fan of the University of Kentucky's men's basketball team. Drake, the "Canadian entertainer," was also a fan. One of the team's recent stars, Jamal Murray, was from Canada. And the coach of the Toronto Raptors, Dwane Casey, had also played at Kentucky.

"All of this might be dismissed as mere trivia. But it's really more than that," Goodale said. "It's a tiny fraction of the mountain of evidence that you find just about everywhere of deep, intricate interconnections between Americans and Canadians in so many dimensions of our lives—in sports, entertainment, family life, business, security, defence, diplomacy . . . and our common values of freedom and democracy."

Rarely, if ever, has American college basketball been framed as a more powerful metaphor. The minister's speechwriters had outdone themselves.

Eventually, Goodale got down to business. "For the Commonwealth of Kentucky, and more than thirty other states, Canada is your number one customer, bar none," he said. "Two-way trade in goods between Canada and Kentucky is valued at $10.9 billion per year. And your exports to us account for nearly 70 percent of that total—$7.5 billion— that's a trade advantage in goods in your favour of more than two-to-one. Plus, there's another $400 million in Kentucky services exported to Canada. Many thousands of Kentuckians enjoy a comfortable life because of a good job here that could conceivably not exist without those trade and investment links with Canada."

He went on. Canadian companies employed 9,500 people in the state, and 113,000 jobs were dependent on trade with Canada. Canadians bought cars and trucks manufactured in Kentucky. They ate ketchup and drank booze that originated there. "Canadians are indeed developing a growing thirst for good Kentucky bourbon, just as you are becoming more fond of Canadian rye," he said.

He thanked the Kentucky business community for joining with other chambers to write a letter to Trump to stress the importance of trade between the two countries. He noted that nearly eighty groups involved in food and agriculture had written a similar letter to Wilbur Ross and urged them to "renew and amplify your message—to promote the exemplary, lucrative, sustainable and vital economic relationship between

Canada and Kentucky and to avoid a trade disruption or roll-back that would hurt Kentucky's economy and cost many middle-class jobs."

The campaign in the United States was matched by efforts to piece together a united front at home. Brian Mulroney, the Progressive Conservative prime minister who led Canada into the original trade deals with the United States and Mexico, was invited to address cabinet. Freeland put together a bipartisan advisory council that included two former members of Stephen Harper's cabinet (Rona Ambrose and James Moore), a former advisor to the late NDP leader Jack Layton (Brian Topp), the national chief of the Assembly of First Nations (Perry Bellegarde) and the president of the Canadian Labour Congress (Hassan Yussuff).

Jerry Dias, the president of Unifor, the largest private-sector union in Canada, offered to help and had lunch with Freeland and Steve Verheul, Canada's lead negotiator, to discuss what he could do. "It was decided that it made more sense for me to be as a part of the team, but basically on the outside throwing the grenades that they couldn't . . . delivering some of the messages that they couldn't say publicly," Dias says.

Dias became a source of running commentary, filling up news reports with his blunt assessments and defiance. "If the United States thinks they can walk in and just say 'here's what we want,' and somehow everybody's going to bow down and say 'yes sir, thank you very much'—not going to happen," he said in July 2017.

In October 2017, Trudeau went to Washington and met with members of the House Ways and Means Committee. Afterwards, Clow asked a member of the committee's staff what good had come from such a meeting. "I said, 'Honestly, did it matter?' Like, 'What did the prime minister's appearance mean for all of this?'" Clow recalls. "She said, 'Brian, the thing that you got out of that was the opportunity for me to have the attention of my members for an hour ahead of time and brief them on what was happening in NAFTA and what the administration was doing.'" That was perhaps sixty minutes more than some members of Congress might have otherwise spent thinking about Canada.

The Trump administration did not always appreciate these efforts.

Robert Lighthizer, the U.S. trade representative, privately complained to Freeland, asking her how she'd feel if he was making trips to Canada to lobby other politicians there. Late in the NAFTA renegotiations, Republican congressman Kevin Cramer of North Dakota, a Trump ally, publicly expressed discomfort with the outreach. "The Canadian government tried to utilize relationships to—I don't want to say undermine, necessarily . . . but at least to leverage the relationships," Cramer told Politico. "I became uncomfortable rather quickly with the notion that somehow, while I don't like tariffs for example or aggressively pursuing this, I was never interested in undermining the president's leveraging once he chose his strategy."

To some extent, Lighthizer had a point. There would have been outcry if it emerged American officials were lobbying premiers or the Conservative opposition. But the American system of government is also fundamentally different: Congress is a co-equal branch of government, with the power to approve or reject international trade agreements. "To ignore the body that has the constitutional role to set tariffs and taxes would be kind of stupid," MacNaughton says.

Lighthizer's complaint also ignores the basic power imbalance. Pierre Trudeau famously said that Canada's proximity to the United States was like a mouse sleeping beside an elephant. Canadian lobbying around NAFTA was like the mouse reaching out to the elephant's friends to explain why the restless elephant should be careful to avoid thrashing around so much that the mouse ends up squished.

"My view on that was whenever they raised it with us, we just had to do more of it because it was obviously having an impact," MacNaughton says. "I mean, you don't raise things like that if it's not causing you some pain."

Regardless, the Liberals couldn't afford to be too polite. However the negotiations were concluded—with a deal or without, with obvious success or debatable concessions—Trudeau and his ministers needed to leave as little room as possible for anyone to suggest they should have done more. It needed to look as if they had tried everything.

CHAPTER 6

THE ART OF
MAKING A DEAL

Chrystia Freeland says she always believed the most likely outcome was a reasonable one.

"I remember Gerry Butts saying to me after we got the deal that he had been surprised at times that I had seemed to be ultimately in my heart so serene. And he said to me afterwards, 'I just, I couldn't, I don't know how you did that.' And I said, 'Well, it was because I really felt at the end of the day we would get to a reasonable outcome, provided we, Canada, didn't score any own goals.' Provided we did things right," she says.

"I don't want to make it sound too simple or be too simplistic," she continues. "But the reason I had that kind of core confidence is I do believe that numbers matter and that facts matter. And any study, for as little as five minutes, of the facts of the Canada-U.S. trading relationship will tell you two things. One, that it's a really important trading relationship. Canada is the single largest market for U.S. exports in the whole world. And the other thing that is also very apparent when you look at the numbers is it is a really balanced trading relationship."

All things being equal, reason should have prevailed. Canada and the United States had been functioning under one free trade agreement or another for nearly thirty years. The two economies were now deeply intertwined. Though proportionally Canada might suffer more, a disruption would do significant damage in both countries. To avoid the public's wrath, political leaders would need to have very good reasons for precipitating such strife. And there simply weren't many reasons, good or bad, to blow up the status quo.

But the post-2016 world was not one in which reason and logic could be taken for granted. A reasonable conclusion to the NAFTA renegotiations was always possible, maybe even probable. But it was not always obvious. At least from the outside.

In the spring of 2017, before formal negotiations began, Freeland met several times with her American counterpart, Robert Lighthizer. "He said, 'Look, we're going to be spending a lot of time together. It would be a good idea for us to get to know each other a little bit before we really start going at it,'" Freeland recalls.

There would be, Freeland says, "many conflicts and many moments of great tension." There was periodic speculation about how well, if at all, they got along. But Freeland says she considers Lighthizer a friend. Several months after the negotiations were concluded, one of Freeland's daughters was involved in a bicycle accident and sustained a mild concussion. When word of that reached Lighthizer—Freeland happened to mention it to an American official she was meeting with—he wrote Freeland to ask how her daughter was doing and to pass on his regards.

Lighthizer was a tall, sixty-nine-year-old trade lawyer who had been the deputy trade representative under Ronald Reagan. His office reportedly features a diorama of a scene from the Revolutionary War that depicts one of his ancestors as a volunteer in George Washington's army.

In March 2008, Lighthizer wrote an op-ed for the *New York Times* in which he cast conservative support for free trade as a relatively new phenomenon, one that betrayed a long history of pragmatic protectionism.

"[President] Reagan often broke with free-trade dogma," Lighthizer wrote. "He arranged for voluntary restraint agreements to limit imports of automobiles and steel. He provided temporary import relief for Harley-Davidson. He limited imports of sugar and textiles. His administration pushed for the 'Plaza accord' of 1985, an agreement that made Japanese imports more expensive by raising the value of the yen. Each of these measures prompted vociferous criticism from free traders. But they worked. By the early 1990s, doubts about Americans' ability to compete had been impressively reduced.

"Reagan's pragmatism contrasted strongly with the utopian dreams of free traders," Lighthizer continued. "Ever since Edmund Burke criticized the French philosophes, Anglo-American conservatism has rejected ivory-tower theories that disregard the realities of everyday life."

Modern free traders, Lighthizer wrote, "see nothing but dogma—no matter how many jobs are lost, how high the trade deficit rises or how low the dollar falls."

A decade later, when Freeland accepted her prize as "diplomat of the year," she argued that technological change was more responsible for the stagnation and uncertainty felt by middle-class families. But she conceded that "even free traders like me have to realize that globalization has contributed as well." Freeland's proposed solution, however, was not protectionism. "When it comes to trade, we need to introduce labour standards with real teeth as Canada and the EU have done in our free trade agreement," she said.

Whatever the differences in world view, Freeland says her conversations with Lighthizer "really reinforced for me that the Americans understood the simple fact that Canada was not at the core of what they perceived to be the imbalanced trading relationship that the U.S. had with the world."

Nonetheless, Freeland chose to prepare Canadians for the possibility that this would not be a perfectly serene endeavour.

"I am confident that this is a story with a happy ending," she said in a speech in Ottawa, days before the start of formal negotiations. "But, and as I am sure Canadians appreciate, the path to getting there could well include some moments of excitement. That is because, while the fine print of such agreements can be rather soporific, trade negotiations themselves tend to offer at least a few moments of drama."

She noted her own example: just ten months earlier, as trade minister, she had made a dramatic show of walking away from the table when talks on the Canada-Europe trade agreement reached an impasse.

Freeland's walkout had a precedent in earlier trade talks between Canada and the United States. "It was during the initial FTA negotiations in 1987 that the late, great Simon Reisman walked out, pulled home by his PM over the Reagan administration's initial refusal to agree to binding binational review of anti-dumping and countervailing duties," Freeland recalled. "Our government will be equally resolute. Just as good fences make good neighbours, strong dispute settlement systems make good trading partners."

This historical note would become relevant again a year later.

In both cases, a breakthrough in negotiations followed and a deal was soon completed: the lesson being that drama is normal and these things usually work out. The problem, of course, is that there is nothing normal or usual about Donald Trump.

In fact, things had already almost gone sideways: in late April, Trump had come close to triggering an American withdrawal from NAFTA.

According to an account in Bob Woodward's *Fear*, a notification letter to that effect was drawn up. Gary Cohn, Trump's economic advisor at the time, was said to have taken the astonishing step of surreptitiously removing the paper from the president's desk, hoping that Trump would forget about it. Sonny Perdue came to the Oval Office with a map and explained to Trump that withdrawing would have negative consequences for people in the states that had supported Trump in 2016. Kushner arranged a call between Trudeau and Trump, and Trump later credited that conversation, and a separate call with Mexican president Enrique Peña Nieto, for persuading him to stand down.

"I was all set to terminate," Trump later told the *Washington Post*. "I looked forward to terminating. I was going to do it."

Even beyond such personal flourishes, this was not to be a standard trade negotiation.

"Ninety-nine times of out a hundred, when you enter into a trade negotiation, the reason you're doing it is because all parties are looking to expand trade, to grow the pie," David MacNaughton says. "The stated purpose of the U.S. in this was not to do that. It was to rebalance the trading relationship. And when they said 'rebalance,' they meant 'What are you going to give us?'"

After an opening round of talks in Washington, there were five days of negotiations in Mexico City, then another five days in Ottawa. At the outset, there was some suggestion the renegotiation could be wrapped up by the end of the year. Then came the fourth round of talks, in Arlington, Virginia, and the first official outbreak of drama. "We have seen proposals that would turn back the clock on twenty-three years of predictability, openness and collaboration," Freeland told reporters afterwards. "I'm surprised and disappointed by the resistance to change from our negotiating partners," Lighthizer said. The fifth round of talks was pushed back to November, and all sides agreed to extend negotiations into the first quarter of 2018.

"It is all quite standard practice in any negotiation to begin with a maximalist position in order that the halfway mark be closer to what you really want," Freeland say now. "And I think, by the summer of 2017, it was also clear to us that that kind of approach was likely to be the approach of this administration. And they didn't disappoint us."

Among the points of friction was an American proposal to change the "rules of origin" that governed automobile manufacturing in North America. Under the existing NAFTA regulations, a vehicle had to have at least 62.5 percent of its parts made in North America to escape tariffs. Lighthizer now proposed an increase to 85 percent and, more importantly, a second requirement that 50 percent of each vehicle be manufactured in the United States.

In that scenario, a significant percentage of business might have set up shop in Mexico. "If they'd been successful, it would have gutted the Canadian auto industry," MacNaughton says.

From the Canadian perspective, the first turning point followed in January. As talks resumed in Montreal, the Canadians countered Lighthizer's bid with a suggestion that some percentage of each vehicle be made by workers earning at least $16 per hour—a wage level that implicitly favoured Canadian and American manufacturers, where most workers were unionized. Lighthizer initially dismissed the suggestion, but later came around. For the first time, in a very significant part of the agreement, Canada was more or less on the same side of the table as the Americans, MacNaughton says.

Nonetheless, a series of deadlines came and went. Negotiators had until March 30 to complete a deal before the Mexican presidential election. Paul Ryan, the Republican Speaker in the House of Representatives, said Congress needed to see the text by mid-May if it was to be voted on before the end of the year. When that didn't happen, he suggested Congress could wait a couple more weeks. That wasn't enough either.

Canada had made a push for a so-called cows and cars deal in May. As Trudeau later disclosed, he called vice-president Mike Pence and offered to go to Washington to seal a deal in person. Pence said the deal would have to include a sunset clause—language that could cause the deal to expire after a certain amount of time, effectively allowing the United States to opt out at some future date. Trudeau refused and the moment passed. "I had to highlight that there was no possibility of any Canadian prime minister signing a NAFTA deal that included a five-year sunset clause, and obviously the visit didn't happen," Trudeau said.

The cows were another matter entirely.

———

HAJDU WAS THE CABINET minister assigned to Wisconsin, but she never made the trip.

There were a few reasons Wisconsin qualified for the original list of eleven states to be targeted for Canadian outreach. Canada was Wisconsin's top international customer, accounting for $6.6 billion in exports. It was a swing state in presidential elections, and Trump had won it narrowly in November 2016. It was also the home state of Paul Ryan.

But then Wisconsin emerged as a crucible for one of the most contested elements of the NAFTA renegotiation. Amid that conflict, it was decided the presence of a Canadian politician on the ground might only exacerbate the tensions.

Over the year and a half of negotiations, Trump would loudly register a few complaints about Canada. He claimed Canadians were purchasing shoes in the United States and then smuggling the footwear back across the border to avoid tariffs. He suggested Canadian lumber exports to the United States were somehow to blame for wildfires in California. He would eventually disclose his lack of fondness for Chrystia Freeland.

But nothing seemed to bother Trump more than Canadian milk.

He first complained publicly about Canada's "very unfair" treatment of American dairy products during an appearance in Wisconsin in April 2017. It was an interesting time for Trump to be in Wisconsin. Two weeks before his visit, news broke that approximately seventy-five farms in Wisconsin had been told that Grassland Dairy, a major processor in the state, would no longer be purchasing their milk. The reason given was that Grassland had just lost its Canadian customers, the result of a recent pricing change within the Canadian dairy industry. Politicians in Wisconsin and New York, where farmers were also impacted, appealed to the Trump administration to do something. In a letter on April 13, the National Milk Producers Federation called for "immediate action." In an editorial that same day, the *Milwaukee Journal Sentinel* concurred. "It is time to see if the 'art of the deal' works in the dairy industry," the editors wrote.

Four days later, Trump was in Wisconsin. And he was suddenly very interested in Canadian dairy policy. "We're going to call Canada, and we're going to say, 'What happened?'" he told supporters in Kenosha. "And they might give us an answer, but we're going to get the solution, not just the answer, okay?"

The next day, MacNaughton fired off a letter to the governors of Wisconsin and New York. The real problem, he said, was a matter of overproduction in the United States. For that matter, he argued, the American dairy industry was more protectionist than its Canadian counterpart. But, for Trump, the welfare of the Wisconsin farmer seemed to become the defining issue of the NAFTA renegotiations.

Trump's grievance seemed to include the entirety of Canada's system of supply management—the combination of quotas and tariffs that are used to protect and maintain Canada's domestic dairy industry against foreign competition. "Prime Minister Trudeau is being so indignant, bringing up the relationship that the U.S. and Canada had over the many years and all sorts of other things . . . but he doesn't bring up the fact that they charge us up to 300% on dairy—hurting our Farmers, killing our Agriculture!" Trump tweeted a day before the G7 summit in Charlevoix. Shortly before departing Quebec, he suggested he wanted the system dismantled completely. "We don't want to pay anything," he told reporters. "Why should we pay?"

In fact, U.S. negotiators had made that demand formally: their opening position in the NAFTA talks was that Canada should abolish supply management.

Whether or not he intended it that way, Trump's complaints about dairy tariffs spoke to a particular preoccupation of the elite political debate in Canada, most notably among a significant segment of columnists who despise supply management.

The finer points of the system are not widely understood. To dismantle it would be costly—the farmers who have operated under the system would have to be compensated. And the political benefit could be limited—Canadian farmers, and the rural communities around those farms, would likely be unhappy with the disruption, while the average family might not notice or appreciate the difference. But for a significant number of commentators, supply management is an illogical and cynical sop to the dairy cartel, a case of cowardly politicians putting noisy farmers and a handful of ridings before the possibility of cheaper milk and more plentiful cheeses. Maxime Bernier, the libertarian conservative and future leader of the People's Party of Canada, had built his claim to being a different kind of politician, a brave truth-teller who will buck the political consensus, on his willingness to say he would abolish supply management. And there are great groans whenever some political leader or another calls for supply management to be protected.

On cue, Trump's rants inspired some commentators to suggest Trudeau seize the moment to kill the sacred cow. That, though, would have looked like capitulation. It also would have gone much further than Canada needed to go.

The degree to which supply management was actually an issue at the negotiating table is also debatable. "I think the United States would rather have a trade deal with Canada, but it has to be a good deal, right? And the word that continues to block the deal is *m-i-l-k*, okay?" Larry Kudlow, Trump's economic advisor, said in September 2018.

"If this comes apart, it will not be because of dairy," Brian Clow said around the same time. "That said, the United States will say it's because of dairy."

When an agreement was finally reached, the Trudeau government did agree to grant American producers access to 3.59 percent of the Canadian market, slightly more than the 3.25 percent that was granted to the countries of the Trans-Pacific Partnership. But the bilateral issues with lactose were more complicated.

"The United States is not about trying to get Canada to ditch its supply management system," U.S. agriculture secretary Sonny Perdue insisted during a visit to Prince Edward Island in June 2018. "What we are saying is if you're going to have a supply management system, you've got to manage the supply, and not over-produce and not over-quota where you dump milk solids on the world market and depress prices from our producers south of the border."

Those farmers in Wisconsin did want more access to the Canadian market. But they were also upset about something called diafiltered milk and a Canadian regulation known as Class 7. Diafiltered milk—a by-product, created by running milk through an extra level of filtration, that is used to make cheese—was developed by American producers after the original NAFTA was agreed to. As a result, it could be legally imported into Canada without being subject to the tariffs that apply to other dairy products. And Wisconsin farmers did well selling the product into Canada. The Canadian dairy industry responded by implementing a new product classification—Class 7—that allowed domestic producers to provide diafiltered milk at a lower price. Those farmers in Wisconsin were unimpressed with the resulting loss of business.

That dispute actually predated the Trump administration: according to MacNaughton, Barack Obama had complained to Trudeau about it. But the Americans also now had another complaint—namely, baby formula.

In 2017, a Chinese company called Feihe International announced plans to open a new factory near Kingston, Ontario, that would produce baby formula. A significant component of that baby formula would be skim milk, which Canadian producers were also now selling under that Class 7 designation. The $225 million investment was expected to create two hundred jobs. Most of the formula produced there would be shipped to China, which, coincidentally, was no longer operating under its one-child policy. In effect, the lower price for skim milk was now not only undercutting American producers in the Canadian market, but also helping Canadian producers make gains in the lucrative Chinese market. The U.S. dairy industry was once again displeased.

"They created this lower price Class 7 in order to compete with our dairy producers and compete on the world export market," Perdue complained at one point. "Frankly, I don't know how we can go forward if Canada insists on a Class 7 part of their program."

In the final deal, the Trudeau government agreed to eliminate Class 7. It also agreed to put a cap on exports, but at a level that would allow the Kingston plant to operate.

"We got into this two-hour discussion about the constituent parts of baby formula and how much of it could be produced by the existing dairy farms within the existing quota around Kingston," Butts recalls of the final frantic weekend of talks. "That took up, honest to god, like half a day of negotiations."

The battle of bovine at least ended in armistice. But by then a new and uglier dispute had emerged.

———

THE TRUMP ADMINISTRATION STARTED looking seriously at the possibility of imposing tariffs on imported steel and aluminum in the spring of 2017. To do so, the United States offered a creative explanation.

Using the exemption in Section 232 of the Trade Expansion Act, the administration pursued the idea that protecting its domestic steel and aluminum industries was a matter of national security.

Those investigations were launched in late April. A month later, Trudeau and Trump saw each other at the G7 summit in Italy, and Trudeau broached the issue of American tariffs on Canadian steel and aluminum. He said such a move would be "insulting." Trump apparently agreed. "He turned to Gary Cohn and said, 'Let's make sure they're not on the list,'" Trudeau recalls.

When Trump finally announced tariffs in March 2018, he granted an exemption to Canada and Mexico, pending the completion of NAFTA negotiations. But even that much had required further lobbying. Freeland credited a "true Team Canada effort" for persuading the U.S. administration, with Sajjan singled out for his lobbying of Defense Secretary Mattis. In all, a dozen American officials were contacted. Trump was said to be concerned that Chinese steel was getting into the United States through Canada. In a phone call, Trudeau told him this would come as some surprise to steelworkers in Canada and reminded the president that Canadian steel was used in American fighter jets and tanks.

But this reprieve would be short-lived. In late May, with NAFTA negotiations still short of a conclusion, Trump's tariffs landed on Canadian steel and aluminum. Freeland said the American move was "totally unacceptable" and "entirely inappropriate." At a news conference to respond to the tariffs, Trudeau was moved to say just about the meanest thing he has so far allowed himself to say in public about the Trump administration: "We will continue to make arguments based on logic and common sense and hope that eventually they will prevail against an administration that doesn't always align itself around those principles."

Trudeau now frames this as a turning point. "For all his unpredictability he had never [not] followed through on a commitment to me on something that he said he'd do or wouldn't do," he says. "I start from a place of confidence, that if someone looks me in the eye and says, 'I will do this for you or I won't do this to you,' I accept it. Once they don't do that, they suddenly go into a different category for me . . . He has moved into a place where whatever he says I need to take with a grain of salt regardless of the handshake and the commitment and the look in the eye."

In 2019, after leaving the Trump administration, Gary Cohn admitted his own opposition to what Trump had done. "When you put tariffs on goods that people in the United States consume every day, it's a consumption tax," Cohn told the Freakonomics podcast. "So all the tariffs did is they made products that Americans were going to buy more expensive." Noting that the United States' trade deficit had actually increased since the tariffs were applied, Cohn put it simply: "tariffs don't work."

Cohn and his interviewer guessed that more than 99 percent of economists agreed with him. But one who didn't—Peter Navarro—was working in the White House. In Cohn's telling, Navarro and Wilbur Ross manoeuvred around him to convince Trump to go forward with the steel and aluminum tariffs.

The other problem with imposing tariffs is that the other country is nearly obligated to respond in kind. And so Canada did, not only on American steel and aluminum, but also American gherkins, toilet paper, hair lacquers, sleeping bags, plywood, coffee, ketchup and several dozen other products. Freeland described it as "the strongest trade action Canada has taken in the postwar era," covering $16.6 billion in American exports: a dollar-for-dollar retaliation for the American tariffs. The Canadian tariffs were coordinated with Europe and Mexico and were aimed, in many cases, at politically important regions. That Kentucky bourbon that Ralph Goodale enthused about? It was hit by a tariff, because Kentucky is the home state of Mitch McConnell, the Senate majority leader.

Canadian consumers would have to either pay these extra costs or find a domestic alternative. But the Liberals also had to account for the damage done to Canadian steel and aluminum producers: by the fall of 2018, the government had set aside $2.4 billion for various measures of support.

It was this dispute that moved Trudeau to say Canada would not be pushed around, which prompted Trump's angry tweets, which scrambled the June 2018 summit of the G7. Three weeks later, the trade war framed Trudeau's approach to Canada Day. Trudeau had pre-recorded a statement for Canada Day while visiting Prince Rupert, British Columbia, for an announcement in late June. But that version was scrapped in favour of a new statement that paid tribute to "Canada's workers" and called for unity. Instead of Parliament Hill, Trudeau spent July 1 visiting a tomato factory in Leamington, Ontario, and steel workers in Regina.

"From Ontario steel to Quebec aluminum, from agriculture and the energy sector in the Prairies and the North, to forestry in British Columbia and fisheries in the Atlantic, Canadians get the job done—and build our communities along the way," Trudeau said in his official statement. "We know we can count on Canadians. We stand with each other, and we will always stand up for each other. Canada's success has always come from its people—lifting each other up, one community at a time."

Later that summer, Abacus Data asked 1,500 Canadians to describe their level of concern about a number of relevant issues. "Donald Trump" came first. A remarkable 73 percent of respondents said they were "extremely" or "very" concerned about Trump, more than were concerned about climate change, health care or housing affordability. Concern was even higher amongst Liberal and NDP supporters, at 81 percent and 86 percent respectively. Canadians were captivated by the show next door, and they were freaked out.

———

THROUGH JULY AND AUGUST of 2018, the United States and Mexico pursued bilateral talks, purportedly because they needed to settle specific differences between the two of them, in particular on the automotive sector.

"We really felt the main thing that was the problem for the U.S. was the trade deficit with Mexico and U.S. rustbelt jobs being lost to low-wage Mexico," Freeland says.

"And our conviction was if the U.S. could achieve a deal that resolved that core issue . . . from their perspective, they would have the lion's share of what they needed. As rational actors and as professionals—and I really want to emphasize Ambassador Lighthizer is both very rational and very professional—their perspective would be that they had most of what they needed. Of course they would fight hard, and they did, to get more out of Canada. But if we were prepared to hold our nerve, if we were prepared for a little more sound and fury, at the end of the day, we would be able to stick to our red line because the U.S. would already have achieved most of what it wanted with Mexico and would therefore be really disinclined to ditch the whole thing."

On August 27, the United States and Mexico announced a deal. According to the new rules of origin, 40 to 45 percent of a vehicle would have to be manufactured by workers earning at least $16 per hour—a version of what Canada had proposed earlier.

But the two countries had gone much further than that. In fact, what they announced was a sweeping agreement that dealt with a range of issues, including dispute resolution, patent protection for pharmaceuticals and duty-free shopping limits. The American demand for a sunset clause had been reduced to a mandatory review. But Chapter 19, the dispute resolution mechanism, was gone.

In announcing the surprising agreement, Trump suggested Canada wasn't necessarily going to be involved, and he repeated a threat to impose a 25 percent tariff on Canadian-made cars. The Mexican ambassador in Ottawa said Mexico was prepared to move on without Canada. The Americans suggested the Canadians had until August 31 to decide.

"We were aware of, involved in to some extent, and supportive of them talking. The only way we were going to get to a deal was if the U.S. and Mexico sorted out their issues. Which they did," Clow said at the time. "But what was not clear to us then, and is now very clear to us, was the extent to which the Mexicans were willing to make significant concessions, to their own detriment, in order to come to that agreement."

Freeland had flown overnight to Frankfurt on August 25 for what was to be several days of meetings in Germany, Ukraine and France.

She made it as far as Berlin before she had to fly to Washington on August 28.

Once in D.C., Freeland confronted Mexico's negotiators during a meeting at the Canadian embassy. "I wouldn't say she was scary. But she was pretty forceful, put it that way. And never lost her temper," MacNaughton says. "She just went through, 'Here's what we had agreed to, here's the kind of efforts I made to keep you in the loop, there were people suggesting and advocating that we throw you under the bus; we never did it. Here's what my expectation was of your discussions with the Americans. That isn't what you did. I am extraordinarily disappointed.'

"Sometimes when people yell at you it's just easier to take than when they're calm and measured. Like my father used to yell at me. My mother never did; she just made me feel like shit," he says.

Freeland will only say that "particularly in private conversations, I think that when you speak for Canada, you need to be prepared to make your displeasure known to your partners if you are displeased."

Ildefonso Guajardo, Mexico's secretary for the economy, turned the Canadian complaint around and blamed MacNaughton for Canada's wage-based proposal on the automotive sector. MacNaughton says it was wrong to suggest he and Lighthizer had come up with the idea, "but I can understand why they thought that put them at a disadvantage."

A source with knowledge of the Mexican government's thinking quibbles with the suggestion that the Canadian side was not kept in the loop, and suggests Canada should not have been surprised with where the United States and Mexico ended up—though Freeland's private reaction would seem to suggest otherwise.

From the Mexican perspective, Mexico deserves more credit than it has received for preserving a trilateral deal. But, according to this account, Mexican officials also believed that there had been a split within Trudeau's cabinet over whether or not to pursue a deal that included Mexico. The Mexican side believed that if Canada eventually faced a choice between a deal with the United States or a trilateral deal with both countries, Canada would have cut Mexico loose.

A Canadian source denies that any such split ever existed.

Regardless, the Canadians needed to deal with the fact that the United States and Mexico had come to an agreement. Included therein were a number of concessions the Canadians were not willing to co-sign, particularly on Chapter 19, which allows for independent arbitration when a company in one country feels it has been subject to an unfair tariff imposed by the other country.

Thirty-one years earlier, it was the Mulroney government's desire for such a dispute resolution process that nearly scuttled the original free trade talks between Canada and the United States. "The dispute settlement issue was vital then, and is now because we are dealing with an economic giant more than ten times our size, one that tends to render decisions on trade that are arbitrary, capricious and contravene U.S. trade law," Derek Burney, the former Canadian ambassador to the United States, recalled in an op-ed in the *Globe and Mail* in September 2018. "It helps temper the raw power imbalance."

Four days of negotiations at the end of August failed to resolve the outstanding differences, but the talks were extended into September. The new deadline became September 30, the last day that would give Mexican negotiators a chance to complete an agreement before their new president, Andrés Manuel López Obrador, was sworn in.

Freeland was joined in Washington by both Katie Telford and Gerry Butts. The prime minister was briefed twice each day by phone. "There was a rhythm to it where we'd go in on Monday or Tuesday where we're kind of testing each other out, developing a good rapport, and then one of us or the other would table an eff-you offer on the Thursday," Butts says. "We would do it one week on dairy and they would do it the next week on 19 and it was like, 'Oh well, I guess there's nothing to talk about' and we'd all go home and come back." At the time, Clow said progress was being made, but it was "achingly slow progress."

Lighthizer rarely spoke publicly, but Freeland had a habit of speaking with the reporters who clustered outside the United States Trade Representative office in Washington as she came and went. For the sake of reminding Canadians that Freeland was hard at work, it was useful to have such a presence. It was also, MacNaughton notes, a prolonged exercise in not saying much. For the final stretch, Lighthizer and Freeland agreed that there would be no negotiating in public and, according to MacNaughton, there was a discussion at the end of each day between both sides as to what Freeland would be saying when she walked out the door.

"She spent several weeks and many, many discussions with journalists saying absolutely nothing. It's a remarkable talent," MacNaughton says.

On September 5, 2018, Trudeau was in Alberta when he and his team decided to send a message to the American negotiators. That afternoon he was to sit down with Alberta premier Rachel Notley to discuss the Federal Court of Appeal's ruling on the Trans Mountain pipeline expansion. But his itinerary also included an interview that morning with CHED, a radio station in Edmonton. If presented with the opportunity, he would say something pointed about Chapter 19.

"One of the dynamics in the negotiations is the dialogue between what the leaders are saying away from the table and what's going on at the table," Butts says. "We said, 'Say something really aggressive on 19 and we'll see what happens at the table.'"

The interviewer was understandably more interested in talking about the pipeline. But near the end of the segment there was a change of topic.

"Do you have time to touch on a couple of NAFTA things this morning as well?" he asked.

"Sure," Trudeau replied.

Trudeau was asked about supply management. After a nod to the actual question, he segued to what he wanted to say.

"One of the things that is clear is that we have red lines that Canadians simply will not accept," he said. "We need to keep the Chapter 19 dispute resolution because that ensures that the rules are actually followed. And we know that we have a president that doesn't always follow the rules as they're laid out."

Trudeau had actually gone a bit further than originally intended. But the Liberals believe the message was heard. "They appreciated how piquant our statement was on it: that the prime minister wouldn't focus the conversation on that issue unless there were strategic reasons for doing so," Butts says.

Trudeau's comments were something that Lighthizer "referenced a number of times," says Telford, "and Jared believed."

Chapter 19 was not the only red line Trudeau drew in that interview: he was also demanding, he said, that any new deal include Canada's existing cultural exemption. Broadly speaking, that clause exempts the foreign ownership rules and targeted subsidies that Canada uses to maintain and protect domestic broadcast, news, arts and cultural industries and producers—the regulations and supports that have been constructed to address the concern that Canadian culture might be swamped by the American behemoth. That too had been a demand of the Mulroney government.

"When it comes to discussing better trade rules for cultural industries, you will have to understand that what we call cultural sovereignty is as vital to our national life as political sovereignty," Brian Mulroney told an audience in Chicago in December 1985, ahead of free trade talks with the United States. "And how could it be otherwise living, as we do, next to a country ten times our size in population."

Now Trudeau was taking up the same cause. "We can't imagine a situation in which an American TV company or network could come up and buy radio stations or buy CTV, for example," he said. "That would not be good for Canada; it would not be good for our identity; it would not be good for our sovereignty."

Kushner had been attending the negotiations in Washington, but had other business on September 20. He called Telford at the end of the day. She told him it hadn't gone well and that the Canadian team was going back to Ottawa. He told her to stick around so they could talk. After they had discussed where things stood, Kushner told her that they should be able to get a deal done. He asked Telford if she would put something down on paper that he could take back to Lighthizer and his negotiators.

The Liberals were unsure about whether to take that step. Things said between officials at the negotiating table are not necessarily locked in, and once something is on paper it becomes harder to take it back.

Kushner also might have been looking for the Canadian side to make concessions, but the Canadians were not ready to give anything.

No formal negotiations were scheduled for the last week of September. On Sunday, Trudeau flew to New York to attend the United Nations General Assembly. Telford went with him. On Tuesday morning, Trudeau had a roundtable meeting scheduled with a dozen major executives, including senior leaders from Ford, Pepsi, Bank of America and FedEx. Discussion predictably turned to NAFTA. "One of the key messages we were delivering is, if you're hearing that dairy is the problem, it's not," says Telford. "That is a big challenge for us, it still has to get resolved, but that is not what is stopping us at the moment from getting a deal."

Stephen Schwarzman, CEO of the Blackstone Group, was one of the executives in that room. Afterwards, Trudeau and Telford met with him privately. The message from Trudeau was that Canada needed Chapter 19 and the cultural exemption.

Trump had also flown to New York, but he and Trudeau crossed paths only once, at a luncheon for world leaders on the Tuesday. Trudeau walked over to where Trump was seated, got the president's attention and there was a quick handshake. A fifteen-second video of the encounter was closely analyzed by media outlets. Trump hadn't stood up to greet Trudeau, but he did stand up later when Mexican president Enrique Peña Nieto stopped by. It had to mean something. "Trump's UN Handshake with Trudeau Suggests Lingering Resentment," reported Bloomberg. Trudeau later suggested there wasn't much to read into the brief exchange.

There was still some debate as to whether or not to put something down on paper. Telford and Trudeau discussed it on a midday flight back from New York on Wednesday. By the time they landed, Telford had decided to make the move.

"Essentially it was laying out where we believed the two sides were on everything," says Telford. "It wasn't making any new big moves . . . but it was showing how close we were."

On Wednesday afternoon, September 26, just before five o'clock, Trump began a news conference at the UN building. After a series of questions about Trump's Supreme Court nominee, Brett Kavanaugh, who was facing multiple accusations of sexual assault, an American reporter asked Trump if he had rejected a one-on-one meeting with Trudeau.

"Yeah, I did," Trump responded. "Because his tariffs are too high, and he doesn't seem to want to move, and I've told him, 'Forget about it.'"

This was apparently news to Trudeau's office, which insisted no such meeting had been requested.

"And frankly, we're thinking about just taxing cars coming in from Canada," Trump continued. "That's the motherlode. That's the big one."

This was probably already enough for two breaking news alerts in Canada. But Trump wasn't done.

"We're very unhappy with the negotiations and the negotiating style of Canada," he said. "We don't like their representative very much."

Trump didn't name this representative, but it was immediately understood that this was about Freeland—it had already been whispered to reporters that Trump was not fond of Trudeau's foreign minister.

There had, perhaps inevitably, been moments of conflict at the negotiating table. "Bob had some moments where he would kind of blow up. And it's hard to know whether that was just part of the negotiating style," MacNaughton says. "But he was clearly frustrated on occasion, no doubt about that."

"We had a lot of very, very, very tough exchanges," Freeland says. "But I never felt it was personal between me and Ambassador Lighthizer."

But there was also that speech in Washington in June—the one Freeland had personally presented a copy of to Lighthizer. "A number of times someone raised that speech with us and particular parts of the speech," MacNaughton says.

On June 29, two weeks after Freeland's speech, the Trudeau government confirmed that it was moving ahead with tariffs to counter the American actions. Trudeau and Trump spoke on the phone that day. According to the official "readout" issued by Trudeau's office, the prime minister "conveyed that Canada has had no choice but to announce reciprocal countermeasures to the steel and aluminum tariffs that the United States imposed on June 1, 2018."

The conversation was slightly more colourful than that. Trump referred to Freeland as a "nasty woman"—a phrase he had previously applied to Hillary Clinton. The president accused Freeland of delivering a "very nasty" speech about him, but he seemed particularly upset about the official release that had gone out from Freeland's office to announce the Canadian tariffs. That release said, "it is inconceivable and completely unacceptable to view any trade with Canada as a national security threat to the United States." Trump said the tone of the release was "nasty." He also accused Freeland of talking about him to other leaders.

Trudeau reminded Trump of the conversation with Cohn in Sicily, but Trump denied agreeing with Trudeau at the time. Trudeau said the two countries were in this position because the Americans had gone forward with tariffs on steel and aluminum. He told the president he was making it personal. Trudeau said the Canadian government had waited to respond and suggested there was a proposal on the table to resolve the tariff dispute. Trump referenced Trudeau's public statements at Charlevoix about not being pushed around, but Trudeau said he had stated his objections directly to the president in private.

Trump maintained his complaints about the tone of the Canadian statement, but the call was not completely unfriendly. Trump told Trudeau that his wife, Melania, said hi. Trudeau expressed his condolences for the deaths suffered in a recent shooting in Annapolis, Maryland.

A few months later, Freeland participated in a panel entitled "Taking on the Tyrant" during a Women in the World conference in Toronto. Technically, there are many world leaders who might be described as tyrannical. And Freeland herself made no mention of Trump in her answers to the moderator's questions. But the organizers of the conference introduced the panel with an ominous, eighty-second video that featured photos and clips of a half-dozen "autocrats" and populists: Rodrigo Duterte of the Philippines, Recep Tayyip Erdoğan of Turkey, Russia's Vladimir Putin, China's Xi Jinping, Bashar al-Assad of Syria and, yes, Donald J. Trump.

Freeland received an extended standing ovation from the audience when the video finished and she was introduced. But that cinematography apparently did not go unnoticed by the American administration. A day after his news conference at the UN, Trump told a crowd of supporters at a fundraiser that Freeland "hates America."

Freeland's feelings for the United States are probably more nuanced than that: she spent a good portion of her adult life working in the United States.

History might look kindly on those who spoke up in this moment and, in the short term, it's possible that a significant number of Canadian voters were eager to see their government stand up to the American president. But it is also not hard to imagine how this all could have gone badly for her and Trudeau. If NAFTA had unravelled and Trump had imposed auto tariffs, the Liberals would have been very vulnerable to a claim they had brought on such tumult and harm, that they had carelessly provoked Trump's wrath.

As it was, Stephen Harper had been heard advancing a theory that the Trudeau government was playing the negotiations out for domestic political gain. "The problem right now is we have two governments that do not want an agreement," Harper told a private luncheon in Montreal in July. "The reality is the government of Canada believes today that it is doing very well; the fight with Trump is good for it politically, it is winning. And so if it can take that fight and continue it, and more importantly, paint Conservatives as linked to Donald Trump, this is great for them. And so right now that is the strategy they are on."

Someone recorded the former prime minister's remarks. And that audio recording somehow found its way to CTV's Ottawa bureau. The resulting story added to a subplot that had begun three weeks earlier when it emerged that Harper would be visiting the White House on July 2, apparently to meet with Larry Kudlow.

No doubt there was some upside for Trudeau as the Canadian prime minister who was faced with Donald Trump. But stringing the Americans along would have also been a dubious use of resources. "I remember when I went out to Saskatoon to brief the prime minister on NAFTA, when we were coming down to the finish line," MacNaughton recalls of a Liberal caucus meeting in mid-September, "and he said at the time, 'I sure hope we can get this behind us because it's consuming most of the time of all of our top people.'"

As it was, all conjecture would soon be rendered moot.

———

ON THURSDAY, SEPTEMBER 27—a day after Trump claimed to have snubbed Trudeau, threatened auto tariffs and publicly stated his dislike for Freeland—the Canadian team's paper was delivered. Freeland was in New York, and a member of her staff was assigned to get it to one of Kushner's assistants.

A day and a half had been spent preparing and reviewing the four-page document. Freeland, Trudeau and Steve Verheul all signed off. The document was entitled "State of Play." Two pages covered outstanding issues related to dairy, and one page dealt with other agriculture issues. The last page listed another dozen outstanding issues, including Chapter 19, the sunset clause, the possibility of auto tariffs, cross-border shopping, culture, government procurement and investor-state dispute resolution.

"There were some in the U.S. who felt that we weren't serious about getting it done. And there was an accusation that we were adding too many things to the list, we were making it too complicated," Clow says. "And the reason why the paper became important is we said, 'Actually we do want to get this done.' Not at any price, but the piece of paper helped convey that we don't have an endless list of asks. We need certain things. We can accommodate on certain other things. And don't just take our word for it, here it is on a piece of paper."

As would become clear afterwards, there were also more obscure conflicts. The Americans, for instance, wanted British Columbia to drop a restriction that kept American wines off regular grocery store shelves. The National Football League wanted Canadian broadcasters to stop airing the commercials that ran on the American broadcast of the Super Bowl. There was also a demand that Canada allow QVC—the American home-shopping channel—to broadcast in Canada.

After receiving the paper, Kushner called Telford on Thursday night and then early on Friday morning to go over what the Trudeau government had put down. He called back a second time on Friday to say he thought he saw a way forward and that they should each get their teams on a call that afternoon. The formal talks then resumed with Telford, Butts, Verheul and John Hannaford, a foreign policy advisor from the Privy Council Office, in Telford's Centre Block office. Freeland and MacNaughton joined by phone.

In the midst of it all, Elton John stopped by. The musician was in town for a concert and had scheduled a meeting with Trudeau to discuss his foundation's work on AIDS prevention and awareness. The Canadians on the NAFTA talks pointed out to the Americans that they were missing out on a chance to meet Elton John for the sake of negotiations.

Lighthizer's office had said it would release the text of the U.S.-Mexico deal that night, but suddenly those plans were off. "In the next forty-eight hours we will know if we are going to get to a trilateral text or if we are going to have to put forward the text of the bilateral agreement," Guajardo announced in Mexico.

The Canadians worked until midnight. Before departing for the night, Trudeau gave his negotiating team a pep talk. He told them he knew they were tired, but he believed they were close to a deal. That they'd shown the Americans they wouldn't roll over and they just needed to keep pushing and holding firm. He said this negotiation might end up being the most important thing the government did and that he had confidence in this team to get it done.

According to a Liberal source, there were broadly two views within the Canadian team. One was that there would not be a deal that weekend because the Americans were not actually interested in making one. It was possible, in this scenario, that Canada would be able to rejoin the talks in the new year, though that could not be guaranteed. The other view was that a deal would only come together at the eleventh hour, in keeping with most negotiations of this sort and bearing in mind that

Lighthizer was an experienced negotiator. In that case, the question was whether that weekend represented a real deadline.

Each side seemingly had to convince the other they were serious about making a deal. "After they did the thing with the Mexicans, I wasn't sure whether they actually wanted to do a deal with us. And I think they weren't sure that we actually wanted to do a deal with them," MacNaughton says. The involvement of Kushner—Trump's son-in-law and senior advisor—suggested the Trump administration was serious. The involvement of Telford and Butts probably should have sent a similar signal to the Americans. "I think both sides finally said, 'Jeez, maybe they actually want to do a deal.' You have to have that if you want to get something done," MacNaughton says.

There were good reasons for both the Trump administration and the Trudeau government to make a deal at the end of September. The midterm elections were five weeks away, and a renegotiated NAFTA would give Trump an accomplishment to boast about. Congressional support for a deal that didn't include Canada couldn't be guaranteed, but nor could the Canadians count on Congress to demand a trilateral deal. The markets would appreciate the elimination of uncertainty. And Trudeau's office would be freed up to worry more about any number of other things, from climate policy to getting a pipeline built.

The Canadian team reconvened at seven on Saturday morning at 80 Wellington Street, the building across from Parliament Hill that houses the prime minister's staff. Freeland's office announced that she would not be delivering Canada's address to the United Nations that afternoon, as scheduled.

The centre of negotiations was Telford's office, with the most senior officials sitting around a speakerphone, including Telford, Butts, Freeland, MacNaughton, Verheul, Clow, Jeremy Broadhurst, Hannaford and Michael Wernick, the clerk of the Privy Council. Over the course of the weekend, the building would fill up with as many as forty-five people, including the chiefs of staff for Bill Morneau, Navdeep Bains and Lawrence MacAulay. Teams prepared for what would happen in the event of a deal and what would happen if the talks collapsed. Telford's husband, Rob Silver, provided food: home-made brisket, jerk chicken and porchetta.

"It was never guaranteed to come together and there were points on every day where talks could have conceivably broken off. But the Americans kept talking, they kept responding," Clow says.

On Friday night, the American side sent back a paper that suggested their demand to eliminate Chapter 19 was off the table. On Saturday, the Canadians received verbal confirmation. In the inside accounts that followed there would be conflicting reports of Freeland's reaction. One account suggested Freeland threw her hands up and exclaimed "yay!" Another report described the exclamation as "woo hoo!"

This was not the entire ballgame, but it was significant for Trudeau's team. The prime minister had tied himself to Chapter 19 and now it was there.

Trump and Lighthizer had publicly linked the steel and aluminum tariffs with the renegotiation of NAFTA, and Trudeau later told reporters that Trump had assured him the tariffs would be removed if a new trade deal was completed. But at some point it became clear that wasn't going to happen. The Americans instead proposed that the tariffs be replaced by quotas on the amount of steel and aluminum that Canada would be able to freely export to the United States. The Trudeau government rejected the suggestion.

"So then we're facing a choice of, do we walk away from the entire deal or not?" MacNaughton says. "Our position was that NAFTA was a totally different thing than the steel and aluminum tariffs and to link them was a mistake. Trump might want to link them, but we do not because we didn't consider the use of 232 a legitimate trade negotiating tactic."

In the meantime, the Trudeau government could at least push to stave off the threat of auto tariffs. Mexico had negotiated a side letter that would allow it to ship 2.4 million vehicles into the United States before such a penalty could be applied. The United States offered to give Canada a buffer of 2.2 million vehicles. Jerry Dias, the president of Unifor, made several visits to 80 Wellington Street that weekend. He told Trudeau's team to ask for 2.8 million, but that 2.6 million would be acceptable. The United States agreed at 2.6 million.

"Frankly, that was Jerry Dias's number," Clow says.

"The 2.6 million is my number," Dias confirms. "In the history of the Canadian industry, the most vehicles we ever shipped to the United States, during our heyday, was 2.2 million. Four assembly plants ago. Right now we ship 1.8 million. So before the U.S. can even contemplate slapping tariffs on Canada, we will have to ship in excess of 2.6 million. I'd say the chances of that are remote at best. So in essence the industry has been protected."

The last swap between the two sides was that auto quota in exchange for an adjustment to an industrial quota on imported cream. Kushner then called back to say the deal had to be called the USMCA: the United States-Mexico-Canada Agreement. (It would be officially registered in Canada as CUSMA, owing to official protocol that puts Canada's name first.)

Trudeau arrived at 80 Wellington shortly before eight on Sunday night. Two hours later, after cabinet had been briefed, word began to leak that a deal was done.

Trump and Trudeau spoke on Monday morning. Trump was apparently in a great mood. Though he also had other things on his mind: according to sources he asked for Trudeau's thoughts on the situation with Brett Kavanaugh, whose nomination was then still facing a vote in the Senate. Trudeau sidestepped the issue and Trump complimented him on his ability to dodge a question.

"There was a lot of tension, I will say, between he and I," Trump told reporters in the Rose Garden after speaking with Trudeau. "But he's a good man. He's a done a good job. And he loves the people of Canada."

Trump was delighted to have a new thing to call his own. "It is my great honour to announce that we have successfully completed negotiations on a brand new deal to terminate and replace NAFTA and the NAFTA trade agreements with an incredible new US-Mexico-Canada Agreement, called USMCA. It, sort of, just works: USMCA," he said. "USMCA. That'll be the name, I guess, that, 99 percent of the time, we'll be hearing: USMCA. It has a good ring to it."

When it was his turn to speak, Lighthizer singled out Trump's son-in-law for thanks. "The president's key advisor and my good friend, Jared Kushner, was my partner in leading the U.S. negotiating team," he said. "I've said before, and I'll say again: this agreement would not have happened if it wasn't for Jared."

Butts similarly recognizes the relationship between Kushner and Telford. "It was huge," he says, though adding that it was a team effort.

Afterwards, MacNaughton acknowledged that his hopes for a deal had risen and fallen throughout the process. "There were days when I was quite discouraged," he says. "There were days when I was quite optimistic."

American commentators were underwhelmed. From the United States, the changes looked like "tweaks."

The Dairy Farmers of Canada were not so placid, declaring themselves "deeply disappointed" as talk quickly turned to compensation.

Andrew Scheer's Conservatives dismissed the deal as a series of concessions and criticized the government for not convincing Trump to remove the tariffs on steel and aluminum. "Would I have signed this deal?" Scheer asked rhetorically at one point. "I would have signed a better one."

How Scheer would have done so was left to the imagination.

The concessions, MacNaughton argues, were "modest," though he acknowledges that if you're a dairy farmer you might feel otherwise. There were gains too, he says, on dispute resolution and automotive rules of origin. But why not refuse to bend at all? "Had we simply been totally intransigent we would have continued to have investment uncertainty," MacNaughton says. And that uncertainty would have likely pulled new investment toward the United States.

At the outset, Freeland had publicly stated a series of "progressive" goals: better labour standards, new environmental protection, a chapter on gender equality and a chapter on Indigenous peoples and elimination of the investor-state dispute mechanism that allowed American companies to sue Canadian governments (and vice versa). She did not get all of that. But the United States did delete the investor-state mechanism, and Freeland could point to at least small gains in each of the other areas.

The broader Canadian reaction seemed mostly to be relief. Public polling was a muddle: 59 percent of respondents in an Abacus Data poll said Trudeau had achieved as much as was possible; 45 percent told the Angus Reid Institute that they were disappointed with the deal.

At any rate, it could have been worse. Matched against a much larger economy and a protectionist president who was obviously willing to use destructive measures and antagonize an ally, Trudeau's negotiators had seemingly contained the damages while getting to a deal. Scenarios might be imagined in which the losses were smaller and the gains were greater. But in conspicuously expending great effort in and around the United States, the Trudeau government at least insulated itself against any charge that it should have done more to swing the negotiations in Canada's favour. That effort also showed a government that was otherwise not always on display: comprehensive, nimble, proactive and well communicated.

But that effort likely came at a cost. If not for having to renegotiate NAFTA, that time and energy and attention could have been put toward literally anything else—as would become clear much later, Justice Minister Jody Wilson-Raybould was already worried by this time about how the Prime Minister's Office was handling questions about a possible remediation agreement for SNC-Lavalin.

A few days after the agreement in principle was completed, MacNaughton was due to deliver a speech. He found himself quoting Churchill: "This is not the end. It is not even the beginning of the end. But it is, perhaps, the end of the beginning." Churchill said this in a speech at the conclusion of the Second Battle of El Alamein in November 1942, a morale-boosting Allied victory over the Axis in North Africa. At that point, the Second World War was only half over.

"Obviously getting the trade agreement done was an important milestone," MacNaughton says. "But it's got to get passed. We've got to get the steel and aluminum tariffs removed. And also, and this is something

I think people need to just be alert to, protectionism is not dead in the United States. And if we take the position that our problem is solved and we go to sleep, then we're going to end up in trouble."

For a while after the new deal was agreed to in principle, both the Canadians and Mexicans suggested they would refuse to participate in a signing ceremony unless the steel and aluminum tariffs were removed. MacNaughton quipped that perhaps the "fourth secretary" from Canada's embassy in Buenos Aires "with a bag over his head" would be put up for the photo opportunity. But both countries eventually relented. At the G20 summit in Argentina, Trudeau, Nieto and Trump appeared together to make remarks and sign copies of the agreement.

When it was his turn to speak, Trudeau told "Donald" that the recent closure of several General Motors plants was "all the more reason why we need to keep working to remove the tariffs on steel and aluminum between our countries."

The free trade deal had survived. But the trade war was still on.

CHAPTER 7

AN UNKEPT PROMISE

C anadian politicians do a better job of keeping their promises than they are probably given credit for.

In a 2015 survey, for instance, 35 percent of respondents said political parties "hardly ever or never" kept their promises. Another 58 percent said "some of the time." Only 3 percent said "most of the time." But it is that 3 percent who have it right. According to academic research that goes back to 1945, the average rate of fulfilment for federal governments is above 70 percent.

Unfortunately, what doesn't get done is often more memorable than what does.

For Justin Trudeau, there were a few things that didn't get done. But none more spectacularly than his promise that the federal election in 2019 would be conducted under a new and better system. It was his most ambitious commitment toward changing the way politics is done in Canada. And then it became another totem for the notion that politicians don't do what they say.

Trudeau has thought quite a lot about electoral reform. "We've covered this so many times in car rides across the country," says Louis-Alexandre Lanthier, Trudeau's executive assistant and campaign manager from 2007 to 2014.

A decade ago, after meeting an Australian at an international conference, Trudeau took an interest in compulsory voting, as is the policy in a handful of Western democracies. In Australia, where it has been the law since 1924, eligible voters who fail to cast a ballot without a suitable excuse can be made to pay a fine of $20 (voters are allowed to spoil their ballot). Turnout for national elections there is typically about 95 percent. In Canada, by comparison, the record turnout for a federal election was 79.4 percent in 1958, and not since 1988 has turnout reached 75 percent. But there are philosophical arguments against requiring a citizen to vote—for that matter, it might not solve the problem of voter disengagement so much as cover it up. In the Canadian context, it's not clear how well mandatory voting would line up with the Charter of Rights and Freedoms.

Trudeau was most assertive in his belief that Canada should adopt a ranked ballot, otherwise known as alternative vote, preferential voting or instant runoff. In such a system, a voter ranks each of the candidates according to preference, putting a number beside each of the names on the ballot. If no candidate is the first choice of at least 50 percent of the voters, the candidate who finished last is dropped from the count and the second choices on those ballots are added to the tally. The process repeats until a candidate goes above 50 percent.

Like many systems of democratic expression, it is more complicated to explain than it actually is in practice. Each of the three major Canadian federal parties uses a ranked ballot to pick its leader. Australia has used a ranked ballot in national elections since 1919, and the municipality of London, Ontario, adopted the system for civic elections in 2018. Federally, it could be implemented as a new feature within the current system.

In theory, a ranked ballot encourages politicians to appeal broadly and avoid alienating those who might be inclined to support someone else. If, for instance, a Conservative was worried they might need the second-choice support of Liberal voters, they might be more careful about slandering the Liberal candidate or platform. That, in turn, would have an impact on the broader shape and form of political debate.

At a Liberal Party convention in 2012, Trudeau spoke in favour of a resolution that called on the party to advocate for a preferential ballot.

"It avoids polarization," he said at the time. A year later, while seeking the Liberal leadership, he included the idea in his platform and argued that it was, in fact, preferable to proportional representation. "The problem with proportional representation is every different model of proportional representation actually increases partisanship, not reduces it," he said during a leadership debate in Halifax. "What we need is a preferential ballot that causes politicians to have to reach out to be the second choice and even the third choice of different political parties. We need people who represent broader voices not narrower interests. And I understand people want proportional representation, but too many people don't understand the polarization and the micro issues that come through proportional representation."

This was a fully formed and distinct position, and it rested comfortably within Trudeau's desire to be seen as a uniter.

There are different models for implementing a system of proportional representation, but the basic idea is the same: the allotment of seats in the legislature should closely match the popular vote across a country or region. So if, for instance, the NDP receives 20 percent of all the votes cast across Canada, New Democrats should get 20 percent of the 338 seats in the House of Commons. Among those who are very interested in the possibility of electoral reform, proportional representation is the most popular option. To its fans, proportional representation is more "fair" than the existing arrangement.

Canada's current system—known as "first-past-the-post"—divides the country into 338 ridings and has voters elect an MP for each. It's fairly straightforward, but it can produce what proportionalists view as a discrepancy. For instance, Liberal candidates were elected in 184 ridings in 2015, or 54 percent of the total. But if you add up the votes cast across all 338 ridings, just 39 percent of all voters cast ballots for Liberal candidates. That difference is deeply aggravating to proponents of proportional representation.

There is an important second level to the discussion though, which concerns how an electoral system impacts the way politics is practised. This is what Trudeau was getting at when he compared a ranked ballot and proportional representation. Some might quibble with his particular analysis, but different systems will inevitably produce different results.

First-past-the-post, for instance, tends to produce single-party governments that hold a majority of seats in the legislature. Proportional representation would likely result in two or more parties having to either share power or co-operate to pass legislation. First-past-the-post tends to create a system that is dominated by two or three major parties. Proportional representation would make it easier for smaller parties to win seats and influence policy. Under first-past-the-post, extreme opinions can end up existing within larger parties. With proportional representation, those with extreme opinions might have an incentive to form their own parties.

Those who like the idea of proportional representation are a passionate and persistent lot. But Trudeau staked out a clear position in favour of a ranked ballot.

If he'd stuck with it, he would have saved himself, and others, a fair bit of trouble.

═══

AT THE LIBERAL PARTY convention in Montreal in February 2014, Trudeau's Liberal caucus put forward a motion that called for the next Liberal government to establish an "all-party process" that would have a year to report to Parliament with recommendations on electoral reforms "including, without limitation, a preferential ballot and/or a form of proportional representation."

Nine months later, the NDP put a motion before the House of Commons, proposing that "the next federal election should be the last conducted under the current first-past-the-post electoral system" and that "a form of mixed-member proportional representation would be the best electoral system for Canada." Trudeau voted against. But the other thirty Liberal MPs who voted on the motion were split: fifteen in favour, fifteen opposed.

Then came June 16, 2015.

It was on June 16, 2015, coincidentally, that Donald Trump descended the golden escalator at Trump Tower in Manhattan and announced his candidacy for president of the United States, setting in motion a series of events that would roil the Western world.

But this was also the day that Justin Trudeau summoned reporters to Ottawa's ornate and historic Château Laurier—the grand hotel named for Canada's second prime minister—and announced his intention to fundamentally restructure Canadian democracy, tying himself to a commitment that would drag along behind him for the first two years of his government and then quietly haunt him as a broken promise after that.

"We need to know that when we cast a ballot, it counts. That when we vote, it matters. So I'm proposing that we make every vote count," he said. "We are committed to ensuring that the 2015 election will be the last federal election using first-past-the-post."

Several dozen Liberal candidates and MPs were lined up behind him in elevated rows. Immediately over Trudeau's right shoulder stood Maryam Monsef, the Liberal candidate for the swing riding of Peterborough, Ontario. Along with her colleagues, Monsef smiled and applauded as the promise was made. She surely had no idea she was going to end up responsible for what Trudeau had just promised.

The Liberal Party had led opinion polls for more than a year after Trudeau became leader in 2013, but the public's enthusiasm had been dissipating for months. According to an aggregate compiled by the CBC, Liberal support on June 16 stood at 26.7 percent. That put them in third place. Even worse for the Liberals, the NDP was now in first place, if narrowly, with 30.4 percent.

The placard affixed to Trudeau's lectern read "Real CHANGE," with "real" underlined. It was the first time the Liberals had used that slogan for a public event. For a while, Trudeau's primary theme had been "fairness"—that was the buzzword in May 2015 when Trudeau announced a package of policies to raise taxes on the richest Canadians and provide greater support for middle-class and lower-income families. But "fairness" wasn't resonating.

In the fall of 2014, Thomas Mulcair and the NDP had debuted their own slogan: the awkwardly worded "change that's ready" (as if change was a roast that had been in the oven for the requisite number of hours). Eventually that became "ready for change." Either way, the message was the same. The NDP was offering a change from the Harper Conservatives and, unlike the youthful and inexperienced Trudeau, the greying and bearded Mulcair was ready to govern. The Conservative Party would later hit on a similar theme of readiness with a series of ads that said Trudeau was "just not ready."

So now Trudeau wanted to talk about the quality and the extent of the change he could offer. "We felt from day one that Harper was most likely going to lose the election and that we were either going to win or disappear," Gerry Butts says. "So the competition was going to be about who was more of a change from Stephen Harper."

The distinction wouldn't fully crystallize until the summer of 2015, when Trudeau announced that a Liberal government would not balance the federal budget in the short term. That was both a dramatic break from recent political orthodoxy and a commitment Mulcair was unwilling to match. For now, on June 16, Trudeau was offering a thirty-two-point plan for "fair and open government," a sweeping suite of promises for new transparency and accountability in government and Parliament (as well as a commitment to halt the Conservative government's plans to end home mail delivery in some regions of the country).

There were a number of interesting items within that agenda, at least if you're into this sort of thing. But the commitment to electoral reform possessed a particular panache—even if it was also an odd combination of definitive and ambiguous. In keeping with the Liberal motion, an all-party committee would be struck to study and consider options for replacing the first-past-the-post electoral system. "Within 18 months of forming government, we will bring forward legislation to enact reform," the Liberals said.

Combine the Liberal and NDP motions in 2014 (and add six months to the timeline) and you get the Liberal promise of 2015. There would be a new electoral system for 2019. Even if the Liberals couldn't say what it would be.

The precise political value of promising electoral reform is debatable. The cynic might believe it was a play to undercut the NDP. Or that it wouldn't have been promised if the Liberals weren't in third place. Liberals point to numbers that suggest it wasn't a significant motivator for voters, though Butts does acknowledge that "it substantiated the real change argument."

Regardless, the promised change itself was potentially seismic. But then little more was said about it. Parliament was dissolved on August 4 and the official campaign was soon dominated by other issues.

The small matter of whether Canada would abandon the federal electoral system that has shaped its politics and national life since Confederation finally returned to the fore when the House of Commons reconvened in December. Near the end of the first Question Period of the new parliament, the Conservatives sent up Scott Reid, a fussy and meticulous backbencher, to query the new minister for democratic institutions. Would it not make more sense, Reid wondered, for the government to allow the public to vote on a new electoral system in a referendum, as had been the recent practice in several provinces?

"Mr. Speaker, in this election, Canadians were clear that they were expecting us to deliver a change," responded Monsef. "This will be the last first-past-the-post federal election in our history."

The Conservatives noticed that Monsef did not actually answer the question. And so, the next day, they asked again. "I will not," Monsef said this time, "prejudice the outcome of that consultation process by committing to a referendum." The Conservatives howled with indignation. "Liberals just said a referendum on electoral reform 'would prejudice public consultations,'" Conservative MP Jason Kenney reported to his followers on Twitter. Granted, Monsef had not actually said that—she had seemingly meant to suggest that the question of a referendum would be left to the special committee. But she had said enough to make clear that the government wasn't committed to calling a referendum, and she had said it awkwardly. "Is she really asserting that

Canadian people are incapable of deciding in a referendum how they should be governed and how our elections should take place?" Reid asked in the House. "Are Canadians too immature to handle a referendum on this subject, yes or no?"

This was just the beginning.

The New Democrats spoke up in February to wonder about the special committee that would be asked to study electoral reform. The ten seats on each standing committee of the House of Commons are traditionally divided amongst the recognized parties according to their share of seats in the House; that is, according to the results of the last election. That election, of course, had been conducted using the first-past-the-post electoral system. The NDP's Nathan Cullen proposed that the number of seats for each party on the special committee should be determined by the share of the popular vote (another NDP MP, Daniel Blaikie, had suggested this to Cullen). After all, the New Democrats argued, if first-past-the-post was a bad system, it shouldn't be used to determine the makeup of the committee that would help choose an alternative.

Undaunted by such warnings, the Liberals tabled a proposal in May for a ten-member committee with six Liberal MPs. In short order, the Liberals were accused of plotting to "rig" the next election: they had given themselves a majority, it was suggested, so that they could pick their preferred system. Two weeks later, after much shouting, the Liberals backed down and adopted the NDP's proposal.

Despite his record of supporting a ranked ballot, Trudeau mostly kept his opinion to himself. After being sworn in as prime minister, he told the Canadian Press he wanted to be careful about "pushing" his own views. That might have shown a refreshingly deferential and open-minded approach to public debate. But if his opinion was going to matter—and ultimately it would—it likely needed to be heard.

While Trudeau stayed quiet, his preferred option was effectively tainted. In December 2015, the Broadbent Institute, a progressive think tank aligned with the NDP, released an analysis that used opinion polling on voter preferences to suggest the Liberals would have done even better in that year's election if a ranked ballot had been used. Such analysis comes with a significant caveat: a change in the electoral system would inevitably lead to changes in the behaviour of political parties and voters. But, from then on, a ranked ballot was tagged as the Liberal-friendly option.

Within that Broadbent poll were other results that should have given a would-be reformer pause. A majority of respondents, for instance, thought the electoral system needed no change or only minor changes. The top priority of respondents was a ballot that was simple and easy to understand. And a plurality (43 percent) preferred the current system to the alternatives of mixed-member proportional representation, pure proportional representation or a ranked ballot. Only 44 percent clearly said the Liberals should follow through on their platform promise.

That last figure matches something the Liberals themselves found. In a survey commissioned by the Liberal Party shortly after the 2015 election, respondents were asked about forty of the Liberal platform commitments and whether each promise should be considered a top, major or low priority. The top choice was increasing taxes on the richest one percent to pay for a middle-class tax cut: 71 percent said it should be a top or major priority. Conversely, only 21 percent of those surveyed said electoral reform was a top or major priority. Of the forty promises tested by the Liberals, electoral reform rated thirty-ninth, ahead of only "reforming Question Period to make it more substantive."

Nonetheless, Trudeau had promised electoral reform. And he was still speaking of it as a priority in the spring of 2016.

"A lot of people I've talked to have said, 'Oh yes, we really, really wanted electoral reform because we had to get rid of Stephen Harper, but now we have a government we sort of like so electoral reform just doesn't seem as much of a priority anymore,'" Trudeau said during a forum at the University of Ottawa in April.

"Well, it's a priority to me. It's a priority to a lot of Canadians who say, You know what, we need to make sure that going forward we have the best possible electoral system. One that values Canadian voices. One that creates good governments. One that makes sure that people can [be] and feel involved in the political process. That they don't have to make impossible choices between options they don't like. That we are able to create the kind of governance that we need in this country."

Though he didn't make a case for a ranked ballot, it was clear that the ramifications of a choice between a ranked ballot and proportional representation were on his mind. "Is it better to create diversity of voices by making as many different political parties as possible so that in the House of Commons there are all sorts of different perspectives reflected?" he asked. "Another way of doing it is to make sure that parties that reach out themselves to fold in a broad diversity of voices and perspectives within their party get rewarded as well."

Then again, a few months later, Trudeau told the *Toronto Star* that "I have moved in my thinking toward a greater degree of openness towards what Canadians actually want."

That openness would turn out to be significantly limited. But that wouldn't become apparent for several more months.

The special committee met through the summer of 2017, travelling outside Ottawa to hold hearings in every province and territory. In all, it heard from a total of 196 witnesses and received 574 briefs. Members from all parties were asked to host town hall meetings in their ridings and 172 reports were filed by MPs from those events—the committee later estimated that more than 12,000 citizens had attended a town hall. In August, Monsef launched her own twenty-four-stop tour across the country. The federal government also posted a thirty-eight-page booklet for citizens who were interested in hosting their own forums. "Your guide to hosting a successful dialogue on Canadian federal electoral reform" included an overview of different voting models, tips on facilitating a worthwhile discussion, and a reminder to buy plates or napkins if refreshments were to be served.

In December 2016, the special committee delivered a 348-page report. It was both a comprehensive survey of electoral reform history, options and considerations, and a dog's breakfast of recommendations.

A majority of members on the committee—presumably including Conservatives and New Democrats—agreed that a referendum should be held on a new system before the next election. But the New Democrats and Green Party MP Elizabeth May also attached a supplemental opinion that suggested a referendum wasn't entirely necessary. "That was meant to be an opening to the Liberals if they wanted to grab a last opportunity," Cullen says. "Because the Liberals suddenly made a big deal out of a referendum." After her initial ambiguity, Monsef had indeed argued that referendums were often divisive experiences.

As for what might be put to Canadians in a referendum, no particular alternative system was specified. Instead, the committee's majority said that the government should choose a model that rated highly on something called the "Gallagher Index," a rating system developed by an Irish political scientist that measures how closely an electoral result matches the popular vote.

In their own supplemental opinion, the Liberal members of the committee argued that the majority was recommending a hasty, and potentially dangerous, course of action. "I was never able to get anything, even a hint, as to what they wanted," Cullen says of the Liberal members.

Monsef might have let the committee's inconclusiveness speak for itself. Instead, she went on the attack—a very unfortunate attack. Brandishing an enlarged copy of the equation that underpins the Gallagher Index, Monsef zealously mocked the committee's report in the House and said she was disappointed in the committee's efforts. "On the main question and the hard choices that we asked the committee to make, the members of the committee took a pass," Monsef lamented. Afterwards, she went into the foyer and repeated her complaints for reporters. The Conservatives and New Democrats were aghast, and they were joined by the husband of Liberal MP Ruby Sahota. "My son saw his mom for a total of 6 hours over 3 weeks, while [the electoral reform committee] toured Canada," Tej Sahota wrote on Twitter. "Try again, Maryam." For a government that was supposed to respect evidence, data and academic expertise, it was a particularly bad look.

The next day, Monsef stood in the House and apologized. The rookie minister was a talented but inexperienced politician. She could handle a public forum with aplomb, but she struggled with Question Period. At times, she could seem too earnest. In this case, she'd been unnecessarily savage. In some ways, she was reminiscent of Trudeau in his earlier years, before he'd fully calibrated his public demeanour. But she had also been assigned what now seems to have been an impossible task.

Days after the algebraic imbroglio, the government launched a new consultation. Fifteen million postcards were mailed to households, directing Canadians to a website—MyDemocracy.ca—where they were asked about what values they wanted to see reflected in an electoral system. Respondents were then grouped into categories that apparently reflected their disposition toward electoral democracy: "co-operators," "guardians," "challengers," "innovators" or "pragmatists." If the government had released such a survey a year earlier, it might've been received as a useful, if somewhat novel, opener to engaging the public on a complicated topic. But at this late date, and in the wake of Monsef's mockery, it became a punchline. "It feels like being on a dating website designed by Fidel Castro," Scott Reid joked.

In the second week of January, Monsef was mercifully shuffled to the Status of Women portfolio, where she would be given an opportunity to rehabilitate her image. A week and a half later, after a two-hour meeting of cabinet, Trudeau decided to abandon his promise.

To make it official, the change was written into the mandate letter for Monsef's successor, Karina Gould. "A clear preference for a new electoral system, let alone a consensus, has not emerged," the prime minister wrote. "Furthermore, without a clear preference or a clear question, a referendum would not be in Canada's interest. Changing the electoral system will not be in your mandate."

After the letter was released on February 1, Trudeau was more specific. "As people in this House know, I have long preferred a preferential ballot," he said, stating an opinion he had mostly suppressed over the previous eighteen months. "The members opposite wanted proportional representation. The Official Opposition wanted a referendum. There is no consensus."

The opposition was united in its scorn.

"What Trudeau proved himself today was to be a liar, was to be of the most cynical variety of politician," fumed Cullen.

"We are in a time of dangerous politics. You must never do anything, as a politician who understands what's at stake, that feeds cynicism," lamented May. "Cynicism has enough to feed itself. It is work to feed hope. It is work to feed faith. And when you break faith you will reap what you sow."

"When they realized that there was no consensus for the system that favoured them, then they simply decided to break their promise," a New Democrat later concluded.

———

SHORTLY AFTER THE DECISION was made public, Trudeau visited Iqaluit. There he encountered a woman asked him about why he'd walked away from his promise.

"Do you think that Kellie Leitch should have her own party?" Trudeau asked her.

Leitch was, at that time, seeking the leadership of the Conservative Party. Months earlier, she had come forward with a Trumpian proposal: all immigrants, she said, should be screened for "anti-Canadian values." The rest of her campaign was devoted to complaining about the "elites" who looked down on such ideas. In a message to supporters, she cheered Trump's victory as an exciting moment that needed to be replicated in Canada.

In a system of proportional representation, Trudeau suggested, such a Leitch party could end up holding the balance of power. "Proportional representation in any form would be bad for Canada," he said. "The strength of our democracy is that we have to pull people into big parties that have all the diversity of Canada and we learn to get along." This was not an entirely abstract concern: in Europe, for instance, systems of proportional representation have allowed far-right parties to gain a foothold in national legislatures.

Trudeau then expanded on such concerns during a town hall in

Yellowknife. He had "always felt," he explained, that a ranked ballot would be a "clear improvement." But others believed it would favour the Liberals and, as a result, he didn't want to push it. "I am not going to do something that everyone is convinced is going to favour one party over another."

A referendum, he said, would be too divisive, noting the recent examples in the United Kingdom and Italy. "At a time when we're look-ing for stability in the face of a very unpredictable and unstable political context around the world, I don't think a referendum is the right way to go," he explained. He could have also noted two early Canadian exam-ples: on the prohibition of alcohol in 1898 and on conscription in 1942. In both cases, voters in Quebec went one way while voters in every other province went the other. A similar split on electoral reform—or perhaps a result that would pit the western provinces against Ontario and Quebec—could have been painful.

"And then there's proportional representation," Trudeau continued. "One of the things that's great about Canada . . . is that we're a country that focuses on common ground."

Trudeau, of course, had given his autobiography that title: *Common Ground*. Little did anyone realize that the answer to the electoral reform adventure was right there on the book's cover.

"We're a country that focuses on the things we have in common with each other even though we're different," he said. "And the differences in Canada—east to west, south to north, English to French, to every background imaginable, Indigenous, non-Indigenous, urban, rural, left, right—there are so many. There are more differences within Can-ada, within Canadians, than within just about any other country in the world and yet, better than any other country in the world we figured out how to make those differences a source of strength."

Our political systems, he argued, have helped us in that regard because they have brought together disparate people to form govern-ments. In effect, he was arguing that the "big tent" parties of Canada's history have reinforced the strength of the country's diversity. In this way, the need to appeal broadly in order to win seats, and thus have influence in governing the country, is a force for national unity and social harmony.

Moving to a system that "that would augment individual voices, that would augment extremist voices and activist voices" could put all that at risk.

The Justin Trudeau of 2017 now sounded a lot like the Justin Trudeau of 2013. If not for the Justin Trudeau of 2015 that wouldn't have been a problem.

Proponents of proportional representation blanch at such comments. Proportional representation might encourage extremist voices to form their own parties, they say, but first-past-the-post gives extremists a chance to form majority governments with less than 50 percent of the popular vote. "First-past-the-post didn't stop Doug Ford from coming into power in Ontario," NDP leader Jagmeet Singh quipped during a speech in September 2018.

Singh has a point. Even if it's also fair to ask whether Ford could have become premier if he'd run on something like Kellie Leitch's platform. On that note, Singh added that "first-past-the-post didn't prevent Maxime Bernier from launching an anti-immigrant political party." But a system of proportional representation likely would have given Bernier's new party a much better chance of winning a significant number of seats in 2019. As it is, the People's Party of Canada might be lucky to win even a single riding.

All of which is worthy of consideration and debate. But that debate never really occurred, in large part because Trudeau didn't engage until after the issue was taken off the table.

Worries about the ramifications of implementing proportional representation or holding a national referendum are also not illegitimate. Indeed, both are very good reasons to avoid making an open-ended commitment to implement electoral reform in the first place.

<hr />

"As I've thought through it many times: How could we have done it differently? I think my mistake was leaving a bit of space open for proportional representation," Trudeau says on a sunny afternoon in September 2018, seated in his office on Wellington Street.

"I was convinced by elements in our caucus of thirty-five people that I had to leave the door open at least a crack for proportional representation if we're going to have a real conversation about this. And I always said, 'Look, I really don't think proportional representation is a good idea but I'm willing to be convinced that I'm wrong on this. It's just no one has been able to convince me that it would be a good idea.' And I left that open a crack and had to leave that open a crack the whole way through, even though I fundamentally believe that ranking your ballots is an elegant and proper solution that would lead to new and different, but better and stable, configurations of Canadian politics that would avoid some of the extremes that we have and would continue to keep a diversity of voices within political parties as opposed to across political parties."

In that respect, Trudeau says he believed he could make the case for a ranked ballot. "I went into it with—and this is the kind of thing that will make people roll their eyes when I say this—but I genuinely went into it with a faith that I could demonstrate that there was a better path of encouraging people to try and be other people's second choices," he says.

But that didn't happen. In fact, the opposite occurred.

"If I had to do it again I would've been making an aggressive case for preferential ballot," he says. "I was perhaps overconfident or overly trusting when I thought that on the merits of things, a preferential ballot is so clearly a better step in the right direction that were I to speak up clearly and aggressively on it, it would harden people against an option that I wanted them to be open to."

Specifically, Trudeau suggests that an aggressive push by him for a ranked ballot could have made it harder for the NDP to agree. As it is, the NDP remained steadfast in its long-standing desire for proportional representation anyway.

There were behind-the-scenes discussions between Liberals and New Democrats. Though the details of those discussions are disputed, such conversations evidently did not come to anything. Mark Holland,

Monsef's parliamentary secretary at the time, says his discussions with New Democrats never led anywhere useful. "There was nothing that I felt that I could've taken up and said, 'Okay, we've got an opening here,'" Holland says.

Trudeau still clearly wants to make a case for his preferred option, even though the matter is officially closed. He suggests, for instance, that he might not have been elected in Papineau in 2008 if a ranked ballot had been used at the time (he won with 41.5 percent of the vote, just 1,200 votes more than the Bloc Québécois incumbent Vivian Barbot). For the NDP, he argues, a ranked ballot in 2015 might have helped Paul Dewar get elected in Ottawa Centre, or Megan Leslie get elected in Halifax, because left-of-centre voters would not have feared splitting the vote.

Proportional representation, he says, might help the Greens and put them in a position to influence government policy, but it could also empower an anti-immigrant party. "We have people along the spectrum— and that's good and that's healthy because it represents Canadians—but there are fringes out there that cannot be accepted by mainstream parties that want to wield power across the country," Trudeau says. "And that's a system that's really important to regulate things."

There is, in fact, a theory that first-past-the-post and the current allotment of federal ridings help to perpetuate political support for multiculturalism and diversity: that, in practical terms, any party seeking to govern must win a significant number of ridings where visible minorities represent a significant number of votes. Using data from the 2016 census, Andrew Griffith, a researcher and former official at the Department of Citizenship and Immigration, has identified fifty-eight ridings where visible minorities make up at least 40 percent of the population. And it would be very difficult to win a majority government without winning some of those seats.

"The other flip side of where you need more proportional representation is in places where individual rights aren't as fully defended as we are under a Charter," Trudeau continues. "I mean, we have a system in which minority voices are, not perfectly, but are better empowered and better respected than anywhere else. And they have an ability to get into mainstream politics in a way that other more tribal or more divided or more homogenous countries simply don't have. So, in extremely homogenous countries, I think proportional representation could work. In extremely repressive societies or divided societies, I think proportional representation is probably reasonable. I just really don't think it works for Canada."

All of which could have made for an interesting discussion in the nearly two years between when Trudeau made his promise and when he announced he was abandoning it. So why didn't Trudeau say all of this then?

"When I proposed, 'Well look, let me go on a tour and let me explain this the way it works,' the way I can. The way in a five-minute conversation I can convince anyone," he says, recalling a conversation with his team of advisors. "They're like, 'Justin, we need you talking about the economic growth strategy that we have. We need you connecting with people on the things that matter to them, not the things that matter to you and a few people here. And you only have so much bandwidth to get your message across, and if you're using a big chunk of it on something that—the people who feel most passionately about it disagree with you and the others just want to trust that you, you know, do it right.'"

"If he could have, he would've gone across the country and sold it. And probably been successful at that. But then we wouldn't have been doing a lot of other things," says Katie Telford.

Trudeau makes a similar admission when asked about one of the popular theories for why the promise was included in the Liberal platform: that it was a cynical attempt to steal votes from the NDP. "It was a promise that was in there because I really cared about it," he says. "And some of the wiser, some of the more experienced or different brilliant heads in my team would have rather, I think, I not make it as firmly, as forcefully. But I thought that being as crystal clear about it and binding myself to it and really being explicit about it was the kind of thing that would mean that it would happen."

Suffice to say, that did not happen. Having committed to a promise he shouldn't have made, he stepped back, kept his opinion to himself and let other voices fill the void. Then, when that failed to achieve something he could support, he walked away.

Even if walking away was a defensible decision, everything about how he got there was a problem. This was not the Trudeau who legalized marijuana, bought a pipeline or put a price on carbon. And his government's meandering pursuit of electoral reform stands in stark contrast to the comprehensive and nimble effort to negotiate a new free trade agreement with the United States and Mexico.

From within the government, there is an acknowledgement that it took too long for everyone to understand that the pursuit of electoral reform was going nowhere good. "It was a combination of early days and knowing how passionate the boss was on this subject, that it took us longer than it probably usually would for us to go, 'We need to put a pin in this somehow,'" Telford says.

Electoral reform was a fatally flawed promise that, once made, was never properly corrected. The result was wasted energy and a self-inflicted wound to Trudeau's credibility.

LESS THAN TWO YEARS after Trudeau abandoned electoral reform, British Columbians were given the opportunity to do what he had not. Somewhat surprisingly, they came to the same conclusion he had.

The referendum that B.C.'s New Democrats and Greens agreed to call was the third time in thirteen years that the people of British Columbia had been asked to consider electoral reform. In 2005, 58 percent of voters endorsed a system of proportional representation known as single transferable vote (STV), but the B.C. Liberal government had established a threshold of 60 percent for moving forward with a new system. A second referendum was held in 2009, but this time STV received only 39 percent of the vote.

In 2018, no single system was put to British Columbians as an alternative. Instead, voters were given a two-part ballot. First, they were asked to decide whether they wished to maintain the current system of first-past-the-post or move to a system of proportional representation. Second, they were asked to rank three possible models for proportional representation. If a simple majority of voters said yes to the first question, an instant run-off would determine the new system.

With the details of a specific alternative put secondary to the basic question of change, the ballot seemed at first to increase the likelihood of a victory for reform. But when the results were released a few days before Christmas, the victory for the status quo was resounding: 61.3 percent voted to keep first-past-the-post. At 38.7 percent, the abstract idea of proportional representation had actually received less support than STV in 2009.

Then, in April 2019, the voters of Prince Edward Island delivered the same verdict. A referendum there in 2016 had produced a messy result: a narrow, run-off victory for mixed-member proportional on a ballot that started with five options and with voter turnout at just 36.5 percent. So the Liberal government in Charlottetown called for a do-over, this time pitting mixed-member proportional against first-past-the-post in a head-to-head contest. The result was a narrow win for first-past-the-post: 51.2 percent to 48.8 percent.

Both results took some of the sting out of attacks on Trudeau for walking away, and somewhat redeemed his decision to not pursue a referendum. It will also now be harder for the NDP to campaign on proportional representation in 2019.

But there remains at least one opening for reform. In Quebec, François Legault's new Coalition Avenir Québec government made a campaign promise to implement mixed-member proportional voting. And with two other parties also supporting that proposed change, Legault might be willing to proceed without a referendum.

If there ever is to be electoral reform, it would make sense for that change to start at the provincial level—that the provinces would serve as the "laboratories of democracy," to borrow a phrase coined by Louis Brandeis, a justice of the U.S. Supreme Court, to refer to American states in 1932.

Trudeau's questions about what reform would mean at the federal level would still stand. The actual arrival of proportional representation in Canada would allow that debate to live on for a while longer.

CHAPTER 8

PIERRE'S SON
BUYS A PIPELINE

In October 2013, Pierre Trudeau's son went to Calgary to condemn Stephen Harper's approach to resource development. The irony was rich. Justin Trudeau noted that he'd recently been to Washington, D.C., where he'd told an audience that he supported plans for the Keystone XL pipeline, which would carry oil from Alberta to the Gulf of Mexico. "It is in keeping with what I believe is a fundamental role of the government of Canada," he said, "to open up markets abroad for Canadian resources, and to help create responsible and sustainable ways to get those resources to those markets."

His words might have flattered his audience at the Petroleum Club, the wood-panelled clubhouse of Alberta's oil industry. But he was also laying down a significant marker for a future Trudeau government.

The president of the United States was reluctant to approve Keystone XL in the fall of 2013. Environmentalists had successfully turned the pipeline into a referendum on Barack Obama's commitment to fighting climate change. Trudeau argued that "Mr. Harper's divisiveness" had only made things worse. The Conservatives had bullied and demonized their critics and taken a "one-sided" approach to regulation. They were unable or unwilling to work with the American president and scoffed at his concerns. And they lacked a clear strategy.

The Liberal leader said he would be clear from the outset: that getting Canada's resources to market is in "the national interest," but that resource development would come within a larger framework that considered climate change. Environmental policy, he said, went together with market access. "If we had stronger environmental policy in this country—stronger oversight, tougher penalties, and yes, some sort of means to price carbon pollution—then I believe the Keystone XL pipeline would have been approved already," he said. "It is the absence of strong policy that makes us an easy target."

There also needed to be diplomacy and partnerships between First Nations, environmentalists and industry. Times had changed, the Liberal leader ventured. "Social licence is more important than ever," he said.

That phrase—"social licence"—had emerged in the late 1990s, coined by a Canadian mining executive to explain the importance of public support for resource projects. By 2013, it was a dominant theme—the words had even crossed the lips of Joe Oliver, the Conservative natural resources minister who also once complained that "environmental and other radical groups" were plotting to "hijack our regulatory system to achieve their radical ideological agenda."

"Governments may be able to issue permits," Trudeau added, "but only communities can grant permission."

This was a tidy bit of rhetoric, and, in the abstract, it contained some logic. But it also did not nearly account for what Trudeau was about to encounter as prime minister.

None of this would be easy, Trudeau granted. It would take hard work. But it could be done. "We know that hope is a fine thing, but without a tireless work ethic, it can be fleeting," he said. "Hope on its own didn't build the [Canadian Pacific Railway], or develop the oil sands. It didn't build the Rideau Canal, or the TransCanada highway." Compared with building a pipeline in the second decade of the twenty-first century, all those things now seem rather easy.

A year and a half later, Trudeau went back to the Petroleum Club, this time to explain what a "stronger environmental policy" would look like if he were prime minister.

Keystone XL was still being blocked, and the resource sector's international reputation was suffering because the Harper government had "failed to deliver . . . a sensible, credible approach to the environment and the economy," Trudeau said. The public needed to be able to trust that Canadian resources were being developed in an environmentally responsible manner.

Indigenous communities needed to be meaningfully consulted. Project approvals had to be subject to adequate oversight. Changes to those regulations shouldn't be buried in omnibus budget bills. And, Trudeau said, "Canada needs to have a price on carbon."

This was no small thing for a Liberal leader to say.

Seven years earlier, Harper's Conservatives had successfully savaged Stéphane Dion for proposing a national carbon tax—it would "screw everybody," threaten national unity and possibly plunge the economy into recession, Harper warned at various points. A few years later, the Conservatives heaped similar scorn on the NDP's proposal for a cap-and-trade system. Never mind that the Conservatives had previously made their own commitment to pursue cap-and-trade, that other options to reduce emissions would likely cost even more to implement, that numerous economists recommend pricing as the smartest and most cost-effective approach, or that the basic issue at hand was the fate of the planet and the welfare of everyone who inhabits it—the Harper government saw something it could exploit and was zealous in doing so.

Some things had changed since Dion's ill-fated campaign in 2008. As Trudeau noted, three provinces—British Columbia, Alberta and Quebec—had implemented pricing mechanisms of one kind of another, and Ontario was likely to go next. That much, he posited, was a tribute to federalism. And that led him to his next point, what he described as one of the most important lessons he had learned during his time in public life: "the federal government does not have all the answers."

Here he invoked his father's National Energy Program (NEP). "When the federal government ignores these regional distinctions, or discounts provincial and territorial perspectives, our country is weakened, not strengthened. This was the case when the federal government pushed the National Energy Program over the strong opposition of Western Canada generally and Alberta in particular." The federal government would be wrong, he said, to impose a "one-size-fits-all solution from Ottawa."

This was not the first time Justin Trudeau had criticized Pierre Trudeau's infamous energy policy. Almost immediately after declaring his candidacy for leadership of the Liberal Party in October 2012, he had gone to Calgary and said the NEP was a mistake. That had been major news—a son's attempt to make peace with those who still fume at his father's memory.

To understand the place of the NEP in popular and political mythology, consider the acidic obituary for Pierre Trudeau, written by a former Reform MP named Stephen Harper, that appeared in the pages of the *National Post* on October 5, 2000.

"By the time Mr. Trudeau embarked on the National Energy Program I was living in the West," Harper recalled. "I witnessed first-hand the movement of an economy from historic boom to deep recession in a matter of months. A radical, interventionist blueprint of economic nationalism, the NEP caused the oil industry to flee, businesses to close and the real estate market to crash. The lives of honest, hard-working Albertans were upended and I came to know many of those who lost their jobs and their homes."

Someone with a master's degree in economics might have been expected to present a more nuanced assessment of the situation, noting, for instance, that the NEP had coincided with a global recession and a drop in world oil prices. But Harper fairly captured Pierre Trudeau's popular stature and legacy in Alberta. And while the province had never been particularly friendly to the Liberal Party of Canada, it became a wasteland for the red team under Pierre's leadership. In 1968, at the height of Trudeaumania, the Liberals won four seats in Alberta. After that, they were completely shut out until Jean Chrétien's Liberals won four seats in 1993. By 2006, they were back to zero.

With a view from Alberta, Harper found his calling: he became a conservative and set about fashioning his political life in opposition to Trudeau's liberalism. The victory of the Harper Conservatives in 2006 would be hailed as the West's arrival within the Canadian political establishment, a bookend to the Western alienation Pierre Trudeau had fostered.

But Pierre's son went to Alberta to denounce the NEP. And then he kept going back.

Some of that was simple politics: Trudeau needed to differentiate himself from his father. He also didn't want to start from the premise that any region of the country could be written off for potential victories. (And, in fact, the Liberals picked up four seats in Alberta in 2015.) But some of it was more than that.

"I think Justin Trudeau has always been determined to not be a Trudeau who cannot see a friendly face west of the Lakehead. He has always been in his public talks, since he was Liberal leader, looking for points of commonality with people in the Prairies and people in the energy business," says Brian Topp, who dealt with the Trudeau government as chief of staff to Alberta premier Rachel Notley. "I have no doubt that one of their political interests is that he just does not want this Liberal government to be demonized the way his father's was."

On a flight to Calgary in November 2018, Trudeau is asked about Topp's analysis.

"I think there are two places in the country where my father's legacy looms larger and in a more challenging way than anywhere else—and that's Alberta and Quebec," Trudeau says. "In Alberta it was the very specific challenge for me to make myself and my approach known as different from my father in a way that I'd settled for myself in all other parts of my political life. I vanquished those challenges in Quebec, and within the Liberal Party and other places. Alberta really kept a key element to their myth around my father very, very much intact. And that's, yes, one of the reasons why I have been so thoughtful about going back."

He says this on the way to his twentieth visit to the province as prime minister.

"But it's not about trying to undo some past wrongs or demonizations like that. It's very much about saying, Look, I'm going to be prime minister for the whole country and I'll keep listening to every-one in the whole country, regardless of whether we do well in elections or have an opportunity to do well in elections. I mean, Alberta is an important place for our economy—so many people go there for work. When Alberta's on tough times, it has impacts on the rest of the coun-try. You can't understand Canada without having a really good grasp of Alberta," he says.

"It's not because I have illusions I'm going to pick up twenty-five seats in the next election in Alberta. It's a sense of, yeah, it's one of those places I need to really understand. The people also need to know that we are listening, we are thinking about them. Because, again, [it speaks to] to my highest imperative around holding the country together, which also involves fighting that easy polarization that domi-nated my childhood between Quebec and the rest of Canada. And it is always present in terms of the thread of Western alienation. And it's not a force that we want to allow to amplify."

But from a purely political standpoint, couldn't he afford to neglect a province where his party might be lucky to hold its four seats?

"I don't think so, because part of my entire political identity is say-ing that everyone matters and that diversity of views, like diversity of everything, is really important," he says. "And I can't authentically and honestly with integrity say, yes, bringing people together and listen-ing—except those guys because, you know, I'm better off fighting for a marginal riding in Central Ontario or something like that."

Back in February 2015, he was pitching a "medicare approach" to climate policy.

"We will set a national standard in partnership with provinces and territories, one that gives them the flexibility to design their own pol-icies to achieve those targets, including their own carbon pricing poli-cies," he told an audience at the Canadian Club in Calgary. "And we will provide targeted federal funding to help the provinces and territories achieve their goals."

In a way, this comparison elevated climate policy to the stature it deserved. A health care system is one of the foundational elements of a functioning society, and universal medicare is central to the modern idea of what Canada is. Climate change, a profound threat to the present and future of humanity on planet Earth, surely should be held in the same regard. At some point, one way or another, it probably will be.

But the history of health care policy in Canada might've offered Trudeau and everyone else a few lessons about how smoothly this might go. National medicare was established only after years of political wrangling and despite cries of objection from provinces such as Ontario and Alberta. Long before the National Energy Program, it was Pierre Trudeau's government that helped push medicare to completion by unilaterally implementing a 2 percent "social development tax," to be paid regardless of whether or not one lived in a province that had joined the federal framework. "Medicare is a glowing example of a Machiavellian scheme that is in my humble opinion one of the greatest political frauds that has been perpetrated on the people of this country," Ontario premier John Robarts fumed at the time.

Fifty years later, there are still complaints—even if there is little to no support for tearing the system apart. Indeed, conservative politicians have had to pledge their allegiance to maintaining the public system. In a national vote in 2004, Tommy Douglas was chosen as the "Greatest Canadian" on the basis that, having established a medicare system in Saskatchewan, he was the "father of medicare" in Canada.

But what Trudeau ended up proposing was even more complicated than medicare. Put together, those two speeches to the Petroleum Club ultimately amounted to a grand bargain: yes, there would be a price on carbon, but there would also be a pipeline. He would seek to reduce emissions for the long term even as he sought to maximize profits for the oil and gas industry in the short term.

There were economic and political arguments for doing each of these things. It might be fun to say that Canada should abandon its oil and gas industry, but it's hard to explain how you would do so while holding together the country and its economy. Albertans, in particular, might not take kindly to their province's primary economic driver being shut down. Oil is still a useful and valuable commodity. For however long oil is being used somewhere in the world, some of it might as well be Canadian. For however long Alberta is going to be producing oil, the province might as well get the best price for it. Meanwhile, if you're going to reduce greenhouse gas emissions, the most efficient way to do so is by putting a price on those emissions—a price that will both take into account the environmental cost of those emissions and encourage the market to make cleaner decisions.

But Trudeau was also proposing to fuse two ideas—fighting climate change and developing fossil fuels—that don't naturally seem to go together. Those who opposed one or the other—pricing carbon or building pipelines—would thus find something to be upset about. To those who would argue it wasn't worth being environmentally friendly to get a pipeline approved or those who would say a pipeline could not be reconciled with caring about the climate, Trudeau would argue that it wasn't so simple, particularly in Canada.

The parties to Trudeau's left and right would pick one or the other: Andrew Scheer's Conservatives would be loud champions of a pipeline, but eventually couldn't even feign interest in meeting Canada's international climate targets; Jagmeet Singh's New Democrats demanded even faster and steeper cuts in Canada's emissions, but have ended up opposed to every pipeline proposal on offer.

Trudeau would be arguing that you didn't need to choose one or the other. You could have both. Maybe that would anger the most passionate opponents of pipelines and carbon taxes, but maybe enough people would find something to support and the spirit of compromise and accommodation would prevail.

It would eventually be argued that, in linking the two ideas, Trudeau was in danger of losing both. That he would have been better off making distinct arguments for two individually defensible ideas.

On that flight to Calgary in November 2018, Trudeau remained convinced of his approach.

"For me, it was never, 'Okay, this is the convenient political narrative that we'll spin.' It was 'This is what we have to figure out as a country and the world.' We have to be a lot more bold on protecting the environment, we have to figure out how to get our jobs now secured and move towards those better jobs of the future," he says.

His conversations with Canadians, he says, reassure him.

"It seems to me that it's always better to have a grand unified theory and not have one for the atomic level and one for the space level. You know, can we bring everything together in something that holds as a cohesive whole. Because I think that's how people think about things. Quite frankly, that's how I think of it. For me everything has to sort of fit in with everything else in a cohesive whole. I don't like isolated little boxes that don't fit into anything else."

In the world beyond Trudeau's head, the fit has not been easy.

―――――――

THE DIFFERENCE BETWEEN THEORY and practice can be measured as the distance between the Petroleum Club in Calgary and the gymnasium at Vancouver Island University in Nanaimo, British Columbia (roughly 1,054 kilometres, if travelling by car). On February 2, 2018, four and a half years after that first speech to the Petroleum Club, Trudeau visited Nanaimo to take questions from the public at a town hall meeting.

Fifteen minutes into the forum, Trudeau called on an elderly woman wearing a knit sweater. "Hey, my handsome, precious one, how are you?" she asked in a singsong voice.

"Thank you, I'm better, now," Trudeau responded, smiling.

"Oh, I'm glad to hear that," said the woman.

Nanaimo is located across the waters of the Strait of Georgia from where the Trans Mountain pipeline comes to an end at the Burnaby refinery. And now, this nice woman in the knit sweater wanted to ask about the Trans Mountain expansion.

Fourteen months earlier—in November 2016—Trudeau's government had approved the expansion, a proposal to twin the existing pipeline to carry diluted bitumen and other oil products from Edmonton. The multi-billion-dollar project would triple the current capacity, allowing for as much as 890,000 barrels each day to reach the west coast. That greater access to international markets would allow

Alberta's oil companies to sell their product at a better price. And that meant greater revenues for the oil industry and billions more in tax revenue for the federal, Alberta and B.C. governments.

What's more, this pipeline was, perhaps counterintuitively, linked to the Trudeau government's national climate strategy.

After taking office in the spring of 2015—following a stunning upset that ended forty-three consecutive years of governing by Alberta's Progressive Conservatives—Rachel Notley's NDP government moved quickly and aggressively to reduce the province's emissions. Without such policies, Canada had little chance of meeting its international climate targets.

But if Alberta was going to significantly curtail its emissions, it wanted the other provinces to follow suit, and it wanted a pipeline to the coast. "In adopting the cap that it did the province has essentially foregone somewhere between half and two-thirds of its daily production potential. It has decided it is not going to be a six to nine million barrel a day producer, it's going to plateau at somewhere around three to four [million barrels a day]," says Brian Topp. "So if that is what's going to happen—because otherwise Canada cannot meet its climate goals—then how can you get more value out of what you produce."

This is a debatable, and somewhat controversial, point. An analysis conducted in 2018 suggested that the cap might be reached in 2030, with production running at 4.1 million barrels per day. But the cap is not officially tied to production. If the oil industry can deploy new technologies to reduce the rate of emissions produced per barrel, the cap would leave more room to produce more oil.

Either way, there was a useful three-way trade-off here, at least in theory. A cap would ensure that, even if another pipeline were constructed, emissions would not be allowed to rise above a certain level, and that would hopefully assuage some concerns about building a pipeline. A pipeline, in turn, would help Notley justify her new environmental policies. Meanwhile, the oil industry and the province would be able to extract more value out of the oil Alberta was producing.

On February 2, 2018, Trans Mountain looked like the last best chance for Trudeau and Notley to get a pipeline built. With Donald Trump in the White House, TransCanada's Keystone XL had a good chance of being revived, but that would still carry oil only to the American market. Trudeau personally opposed Northern Gateway, a proposal to carry oil from Alberta to the coast across northern British Columbia, on the grounds that it would have cut through the Great Bear Rainforest. After the Federal Court of Appeal ruled that the Harper government had not done enough to consult Indigenous groups on that project, the Liberals killed it and then moved to ban large tankers from transporting crude oil to or from ports along the northern coast of British Columbia. Meanwhile, regulatory and political challenges, as well as a preference for the Keystone proposal, convinced TransCanada to walk away from a proposal known as Energy East, which would have carried oil from Alberta to refineries in Quebec and New Brunswick.

That left the Trans Mountain expansion. There were good political and economic reasons to proceed. But, of course, a pipeline is not a perfectly benign source of wealth. It might be safer to transport oil by pipeline than by rail—forty-seven people died when a train carrying crude oil crashed in Lac-Mégantic, Quebec, in 2013—but a pipeline will still periodically spring a leak. Exporting that oil would require an increase in tanker traffic around the port of Vancouver. And, in this case, the oil was originating from Alberta's oil sands, a development portrayed by environmentalists as a noxious blight on the natural world.

There was also the question of Indigenous consultation and support. Kinder Morgan, the pipeline's proponent, identified more than a hundred Indigenous communities as having an interest in the Trans Mountain expansion. Of those, the company signed benefit agreements with forty-three. But more than a dozen launched legal challenges.

Kinder Morgan had first applied for approval of the Trans Mountain expansion in 2013 and, despite his own criticism of Harper's regulatory changes, Trudeau did not ask that the company start all over under a new process once the Liberals came to power in November 2015.

Instead, a ministerial panel was struck to review the project, and Environment Canada was asked to produce an analysis of potential upstream emissions. A new round of consultations with Indigenous groups was conducted. Then, in November 2016, Trudeau travelled to Vancouver to announce an investment of $1.5 billion over five years to improve marine safety and spill response, including measures to protect and support the southern resident killer whale, an endangered population that was located in the waters around Vancouver Island.

As premier of British Columbia, Christy Clark had set out five conditions that needed to be satisfied before her government would accept any pipeline: completion of an environmental review, a plan to respond effectively to an oil spill on water, measures to mitigate the risk of a spill on land, consultation with Indigenous communities and assurances that British Columbia would receive a "fair share of the fiscal and economic benefits" derived from a project. For the Trans Mountain expansion, the last of those was satisfied when Kinder Morgan agreed to a twenty-year revenue-sharing deal that would pay the province between $500 million and $1 billion.

Thus, as of January 2017, the government of British Columbia was officially on side. But the government of British Columbia was not guaranteed to continue being the government of British Columbia for much longer—an election was set to be called for May. The province's voters then produced a tantalizing result: forty-three Liberal members of the legislative assembly were elected alongside forty-one New Democrats and three Greens. Clark's side had the most seats, but was one short of holding a majority. And that gave NDP leader John Horgan an opening to make a deal with the Greens.

As luck would have it, the Trans Mountain expansion was among the issues on which the B.C. New Democrats and Greens could agree: they both opposed it. Building on language in the NDP's campaign platform, the ten-page confidence and supply accord between the two parties set out that an NDP government would "immediately employ every tool available to the new government to stop the expansion of the Kinder Morgan pipeline." Horgan and Green Party leader Andrew Weaver signed that agreement on May 30, 2017. After turning down

Clark's request for a new election, British Columbia's lieutenant governor invited Horgan to form a government.

A week after he was sworn in, the new premier went to Ottawa to meet with Trudeau. "Difficult issues come up. We're going to work together to resolve them," Trudeau told reporters.

Inside that meeting, according to a Liberal source, Trudeau suggested he and Horgan agreed about more than they disagreed about. They had both been elected to invest in transit, housing and infrastructure. And they should try to minimize their fights over Trans Mountain. But, Trudeau explained, the pipeline was going to be built and his government was going to do everything in its power to make sure it did. What Trudeau hoped was that, at some point, he could provide Horgan with an "off-ramp"—maybe more money for ocean protection or a higher percentage of unionized contracts for the construction. Two or three things that Horgan could point to while conceding defeat and assigning all responsibility for the pipeline to Trudeau. Discussions between the federal and B.C. governments continued along those lines over the next six months. "Prime Minister Trudeau stated his belief the pipeline was necessary, Premier Horgan disagreed and they left it at that," says an official in Horgan's office.

Once in office, Horgan's government realized some tools were better left unused. Withholding permits for the pipeline, for instance, could expose the B.C. government to a lawsuit. But the provincial government applied for and was granted intervener status in a legal challenge mounted by Indigenous groups. Later, it asked the Federal Court of Appeal to reconsider a decision of the National Energy Board (NEB) that Kinder Morgan did not have to abide by certain municipal by-laws.

Neither of those two moves was particularly provocative. But then, on January 30, 2018, British Columbia's environment minister, George Heyman, announced he would be seeking public input on "additional measures" to "protect B.C.'s environment from spills." Five possible "measures" were listed, the fifth of which was "restrictions on the increase of diluted bitumen ('dilbit') transportation until the behaviour of spilled bitumen can be better understood and there is certainty regarding the ability to adequately mitigate spills."

Trudeau now describes this as "accidental overreach."

The official news release did not mention the Trans Mountain pipeline. But the primary source of "dilbit" in Canada is Alberta's oil sands. And there was only one existing proposal to "increase" the transport of dilbit through British Columbia: the Trans Mountain expansion. As one environmentalist observed at the time, "Even if Kinder Morgan and the federal government keep pushing to build the pipeline, they could build their pipeline, but with these new regulations they won't be able to turn the tap on."

This, in other words, was a suggestion that one province might restrict the transportation of another province's natural resources. Notley understandably saw red. "The B.C. government has every right to consult on whatever it pleases with its citizens," she told reporters. "It does not have the right to rewrite our Constitution and assume powers for itself that it does not have. If it did, our Confederation would be meaningless." Before an emergency cabinet meeting on January 31, she threatened retaliation.

Two days later, Trudeau was in Nanaimo. And the nice lady in the knit sweater wanted to have a word.

She'd voted for him, she said, in part because she thought he was against pipelines. She was "so upset" when he approved the Trans Mountain expansion. She was worried about the wildlife and the coastline. Trudeau nodded as he listened. Some in the audience applauded. "So please, please, oh please, please," she pleaded. She began to move forward and two members of the prime minister's security detail sprang up from their seats and put their hands in front of her. "I just want to give him a hug," she protested.

Trudeau moved forward toward her. "I think I'm okay," he said. They hugged and she finished her plea. "Please don't approve it," she said.

The woman returned to her seat and Trudeau went back to where he'd been standing to respond. He thanked her for her question and her passion. He then corrected her: he'd never said he was against all pipeline development.

He understood, he said, something that "most Canadians understand, which is you can no longer make a choice between good for the environment and good for the economy, we have to do them both together."

There were jeers from the crowd.

"And I think there are folks here demonstrating my point that some people still think there is a choice to be made, either environment or economy, but most Canadians understand that we need to build both a stronger economy, in sustainable ways, while protecting the environment at the same time."

The jeers continued, but now there was some applause.

"That's actually something that the previous government didn't get and didn't do a very good job of," Trudeau continued. "I think we can all agree on that."

He proceeded to try to explain his government's commitment to act in a "responsible way," but he became distracted by a heckler nearby.

"See, the thing is you have folks who have all the answers," Trudeau said, "who are not interested even in hearing the reflections that led their government to do what it did."

The police removed a young man with a goatee and ponytail, but then a young woman wearing purple stood up and started shouting, and she was soon joined by a young woman wearing a wide-brimmed hat. Trudeau asked them to be respectful of everyone else in the room. When they persisted, he asked them to leave. That seemed to restore order, but when the first woman popped up again and resumed heckling, the prime minister lost his temper. "Oh, come on," he snapped. "Come on! Really?" Then the second woman appeared again. "You're still here?" Trudeau sighed, laughing to himself. Finally, he put it to a vote, and a show of hands demonstrated that the room was ready for the young women to leave. They were escorted away by police.

"Okay, we're going to try answering the pipeline question," Trudeau said when they were gone.

"We brought in a national carbon reduction plan that's going to allow us to reach our climate goals, to reach our Paris commitments. But in order to do that, part of moving forward is approving the Kinder Morgan pipeline, which will be able to get our resources, responsibly and safely, to new markets across the Pacific."

Behind him, two people held a yellow sign that read "Climate leaders don't build pipelines." One woman shook her head. Another pointed her thumb downwards.

"It is something that some people, many people, feel very strongly about, on either side, but that is the nature of the compromise we had to make in the best interests of Canada. To grow the economy, to protect the environment at the same time, we have to make tough decisions. That's exactly what I did. It is in the national interest to move forward with the Kinder Morgan pipeline and we will be moving forward with the Kinder Morgan pipeline."

He stood and took a sip of water as boos rained down. Extending his arms slightly, he shrugged, one of his father's quintessential gestures— that move of nonchalant defiance and confident commiseration.

"Although Justin Trudeau scans differently than his father, every once in a while he reaches up into his hair and he finds a zipper that's up there and he pulls it down and he unzips himself and Justin Trudeau falls away and his father steps out and makes a really hard, clear, clean decision because he thinks it's the right thing to do," Topp says, speaking of Trudeau's decision to approve Trans Mountain. "And then he goes back in the suit."

———

PROBABLY NO ONE IN that room, including Trudeau, had any idea they would all soon own that pipeline.

A week after the B.C. government said it would be consulting about new regulations on dilbit, Notley announced Alberta was banning the import of B.C. wines. According to an Alberta source, internal polling suggested support for the pipeline in British Columbia had steadily been increasing, up until the wine ban was implemented. That move caused support to dip slightly.

The wine ban was rescinded in late February, after Horgan announced his government would seek a court reference to determine the extent of its authority to regulate the flow of oil through the province. But Notley's government then used a throne speech to suggest it might cut off oil and gas exports to B.C.'s refineries, a move that would drive up gas prices in the province.

Unbeknownst to the public, Kinder Morgan was getting antsy. On March 6, 2018, representatives from the company met with Jim Carr, minister of natural resources at the time, and Carr's chief of staff, Zoë Caron. Kinder Morgan wanted federal legislation that would override anything British Columbia did to obstruct construction of the Trans Mountain expansion, and a federally financed backstop that would protect shareholders against any loss resulting from the suspension or stoppage of the project.

Throughout the Trans Mountain saga there had been suggestions that, through Parliament, the federal government could do something to explicitly assert its authority to approve the pipeline—Trudeau himself once suggested that the government was pursuing "legislative options." But no such action was ever taken. "The problem with doing that is that then you are, for no reason, putting to an eventual court challenge the widely accepted truth that the federal government has paramountcy on these things," says a senior Liberal. "So basically, the people who are calling for that are saying, roll the dice on reasserting federal paramountcy. And not to mention it's potentially very disruptive for the country, doing that. Because maybe Quebec would join in it. Regionally, you don't know what the result of that is going to be."

Notley's government pressed the Trudeau government to do more to get Horgan out of the way. The Liberals could, for instance, withhold funds for infrastructure or support for liquefied natural gas development in British Columbia. According to both federal and B.C. sources, no such threat was ever made.

Discussions between the federal government and Kinder Morgan continued through March, with the finance minister's office and the Prime Minister's Office getting involved. In exchange for indemnifying shareholders against potential losses, the company proposed that the government would receive an option to purchase a 5 percent ownership interest in the pipeline expansion. By late March, Kinder Morgan later told its shareholders, the federal government "had expressed a willingness to provide some form of a limited backstop, subject to numerous conditions, pursuant to which it would compensate the company for a portion of its TMEP [Trans Mountain Expansion Project]-related costs, and potentially step into ownership of the TMEP, in order to see the TMEP to completion."

At 5 p.m. on April 8, Kinder Morgan went public with its concern: the company announced it was suspending all non-essential spending on the project and it set a deadline of May 31 for assurances that its pipeline would proceed and its shareholders would be protected.

"All options are on the table for the government of Canada," Carr told reporters on Parliament Hill, while declining to specify what those options might be.

On April 10, Notley said her government was willing to purchase the pipeline. During a conference call with Kinder Morgan that same day, federal officials raised the possibility of purchasing a 51 percent stake in the pipeline. On April 13, Kinder Morgan came back and suggested that the federal government buy 100 percent. The government maintained that a backstop was its preferred option. But the board of Kinder Morgan met and confirmed that it would rather sell the project.

"I think the general principle, whether it was indemnity or partial ownership or all the way up to buying the whole thing, is let's not do anything we don't have to do," says the senior Liberal.

Trudeau was set to fly to Peru for the Summit of the Americas on April 12 and then to Paris for an official visit, but it was decided he would stop in Ottawa on his way to France for a meeting on Parliament Hill with Notley and Horgan. In that meeting, Trudeau pressed Horgan about what the federal government could do to allay his concerns about the pipeline. But Horgan could not offer a definitive answer.

It's possible that Horgan simply couldn't afford, politically, to take an off-ramp, either because his own caucus would not accept such a move or because the Greens would withdraw their support for Horgan's government if he did. A year after this summit in Ottawa, five judges from British Columbia's court of appeal unanimously agreed that it would be unconstitutional for the provincial government to restrict the flow of diluted bitumen from Alberta. Even then, Horgan's government persisted, asking the Supreme Court to review the court of appeal's decision.

On April 30, Kinder Morgan's representatives proposed a price for the pipeline: $6.5 billion. Eight days later, a Canadian delegation flew to Houston: Bill Morneau, Gerry Butts, Ben Chin (Morneau's chief of staff), Tim Duncanson (a former investment banker now working for the Finance Department) and Ava Yaskiel (a corporate lawyer who was on a two-year leave to serve as associate deputy minister at Finance). They presented Kinder Morgan with two possibilities. In the first scenario, the company would proceed with the pipeline while the federal government would provide a limited indemnity to cover increased costs resulting from British Columbia's actions and, if the project was abandoned or unable to be completed by a certain date, the federal government would cover construction costs and retain an option to acquire ownership. In the second scenario, the federal government would agree to provide a backstop and would help Kinder Morgan seek another buyer. If no buyer was found, the federal government would buy the pipeline for a little over $2.3 billion.

"In other words, if you really think you can get $6.5 billion for it, go find that," says a senior Liberal.

Morneau says that as soon as the negotiations began he realized that a purchase was a "high-potential outcome." But he also didn't want to get to that discussion too fast.

"We needed them to know that we had more options than just one to get to an answer. And that [just] because we had a really important objective of de-risking the project, that wasn't going to give them extra value. But from their perspective they had come to the conclusion probably relatively early on that while there might be other ways to do it, their preferred way would be to move on," he says. "So I understood that that was their preferred way. But if we just immediately acquiesced

I think we would've ended up in a price negotiation that wouldn't have been to our advantage."

On May 10, Kinder Morgan's CEO, Steve Kean, informed Morneau that the board had rejected those proposals. Nonetheless, on May 16, Morneau went public with the government's offer to indemnify the project. On May 21, Kinder Morgan came back with a new demand for what it would need in terms of a backstop. On May 22, the government rejected that proposal and came back with an offer of $3.85 billion for the pipeline and expansion project. Meeting with Kean in Toronto, Morneau made the case that the government of Canada was not a typical buyer. It would be spending public money. And Morneau would have to stand up in Question Period and defend any purchase. He couldn't be seen as overpaying.

On May 23, the two sides met and Kinder Morgan said it could accept nothing less than $4.5 billion, while also noting that it would end up paying $325 million in capital gains taxes, effectively lowering the purchase price for the federal government. The federal negotiating team—including Morneau, Chin, Duncanson and Evan Siddall, the president and CEO of the Canada Mortgage and Housing Corporation and a friend of Morneau's—stepped out to consider the offer. "We really liked their offer and we just needed to all have a gut check with each other," says the senior official. "But we took our time. You don't want to go out and then come right back in."

When the federal officials returned, they asked for three conditions: six weeks to seek a third-party buyer, an agreement to restart construction during the transition period and a commitment by the company to pay at least $325 million in capital gains taxes. The Kinder Morgan officials agreed.

With that, the Trudeau government had an agreement in principle to purchase a pipeline and, with it, the right to spend billions more to build an expansion. It took another six days to work through the details. On May 29 the deal was presented to cabinet.

Viewed from certain angles, this was an astonishing turn of events. The government of Canada would now own and operate a pipeline to the west coast. Justin Trudeau—son of Pierre, and a leader committed to combating climate change—had bought a pipeline to carry Alberta's oil.

The plan is to one day sell it, and several interested parties are said to have been in touch. But a sale—perhaps with some amount of Indigenous ownership—would likely not occur until after the expansion has been completed. Federal ownership is thought to better safeguard the project against legal challenges.

Conservatives had already begun spinning public investment as proof of Trudeau's failure. "Before Justin Trudeau became prime minister, energy projects didn't need government money to succeed," Andrew Scheer claimed at one point.

This ignored significant portions of Canadian history. More than a century ago, for instance, Wilfrid Laurier's government paid a bounty for oil discoveries in the west. Later, it was a federal engineer who played a pivotal role in surveying and investigating the oil sands. As minister of trade and commerce in 1956, C.D. Howe infamously extended loan guarantees to get the TransCanada pipeline built—the resulting debate in the House is considered one of the most fractious moments in the history of Parliament (and contributed to the defeat of that Liberal government). In partnership with Alberta and Ontario, Pierre Trudeau's government helped bail out Alberta's Syncrude in 1975. Brian Mulroney backed up Newfoundland's Hibernia project with $2.6 billion in 1993. Jean Chrétien extended tax breaks in 1996 that helped propel the oil sands to the major development it is now.

The outright purchase of a pipeline—along with the promise to build another—was perhaps a new level of commitment. But then it was also roughly in line with what Trudeau had told the Petroleum Club in 2013: it was the federal government's responsibility to get the country's resources to market. He presumably meant that in the broad sense. Now he would be doing it in the literal sense.

Ultimately, Trudeau says, it simply became obvious that buying the pipeline was the only answer. "It wasn't something that I quailed at in an instinctive or the most prudish way, sort of, 'Oh no, heavens!' It was like 'No, what is the solution to get our oil resources to markets other than the U.S.?'" he says.

"People were like, 'I can't believe you bought a pipeline!' But it was the logical thing and the responsible thing to do that is entirely consistent with the frame I've been putting forward for three years. It's important."

By cancelling Northern Gateway and imposing a tanker ban in northern British Columbia, the Trudeau government had left itself with only one option for completing that frame. In hindsight, that had been a gamble—even if the Liberals felt strongly about each of the individual decisions that got them there.

Could Trudeau have pressed harder on Horgan? Maybe. But punitive measures against British Columbia also would have risked inflaming opposition to the pipeline.

In January 2019, the office of the parliamentary budget officer released its analysis of the purchase. In its estimation, the pipeline was worth somewhere between $3.6 billion and $4.6 billion. The final purchase, after some adjustments, had come in at $4.4 billion, and the government argued that, once the revenue from the capital gains taxes was factored in, the price was more like $4.1 billion. But the parliamentary budget officer, Yves Giroux, suggested Morneau had paid more than he needed to. "If it was a car, we would say they paid sticker price. They didn't negotiate very much, they didn't get that many deals or manufacturers' rebates—quite the opposite," Giroux told reporters.

Morneau tried to defend himself, but pointlessly claimed he had never said the price was $4.5 billion, a contention that was easily disproven by the CBC with a clip of him saying exactly that when he announced the purchase.

If the expansion is completed and oil starts flowing through it, the question of whether the government should have gotten a better deal will be a historical footnote. For the sake of national unity, it might've been worth paying a bit more.

======

KINDER MORGAN CANADA'S SHAREHOLDERS voted overwhelmingly to approve the transaction on August 30, 2018. Their timing was impeccable.

That same morning, the Federal Court of Appeal returned a ruling in the case of *Tsleil-Waututh Nation v. Canada*. The Tsleil-Waututh Nation, a community of five hundred people living on a reserve in Burrard Inlet, had joined with a number of other bands and tribes, as well as the cities of Vancouver and Burnaby, to challenge the federal government's approval of the Trans Mountain expansion. Shortly before the shareholders signed off, the verdict was released: the three judges had ruled unanimously in the applicants' favour.

Justice Eleanor Dawson, writing for the majority, explained that the National Energy Board had incorrectly declined to consider the increase in tanker traffic related to the project. Further, the Trudeau government's additional consultations with Indigenous groups were insufficient: the federal government had listened, but it had failed to engage in a meaningful "two-way dialogue" that responded to and grappled with the concerns raised by the Indigenous applicants. For those reasons, the federal cabinet's approval of the project was quashed and construction would have to be suspended. Justice Dawson suggested, perhaps optimistically, that addressing the shortcomings might require only a "short delay."

Butts and Telford were, coincidentally, at the Canadian embassy in Washington, on a break from negotiations at the offices of the U.S. trade representative. Four days earlier, Donald Trump had announced a surprising bilateral trade agreement with Mexico. Canadian officials had flown to D.C. to deal with the ramifications. Butts concedes he was hit with a wave of depression when the news broke of the court ruling: he could see how Notley was going to react, how the Opposition would respond and what the front page of the *National Post* would look like. Everything would now be harder and the government's margin for error would shrink.

The errors were correctable, though also perhaps avoidable. But Trudeau was apparently less interested in being upset about what went wrong.

"'Okay, so what's our path forward?' is always my question," Trudeau says. "I actually had a conversation with Sophie afterwards where she was like, 'Okay, so what happened in this court case?' And I explain it, and I want to get into, 'Okay, but this is what we're going to do and this is the challenge that we'd be facing if we go down the appeal path, this is the challenge if we go the legislative path.' And Sophie instead said, 'Well, who messed up? What was the mistake, whose fault was it? Is somebody going to get fired because you didn't do this the right way?' And it was actually a really frustrating conversation because my brain doesn't go there. I'm not saying I don't ever go there. Sometimes when things mess up, I'm like, 'That person needs to lose their job' or whatever. I do get that way. But this was almost too big for that, and there are too many moving pieces and too much we inherited."

Notley's chief of staff, Nathan Rotman, called Ben Chin to tell him how the Alberta premier was going to respond. Notley wanted the federal government to appeal the Federal Court of Appeal's ruling, but she would also demand that Trudeau recall Parliament. The Alberta proposal was that the federal government introduce legislation to retroactively declare that the NEB was not required to consider marine shipping impacts, effectively turning back time to render moot one portion of the ruling. In her public statement, Notley suggested this course of action could have construction restarted by "early in the new year." In the meantime, Notley would refuse to raise her province's price on carbon above $30 per tonne, as the federal framework required after 2020.

The latter move was mostly symbolic—and Notley no doubt needed to show resolve and strength—but federal officials were surprised when Notley later framed it as a full withdrawal from the national framework. "Until the federal government gets its act together, Alberta is pulling out of the federal climate plan," Notley said at a news conference that evening. "And let's be clear—without Alberta, that plan isn't worth the paper it's written on."

"There is an electoral urgency and a challenge for Rachel that I totally get and I want to be helpful with," Trudeau says in a conversation in the fall of 2018, "but I am also not going to miss this opportunity of a publicly controlled project where we can demonstrate the path and that it works to all global investors who then want to do a project and say, 'Look, if you go through these things, you will get it built.'"

Instead of Alberta's proposed legislative manoeuvre, the Liberals mandated the NEB to complete a review of marine impacts within twenty-two weeks. Former Supreme Court justice Frank Iacobucci was appointed to design and oversee a new round of consultation with Indigenous groups. The Liberals stressed they were committed to moving forward in the "right way." But that would mean not moving forward until after a spring election in Alberta. By which time it would be too late for Rachel Notley.

===

TRUDEAU'S TWENTIETH VISIT TO Alberta as prime minister coincided with a steep drop in the market price for Alberta's oil. Notley said the province was losing $80 million each day. Trudeau would be coaxed into calling it a "crisis." How it got to that point is a complicated story—including the political failure of successive governments to address climate change and the national failure to reconcile this country with Indigenous peoples. And there was now no easy or immediate fix. But in Trudeau the aggrieved found a convenient target for blame. As Trudeau's motorcade pulled into the garage of a downtown Calgary hotel, a middle-aged man, stopping on the sidewalk to let the cars pass, quietly extended both of his middle fingers. The crowd inside, invited by the chamber of commerce to hear from the prime minister, politely clapped when Trudeau was introduced and again when he departed, but otherwise sat in silence.

"For many people in this province, they don't know what their next job looks like, or when they're going to find it," Trudeau said. "I want you to know that I feel that frustration and I understand that anxiety, the status quo cannot continue."

Outside the hotel where Trudeau was speaking, 2,000 protestors chanted "build the pipe." Of course, Trudeau basically agreed with them.

As prime minister, Trudeau has not always endeared himself to Albertans. During a town hall forum in 2017, he suggested there was a need to "phase out" development of the oil sands. Trudeau had spoken previously of the need to transition away from fossil fuels, a goal that even Stephen Harper had been willing to recognize, but in this case he was perhaps a bit too specific, and the result was outrage (he quickly retracted the statement). Six months later, he forgot to mention Alberta during a portion of his Canada Day remarks that otherwise referenced every province (Alberta was mentioned in the prepared text, but Trudeau's eyes skipped over it). By the time he made his twentieth visit, there were other complaints: he'd allowed Northern Gateway to die, and his government's proposed regulatory reforms were being panned by proponents of the energy sector.

But, still, there was that pipeline. Trudeau had used the fiscal and political power of the federal government to purchase the Trans Mountain pipeline and proceed with its expansion, burning some amount of his own political capital in the process. He had launched a new round of consultations with Indigenous communities to satisfy the government's legal obligation. All that on top of the resources put toward marine protection in hopes of satisfying environmental concerns in British Columbia. If he truly disliked Albertans or didn't care for their province, he had an odd way of showing it.

———

LOST IN THE PUBLIC frustration, political manoeuvring and legal realities was a relatively remarkable development: that pipeline had actually become more popular.

In November 2014, the Angus Reid Institute asked 1,500 people about Kinder Morgan's proposal to build a pipeline through Burnaby. Across the country, 51 percent were supportive, 48 percent opposed. In British Columbia, 46 percent were in favour, 54 percent against.

In June 2016, two weeks after the National Energy Board approved Kinder Morgan's application, the Angus Reid Institute asked again. By that point, 41 percent of all respondents believed it was the right decision, and 24 percent said it was the wrong decision. In British Columbia, 41 percent thought it was the right decision, while 34 percent said it was wrong.

Nearly two years later, in February 2018, national support for the pipeline was at 49 percent, with 33 percent opposed. In April 2018, the split was wider. Nationally, 55 percent supported the project, while 26 percent were opposed. In British Columbia, it was 54 percent to 38 percent.

By June 2018, national support was up to 57 percent. On the federal government's decision to purchase the pipeline, respondents were split: 37 percent in favour and 37 percent against. But they took a dim view of the B.C. government's position: 61 percent said the Horgan government was wrong to oppose the pipeline.

It would be too much to credit Trudeau and his government for moving those numbers on their own. It was Notley's government that implemented a price on carbon and a cap on emissions from the oil sands. The Alberta government had also launched a national advertising campaign—"Keep Canada Working"—to promote the Trans Mountain expansion, with ads targeted at viewers in both British Columbia and the Liberal bastion of Toronto.

But that a majority of Canadians supported the pipeline—and that support for the pipeline had increased over time—would seem to suggest there was some merit in the Trudeau-Notley approach.

"People aren't unreasonable—if they see an economic plan that goes with an environmental plan that involves communities, particularly Indigenous communities, people will say, 'Okay, that makes sense,'" Trudeau says. "And setting that narrative instead of the people are in two camps and there is no bridge—it's really hard to build a bridge between those two things, but if you want Canada to work in the long term, like, I've got to try and build that bridge, because if not me, who?"

Nonetheless, at the end of 2018, Abacus Data asked Canadians to grade Trudeau's handling of a dozen issues. He received a decent grade on climate change: 31 percent said he was doing a "good" or "very good" job, and 35 percent said it was acceptable. But just 18 percent said Trudeau was doing a "good" or "very good" job on Trans Mountain. Forty-nine percent said it was "poor" or "very poor." Of the twelve files that Abacus asked about, the pipeline was Trudeau's worst.

That might have been a reflection of the Federal Court of Appeal ruling. Trudeau's score might improve if or when construction resumes. Or if and when the pipeline is sold to new investors.

Or it might be that no one will ever be particularly happy that it came to this. It is ironic enough that Pierre Trudeau's son bought a pipeline. It would be that much more ironic if he never gets much credit for doing so.

CHAPTER 9

HARD THINGS ARE HARD

Eight days after he was sworn in as prime minister, Justin Trudeau announced he would be convening a meeting with the premiers to discuss the future of the planet.

In its staging, that conference at the Canadian Museum of Nature in Ottawa was a spectacle of change. For one thing, a prime minister was sitting down with all his provincial and territorial counterparts. Stephen Harper had participated in just two first ministers' conferences during his nine years as prime minister and had last met the premiers as a group in January 2009. For another, it was a discussion about climate change, a policy area to which Harper had demonstrated only a passing commitment.

For good measure, two scientists—including a senior researcher with Environment Canada—were invited to open the meeting with a public presentation on the realities of climate change. An astronaut, Jeremy Hansen, moderated the briefing, and it was streamed to high schools across the country. The Harper government's interest in science and evidence had been intermittent, at best. Its reluctance to let federal researchers speak publicly was notorious. The Trudeau government was practically begging everyone to notice the difference.

The slides of that presentation laid out the facts, both basic and worrisome. The planet was getting warmer. This was "indisputable" and "largely due to human activity." There was an illustration explaining the greenhouse effect. There were graphs showing a century of warmer annual temperatures, a decline in Arctic sea ice and a rise in water levels. There were slides showing the impacts in Canada: wildfires, drought, heat waves, infrastructure failures. Global emissions, it was explained, would have to be reduced sharply and quickly to limit the damage.

It was no doubt good and important to have these realities front and centre—even if it was also a shame that any of it still needed to be said. Twenty-seven years earlier, on June 23, 1988, a NASA scientist named James Hansen had testified before the U.S. Senate. "The greenhouse effect has been detected and it is changing our climate now," he declared. That warning, offered amidst a scorching heat wave, made it to the top of the front page of the next day's *New York Times*.

Three days later, a few hundred leaders and thinkers—politicians, scientists and activists, including representatives from four dozen countries—gathered at the convention centre in downtown Toronto for a conference entitled "The Changing Atmosphere: Implications for Global Security," one of the first major international meetings on the global climate. The government of Canada was a co-host. The prime minister, Brian Mulroney, delivered opening remarks, and Stephen Lewis, Canada's ambassador to the United Nations, chaired the discussions.

There were three main concerns: the depletion of the ozone layer, the acidification of water and soil, and the threat of "climate warming." At the conclusion of those meetings, a consensus statement was released. It began with a stark and enduring message for the world: "Humanity is conducting an unintended, uncontrolled, globally pervasive experiment whose ultimate consequences could be second only to a global nuclear war."

The Cold War—an era in which mutually assured destruction was both a threat and a deterrent—was nearing an end. Within seventeen months, the Berlin Wall would come down. But a new existential threat was now apparent.

"Far-reaching impacts will be caused by global warming and sea-level rise, which are becoming increasingly evident as a result of continued growth in atmospheric concentrations of carbon dioxide and other greenhouse gases," the statement continued. "The best predictions available indicate potentially severe economic and social dislocation for present and future generations, which will worsen international tensions and increase risk of conflicts among and within nations. It is imperative to act now."

Delay would only increase the size and scope of the challenge. "If rapid action is not taken now by the countries of the world, these problems will become progressively more serious, more difficult to reverse, and more costly to address."

The following years were not without progress. The Montreal Protocol, an international agreement signed in 1987, succeeded in reducing the worldwide use of the chemicals that were eroding the ozone layer. In 1991, Mulroney and President George H.W. Bush signed an air quality agreement that substantially curtailed the sulphur and nitrate emissions that were causing acid rain in North America. Both problems are rarely spoken of now.

But the greater threat was not much diminished. Global carbon dioxide emissions continued to increase. The planet continued to warm. The impacts began to become apparent. And the potential for catastrophe grew.

The Toronto conference recommended an initial goal of reducing greenhouse gas emissions by approximately 20 percent by 2005. As later calculated by the National Round Table on the Environment and the Economy—a federal commission established by Mulroney and disbanded by Harper—that would have required Canada to cut its annual emissions by 118 megatonnes—from 588 megatonnes to 470 megatonnes—over the course of seventeen years. In hindsight, that was a pretty good deal.

Mulroney picked a new target in 1990: to stabilize emissions at current levels by 2005. Three years later, Jean Chrétien recommitted Canada to the target from the Toronto conference. Once again, that target only lasted two years. Under Chrétien, the federal government set new targets in 1995, 1998 and 2002 (as part of ratifying the Kyoto Protocol).

Stephen Harper became prime minister in 2006 and then committed Canada to different targets in 2007, 2010 and 2014. Hypothetical reductions were cast further and further into the future.

Successive federal and provincial governments did not completely fail to take action—British Columbia implemented a carbon tax in 2008, and Ontario began a phase-out of coal-fired electricity generation in 2005—but a comprehensive set of policies to reach Canada's international targets was never implemented. Canada was hardly the only nation to fail in that regard. But future generations might not accept that as much of an excuse.

In a candid moment in December 2007, Stephen Harper tried to explain why it was so hard for governments to make good on these commitments.

"I know that whatever we do, the radical edge of the environmental movement that gets most of the press will not think it's enough. And I also know that as soon as we impose costs on the economy—and there is no way of making progress without some short-term costs—that others, industry and others, will complain we're going too far. That's why the previous government was paralyzed with inaction for a decade, because they couldn't square the circle," Harper told two Postmedia journalists as part of a year-end interview. "There is no squaring the circle. Sometimes you have to make a decision . . . you have to stand by the decision and see it through, and encourage people to judge you by the results."

That was apparently what Harper intended to do. Eight months earlier, his government had released its own plan, entitled "Turning the Corner."

"I don't think it's feasible that we keep deciding—well, hey, let's float another plan. That's what the Liberals did. As soon as you're getting close to actually implementing you say, well hold on, we're getting some kickback here, so let's float a whole new plan and do consultations on that. So you do what the Liberals did for a decade—a series of rolling consultations that never actually end," Harper said.

"You know, we inherited the worst record of greenhouse gas emissions of any industrialized country, at least relative to the commitments we took on in [the Kyoto Protocol]. It's a terrible record. Now we have to do something. We can't just keep saying, we're just going to keep consulting."

And yet, history repeated itself. The "corner" remained unturned. In fact, the plan to turn it was abandoned. A subsequent promise to take a sectoral approach to regulating different industries was also never completed. In lieu of action, the Conservatives put their time and energy toward condemning successive Liberal and NDP plans to reduce emissions, loudly criticizing the cost that Harper himself had said was unavoidable.

The most recent national target—adopted by the Conservatives in 2014—aimed for a 30 percent reduction in emissions below 2005 levels by 2030. At the time, annual emissions had reached 699 megatonnes, a slight decrease as compared to 2005. But when the Harper government was defeated in 2015, its latest projection showed Canada was on track to *increase* emissions by 10 percent above 2005 levels by 2030. In simple math: Canada needed to cut its annual emissions to 516 megatonnes, but it was on its way to reaching 815 megatonnes.

That was the challenge Trudeau inherited. For a brief moment after assuming office, his government seemed as if it might try to do even more. Two weeks before the meeting with the premiers in the fall of 2015, Environment Minister Catherine McKenna suggested the Conservative target would be the "floor" for Liberal ambitions. Sometime thereafter, the Liberals realized reaching the floor was going to be hard enough. But New Democrats and Greens would loudly complain that the Liberals were not aiming low enough.

———

JUSTIN TRUDEAU HAD AT least one thing going for him in November 2015: Rachel Notley was the premier of Alberta.

The NDP's victory in Alberta in April 2015 was a historic turn of events. The province's Progressive Conservatives had been in power for nearly forty-four years, and federal conservative parties had been dominant in Alberta for decades. But Canada's bluest province was now orange. Even more remarkably, Notley's government was intent on making the oil patch green.

A day before the first ministers met in Ottawa, Notley convened a news conference in Edmonton. Flanked by both oil executives and environmentalists, she announced a sweeping new climate plan, including a carbon tax, a cap on emissions from the oil sands and a plan to phase out coal power. Two and a half weeks earlier, Barack Obama had rejected the Keystone XL pipeline, citing a desire to show climate leadership and an aversion to importing "dirtier crude oil" from Alberta. Now, under Notley's plan, Alberta would be at the forefront of climate policy in North America. "I'm hopeful that these policies, taken overall, will lead to a new collaborative conversation about Canada's energy infrastructure on its merits," she said, "and to a significant de-escalation of conflict worldwide about the Alberta oil sands."

For the sake of crafting a national climate plan, Notley's contribution was profound. In 2015, Alberta was the highest-emitting province, accounting for 38 percent of all greenhouse gas emissions in Canada. But with Alberta joining British Columbia, Quebec and Ontario, the four largest provinces would now have robust carbon-pricing policies. And with a government in Alberta willing to act, Trudeau wouldn't have to worry about imposing a policy on a province that reflexively associated his surname with unwelcome federal intrusion.

Notley had been prepared to act regardless of who was in power in Ottawa. But the arrival of Trudeau also presented an opportunity for her to nest the Alberta approach within a system of comparable policies across the country.

"When the Trudeau government appeared we engaged with them with a finished plan and pitched them to adopt a complementary federal framework," Brian Topp, Notley's former chief of staff, says. "From Edmonton's perspective it was helpful for the feds to do so because it held out the prospect that Alberta would not be out by itself with these policies. Their obvious interest was to find a federal plan that Alberta supported."

For Trudeau, the meeting in Ottawa was also his debut as chairman of the federation, the young prime minister suddenly sitting at the head of the table, surrounded by older and more experienced counterparts. "He was impressive in that meeting room. I think it surprised people . . . how well he could run a meeting and run the room," says a senior Ontario Liberal. "It was impressive as well because he was quite naturally conversant in the subject matter, again, I think, more so than people probably would have expected. He wasn't just reading from notes, especially in responses. He knew what he was talking about."

Not everyone sounded excited to be in Ottawa, mind you. Facing reporters before the official proceedings, Saskatchewan's Brad Wall made a point of sounding skeptical, deviating from the questions that were asked to offer an unbidden comment on the recent struggles of Canada's resource industries. "We need to do better in terms of our record on climate change, but we can't forget the economy," Wall said.

Several months of shadowboxing ensued. Wall's hint of concern evolved into an argument that it was "not the time" to implement a price on carbon. If the Trudeau government tried to impose a price, he suggested, Saskatchewan would challenge the policy in court.

But then, in October 2016, Trudeau made a dramatic show of making a move. Standing in the House of Commons to deliver a speech on the Paris Agreement, he announced a federal plan to price carbon. This was the Trudeau who had kicked senators out of his caucus in 2014, making a sudden and dramatic announcement to move the public debate.

If provinces did not adopt either a carbon tax or a cap-and-trade system, the Trudeau government would step in to fill the gap. Whether provincially or federally administered, the price would start at $10 per tonne and rise to $50 per tonne by 2022. In the case of the federal backstop, all revenue from the price would be returned to the province from which it originated. On price, and later in terms of design, Trudeau's approach lined up neatly with the Alberta plan.

The prime minister's announcement nonetheless came as some surprise to the provincial environment ministers who were meeting in Montreal to continue negotiations with their federal counterpart. The ministers from Saskatchewan, Newfoundland and Labrador, and Nova

Scotia walked out in protest. Afterwards, Wall and Trudeau had what was described as a "spirited" conversation by phone.

Two months later, Wall refused to sign on to the framework and publicly sparred with Trudeau at the joint news conference that followed that first ministers' meeting.

There were other quibbles, but nothing that couldn't presumably be worked out. Manitoba's Brian Pallister held off on signing, and then introduced a plan to price emissions in his province at $25 per tonne, while insisting his government would not go higher. British Columbia's Christy Clark wanted to be able to opt out of the framework at a later date if an independent review showed the cap-and-trade systems in Ontario and Quebec weren't pricing carbon at the same level as British Columbia's carbon tax. New Brunswick's Brian Gallant suggested he would implement a carbon tax, but also cut the province's excise tax on fuel, an approach McKenna rejected. After some negotiation, an equivalency agreement was signed with Nova Scotia to allow its coal-fired electricity plants to remain in use beyond a federal deadline of 2030.

Wall's successor, Scott Moe, eventually made good on a threat to challenge the federal plan in court. But most observers believed the federal government was empowered to impose this new tax (an independent legal opinion, commissioned by Pallister, stated as much). Casting forward, there was a very real possibility that Notley would be replaced by Jason Kenney, who, having returned to Alberta to lead the province's conservatives, was intent on styling himself as a crusader against both the carbon tax and Trudeau.

That would not be ideal. Trudeau would surely prefer to avoid a fight with the prairies. But the challenge could at least be contained. In no small part because there was a conservative leader in Ontario who was ready to put a price on carbon.

And then there wasn't.

———

PATRICK BROWN'S PLAN TO become the next premier of Ontario unravelled in spectacular fashion on the evening of January 24, 2018.

Brown had been a relatively unremarkable Conservative back-bencher during the Harper government's years in power. But then he had entered himself in the 2015 race to be leader of Ontario's Progressive Conservative Party. And then, somewhat surprisingly, he won. By January 2018, with Kathleen Wynne's Liberal government looking increasingly tired and beaten down, Brown was in a very good position to become the twenty-sixth premier of Ontario.

As leader of the PCs, Brown had also done something potentially significant for the future of climate policy in Canada: he had promised to replace the Wynne government's existing cap-and-trade system with a broad-based carbon tax. His party was not particularly enthusiastic about it. But Brown was apparently keen to show he could be trusted to do something serious about climate change. In doing so, he seemingly ensured that, whoever was premier after Ontario's June 2018 election, a provincially administered price on carbon would be in place in Canada's most populous province.

And then came the evening of January 24. That night, CTV reported the allegations of two women who said Brown had made inappropriate sexual advances. The #MeToo movement—the reckoning that had already come for powerful men in American entertainment and business—had arrived in Canadian politics. Brown insisted he was unfairly accused. But, within hours, he was compelled to resign as leader.

Into the breach stepped a handful of contenders. Two of them—Caroline Mulroney and Christine Elliott—had already been preparing to run as candidates for Brown and his carbon-pricing policy. But each was now competing for the votes of the PC Party's most ardent supporters. Doug Ford, the loud and brash brother of the late Toronto mayor Rob Ford, quickly declared his opposition to both the Liberal cap-and-trade system and Brown's promise of a carbon tax. Mulroney and Elliott followed suit. But they were no match for the real populist. By mid-March, Ford was the new leader of the party (in the leadership vote, Elliott won more votes and more ridings, but Ford won more points in the party's weighted system).

On June 29—after an inelegant but ultimately successful election campaign—Ford was sworn in as premier. In short order, his government introduced legislation to repeal Ontario's cap-and-trade system and announced its intention to challenge the federal plan in court.

Then things changed in two other provincial capitals. In September, Gallant's Liberals in New Brunswick won just twenty-one of forty-nine seats in that province's election, opening the door for a Progressive Conservative government, led by Blaine Higgs, that opposed the federal plan.

In the middle of that same month, Trudeau visited Pallister in Winnipeg. The prime minister acknowledged that he and the premier still had to work out their differences on a price schedule, but otherwise Trudeau enthused about Pallister's co-operation. "To see a leader, indeed a conservative leader, who understands the need to have a concrete plan to fight climate change . . . is something I very much welcome," Trudeau said. "I wish he would encourage some of the other conservative provinces across the country to recognize that having a plan to fight climate change is something that all Canadians, regardless of where they are on the political spectrum, have the right to expect."

Less than a month later, Pallister bailed. "I don't think anybody likes to be used as a prop, and I certainly am not inclined that way," he said. Sounding like a modern-day Robarts, Pallister called the Liberal plan "hucksterism of the worst kind."

On the day the federal backstop came into effect, the medicare approach to climate change had produced a split. Five provinces had systems that met the federal standards: British Columbia, Alberta, Quebec, Newfoundland and Nova Scotia. Four provinces had the federal system imposed upon them: Saskatchewan, Manitoba, Ontario and New Brunswick. And one province, Prince Edward Island, opted for a combination of its own plan and elements of the federal backstop. By population, about 47 percent of Canadians lived in provinces covered by the federal price.

"It was always tenuous because it involved too many moving parts," says David McLaughlin, a former chair of the National Round Table on the Environment and the Economy and an advisor to Pallister on the

Manitoba plan. "It involved provinces, which had their own constituencies. It involved existing plans; it involved new plans. It relied on an awkward cocktail of threats, carrots and sticks that, in many ways, have backfired and were not sufficient to do the business. And, for me, the ultimate conclusion is, if you were starting today, would you build it via this model, and the answer is a resounding no."

Which is to say, with perfect hindsight, Trudeau might've been better off starting with a federal plan and working backwards.

The medicare comparison was always more complicated than it seemed. With the Canada Health Act, the federal government has established principles that the provinces must adhere to when delivering medical services. But, in that case, the federal government has both a political advantage (it's pretty easy to like getting health care) and a significant financial incentive it can withhold from provinces that don't follow the rules (the Canada Health Transfer totalled $38.5 billion in 2018–19).

In the case of carbon pricing, the service would be a bit more of an imposition. And the incentives were relatively small: provinces that implemented their own systems would have access to a share of a $2 billion federal fund for low-emission projects and the ability to control the revenue raised by a carbon tax or cap-and-trade system. In Saskatchewan, Alberta, Ontario and New Brunswick, conservatives decided it was to their advantage to run against a new tax (even if the revenues were going to be rebated to the public).

A fully federal price would have meant figuring out how to accommodate systems in at least British Columbia, Quebec and Alberta. But it might've at least produced a quicker resolution. Nearly two years elapsed between the first ministers' meeting to sign the pan-Canadian framework in December 2016 and Trudeau's announcement of the federal backstop in October 2018. That delay allowed the issue to remain an open question. And, in the meantime, the framework seemed to fall apart.

But it is also surely worth pausing to consider how much of even that narrative depends on luck, or the lack thereof. In an alternate timeline, Patrick Brown's private life is perfectly beyond reproach and Trudeau's climate plan is relatively secure.

SHORTLY BEFORE TRUDEAU WALKED down to the House of Commons to announce his government would move forward with a federal price on carbon, as he and his advisors were gathered together around the prime minister's suite of offices in Centre Block, Gerry Butts leaned over to Trudeau. "We're doing the right thing," he said. "Hard things are hard."

"I was excited to be able to lay out the principles, the examples, have the actual conversation in a very direct and clear way. For me to be able to say, 'This is us, this is where we're going, this is what we believe in. Bring it on and we'll figure out whether or not Canadians are against us or with someone else,'" Trudeau says. "I always look for those moments of, 'Here, let me give a big speech on this and lay out where we are and where we stand and over the coming months we'll develop and defend it.' People will know exactly where I stand and be able to choose to listen to my arguments or listen to the counter-arguments."

In that speech, Trudeau referenced his three children by name—Xavier, Ella-Grace and Hadrien—as his motivation for acting. Two and a half years later, Butts made a similar appeal in the midst of announcing his resignation from Trudeau's office. "I also need to say this (and I know it's a non sequitur)," he wrote. "Our kids and grandkids will judge us on one issue above all others. That issue is climate change."

"Hard things are hard" is a credo borrowed from Barack Obama's presidency. David Axelrod, an advisor to the president and a friend to Butts, offered that wisdom to Obama during the administration's fight to pass health care reform. It was later inscribed on a plaque that sat on Obama's desk. That battle dominated the first two years of Obama's first term. The legislation was loudly opposed, just barely passed and likely contributed to Democratic losses in the 2010 midterm elections. It was challenged in court and Republicans vowed to repeal it. Its launch, via an online portal, was riddled with technical failures.

"Sometimes we get disappointed, in this age of instant gratification, when we don't feel as if everything is solved," Obama remarked in a speech in 2016, reflecting on Axelrod's wisdom.

Hard things are hard. Progress is rarely perfect and not always linear. Nothing is ever solved in a day. Crafting national policy is a lot harder than sending a tweet.

After coming to office in 2017, the Trump administration took various steps to weaken "Obamacare." And yet, more than eight years after the Affordable Care Act was signed into law, Obamacare still exists. As of 2019, it was still helping people access vital services and it loomed as a standard by which any effort to reduce public care would be measured. Indeed, both its successes and shortcomings seem to have inspired a new generation of Democratic Party leaders to push for a further expansion of public medicare.

Designing a national approach to climate change in Canada is, similarly, not simple. Allowing each province to decide on its own emissions reductions would invariably lead to varying levels of ambition, with no guarantee that those provincial targets would necessarily add up to a responsible national target. Applying a uniform target to every province would invariably result in disagreements over local differences in industry and energy usage. Attempting to set different targets for each province would require prolonged and messy negotiations.

The Liberals opted to focus on establishing a common standard of policy—a price on carbon, with a federal backstop for provinces with recalcitrant premiers. The courts will decide whether the law is on their side. In the meantime, economists will line up to say that putting a price on carbon is the most efficient method for reducing emissions— that it will achieve those reductions at the lowest possible cost to the economy. Broad regulations—whereby governments simply declare a limit on emissions or a requirement for production—tend to actually cost the economy, and consumers, more. But with regulations, the cost is obscured. With carbon pricing, the charge is explicit. And therein lies the politics.

Trudeau was at least well acquainted with the political challenge— he was a rookie candidate in 2008 when Stéphane Dion put a carbon tax at the centre of the Liberal campaign. Dion "picked the right thing, the principle that we tax pollution more and reduce personal taxes. For me, [it's] the right thing and it's something we're going to do within the decade," Trudeau said in an interview with *Maclean's* after that election. "It's a no-brainer. It's the right thing to do, but it also is going to be a difficult thing to do, politically."

The Liberal result in that election was not entirely attributable to the carbon tax. Dion was a flawed leader. And the Liberal Party was a flawed organization. "It's lack of resources, lack of ability to counteract—I mean, you can counteract a highly negative personal-attack-based ad campaign without being highly negative and attacking personally yourself. But it takes similar amounts of funds. And it takes a coherent strategy that everyone's working together. And it takes a strong, resilient organization that can reach out at every grassroots level," Trudeau said in 2008. "And those three things we didn't have, and that's what we know now."

The problem, Trudeau suggested, was that voters looked at Dion and just couldn't see him as a prime minister. "It's that 'we just don't see him as' that killed us. That's our job as communicators, to be getting that out."

Dion was a fussy academic, stuffy and awkward and inelegant in English, his second language. What he proposed in 2008 was a "Green Shift." "We need to make polluters pay," Dion said, "and put every single penny back into the hands of Canadians." But it was not a straight swap.

A price on carbon would be implemented at $10 per tonne, gradually increasing to $40 per tonne. The revenue from that price would be directed toward a combination of tax relief, poverty reduction and environmentally friendly investment: three cuts to personal income tax rates, the creation of a new child benefit, increases to two employment benefits, targeted allowances for rural and northern residents, a corporate tax cut, a small business tax cut and two business investment incentives. That inclusion of measures to fight poverty added an element of social spending to Dion's plan. And there was no mechanism to account for provincial disparities in emissions.

A decade later, things were different. Trudeau, for one, was everything Dion was not. The Liberal promise in 2015 was merely to work with the provinces to put a price on carbon. And that was just one element of an expansive platform that was primarily focused on other concerns.

By the time Trudeau stood in the House of Commons to announce a federal backstop, the four biggest provinces were already putting a price on carbon. And when it came time to apply the federal policy, the Liberals chose to return 90 percent of the revenue directly to the residents of each province through a rebate. The remaining 10 percent would be directed to schools, businesses and hospitals. The government estimated that approximately 70 percent of residents in the four provinces would receive more via the rebate than they would end up paying in increased costs. The parliamentary budget officer later estimated that only those in the top 20 percent of income earners would end up paying more than they received.

An Angus Reid poll conducted immediately after Trudeau announced the rebate found a significant shift in public opinion. In July 2018, 45 percent of respondents supported the plan, against 55 percent opposed. By late October the numbers had flipped: 54 percent in favour, 46 percent against. Support increased 11 points in Ontario.

"I think both the way we're telling this story and the readiness of Canadians to hear the story have changed," Trudeau says now when asked about Dion. "I also think we have made different policy choices that instead of the environmental combination of doom and gloom and take your medicine, we know what's best for you, we're saying, 'We're going to do the right things to protect the environment for future generations, but we are going to make sure that ordinary families succeed through this transition we have to do.'"

The Liberals also found a new way to talk about what they were doing. Dion had talked about a "carbon tax." Trudeau spoke initially of a "price on carbon." Then, two and a half years into governing, Liberal ministers and MPs started talking about a "price on pollution."

This was about marketing and persuasion. But it was also, arguably, a clearer description of what the policy is supposed to do. "Canadians realize that polluting isn't free," McKenna had said. That is, Canadians should understand that greenhouse gas emissions have a cost: that the carbon emissions we produce ultimately contribute to damages to the environment, human lives and property.

Going back to 2012, when Stephen Harper's Conservatives were in office, the federal government has calculated a "social cost of carbon" to account for those damages when assessing policy. In 2016, it was set at $40.70 per tonne. The free market does not account for that cost. Which is where, in theory, government policy should step in.

The professional opposition was nonetheless loud. Andrew Scheer, Ford, Kenney, Pallister and Moe formed a barbershop quintet of Conservative leaders who, without quite being able to explain how Canada would otherwise meet its international targets, were happy to sing the same dire tune about carbon pricing. Though a few are willing to dissent—most notably, Harper's former director of policy, Mark Cameron— it became an article of faith in post-Harper conservative circles that implementing a price on carbon would bring about economic ruin. Ford travelled to Saskatoon and Calgary to appear alongside Moe and Kenney, while Scheer visited Queen's Park in Toronto to be seen with Ford. All five leaders posed for the cover of *Maclean's*—as "the resistance"—with Kenney claiming credit for bringing the coalition together.

At their most ambitious, Conservatives claimed that putting a price on carbon wouldn't reduce emissions anyway. The basic law of demand—that the quantity purchased tends to decline as the price increases—would suggest otherwise, and this is confirmed by a number of studies that have found British Columbia's carbon tax, in place since 2008, successfully reduced fuel consumption and emissions.

Sitting in his office, shortly after Notley had announced Alberta's withdrawal from the federal framework, Trudeau frames the 2019 election as a contest between action and inaction, one with potentially profound ramifications.

"I find it difficult because it is both having a consequence on folks in B.C. who said, 'No, no, we were accepting the pipeline because it was part of the framework,' but the other piece is it has emboldened other provinces to say, 'See, the whole thing's collapsing.' And it enables the pundits on the right to sort of say, 'See, his careful balance is now completely . . .' Again, that's why we have a federal backstop, you know. I'd rather do it with the provinces, but I'm fully within my rights to do it anyway and I will," he says, reflecting on Notley's announcement.

"But it also makes this part of our upcoming election a really important fight, because if we don't demonstrate that we can take real, tangible actions on the environment and continue to get the support of Canadians, no Canadian government's going to bother defending the environment anymore. It'll be seen as an electoral loser. And I can't have that, we can't have that, we can't afford—Canada can't afford that. Not because Canada's emissions are so big, proportional to everyone else, but because we're one of those places that is going to figure out solutions that other people can say, 'Well, if Canada can do it—a cold and energy-resource-rich country can figure out how to reach their Paris targets—then we have a path for everyone else.'"

That is both a plea for support and the self-assignment of incredible responsibility.

There is still a gap. Based on that last estimate from the Harper era, Canada needed to reduce its projected emissions for 2030 by 302 megatonnes. In December 2018, the federal government projected that 199 megatonnes would be eliminated by federal and provincial policies announced since 2015. A further reduction of 24 megatonnes would be accomplished through changes in land use. That left 79 megatonnes to be covered by some combination of unmodelled initiatives (planned investments in clean technology, innovation and public transit) and future policies. At least some of that could also conceivably be covered by the purchase of international credits.

Depending on one's perspective, the glass is thus either 223 megatonnes full or 79 megatonnes empty. But, from either view, this is also the closest any prime minister has come to implementing a plan sufficient to meet one of Canada's international climate commitments. After thirty years of setting targets—a total of eight targets, committed to by three different prime ministers—there is at least a chance that Canada might follow through.

Though initially committed to tabling a plan that would get Canada to its 2030 target—while repealing the national carbon price—Scheer had backtracked by the end of 2018, instead promising only that reductions would be "meaningful." The New Democrats, conversely, seemed eager to promise to do more on emissions, while also criticizing Trudeau's willingness to build a new pipeline to the West Coast. Between the two of them, Scheer and Singh might try to pull apart Trudeau's attempt to knit together a national approach around Alberta.

The spring of 2019 brought another complication. On April 16, Jason Kenney's United Conservatives won sixty-three of eighty-seven seats in Alberta's legislature.

Kenney came to office with a promise to repeal the NDP's broad carbon tax. Large emitters would be made to pay a levy of $20 per tonne, but the Alberta plan would no longer meet Trudeau's national standard. That would compel the Trudeau government to step in and apply the federal backstop.

Kenney had also pledged to abandon Notley's plans for a cap on emissions from the oil sands. When Justin Trudeau stood on the floor of that gymnasium at Vancouver Island University in Nanaimo in February 2018 and tried to explain to that nice lady in the knit sweater why his government had approved the Trans Mountain expansion, that cap had been one of his reasons. A pipeline could be approved because, no matter what, emissions from the oil sands would not rise above a certain level.

A potential point of conflict seemed to pass when Kenney, moments after being sworn in as premier, suggested he actually wasn't all that worried about the cap and would be willing to leave it in place.

Meanwhile, another sea change also began to play out as these opponents of the carbon tax came to power: provincial targets for reducing emissions weakened.

In Ontario, Kathleen Wynne's government had been aiming to reduce emissions to 37 percent below 1990 levels by 2030. Doug Ford's government now pledges reductions of 30 percent below 2005 levels by 2030. The difference between those two targets amounts to 37 megatonnes.

In New Brunswick, Brian Gallant's government had put into legislation a target of reducing emissions to 10.7 megatonnes. Blaine Higgs's new government decided it would aim to get to 14.1 megatonnes.

In Alberta, Rachel Notley believed her government could reduce the province's emissions by 50 megatonnes. Jason Kenney seems to be shooting for something less than that.

In a way, this was clarifying. No longer were Canadian conservatives claiming they could achieve the same level of reductions—and meet international targets—at a lower cost. No longer was it a choice between carbon pricing and some unspecified but apparently magical alternative. More than thirty years after the Toronto conference, the question was whether Canadians were interested in trying to fulfill Canada's international commitment for 2030.

"We are the first generation who has known how to fix this problem, but we are the last generation that will actually be able to do something about it," Trudeau said on October 23, 2018, almost exactly a year out from the next election. He was announcing the details of the federal backstop that would be applied in Ontario, Saskatchewan, New Brunswick and Manitoba. Butts had come up with the line. It was a twist on something Barack Obama had said in 2014: "We are the first generation to feel the effect of climate change and the last generation who can do something about it."

Two weeks before Trudeau's announcement there had been a remarkable confluence of events. On October 8, the Nobel Prize in Economics was awarded to William Nordhaus for "integrating climate change into long-run macroeconomic analysis." Nordhaus was a pioneer in the field of environmental economics, and his work had shown that carbon pricing would be the most efficient policy response. That same day, the Intergovernmental Panel on Climate Change issued a report on the potential for future global warming. The study's ninety-one authors concluded that the world had just twelve years left to take the action necessary to limit warming to 1.5 degrees Celsius.

So now Trudeau could lean on both economics and science. But the politics would be solely his responsibility.

CHAPTER 10

"North Star"

Malala Yousafzai was a young girl living in the Swat district of Pakistan when the Taliban seized control of the area. She emerged first as a voice from within that occupation and then as an activist for education and the rights of girls. As her national and international stature grew, the Taliban sought to silence her. She survived an assassination attempt in 2012, when she was just fifteen, and both she and her cause were elevated by the attack. In 2014, she became the youngest person to ever receive the Nobel Peace Prize, which she shared with Kailash Satyarthi, an activist for children's rights in India, who was credited with saving more than 80,000 children from slave labour.

Two weeks after becoming a Nobel laureate, Yousafzai was scheduled to be in Ottawa to receive the award of honorary Canadian citizenship, accepting an offer the Harper government made in 2013. A gunman's attack on Parliament Hill scuttled those plans. When she finally made it to Ottawa in April 2017, she was received by a new prime minister, one still basking in his own kind of international acclaim.

"Your motto and your stand of 'welcome to Canada' is more than a headline or a hashtag," she said, addressing a special joint session of Parliament. "It is the spirit of humanity that every single one of us would yearn for if our family was in crisis. I pray that you continue to open your homes and your hearts to the world's most defenceless children and families, and I hope your neighbours will follow your example."

She was "very happy" to meet the prime minister and "amazed by his embrace of refugees, his commitment to appointing Canada's first gender-balanced cabinet, and his dedication to keeping women and girls at the centre of your development strategy."

She was also familiar with less-substantive matters related to Canada's head of government. "We have heard so much about Prime Minister Trudeau," she continued. "People are always talking about how young he is. They say that he is the second-youngest prime minister in Canadian history. He does yoga. He has tattoos, and a large mole."

Such was the extent of Trudeau's fame in the spring of 2017.

"While I was coming here," Yousafzai said, "everyone was telling me to shake the prime minister's hand and let us know how he looks in reality." The audience laughed. Sophie Grégoire Trudeau, seated beside her husband in the centre aisle of the House, shook her head.

This was back before the trip to India. Before thousands of people were showing up at the Canadian border. And before anyone had reason to know what a "deferred prosecution agreement" was.

"People are just so excited about my meeting Prime Minister Trudeau," Yousafzai continued, "that I do not think anyone cared about the honorary Canadian citizenship." Both Trudeau and his wife looked down and brought their hands to their faces as others in attendance chuckled.

The Trudeau phenomenon was driven by a combination of old-media storytelling and new-media glee.

The international press was immediately intrigued by the arrival of a handsome young man bearing progressive values. There was a feature in the *New York Times* ("Trudeau's Canada, again"), a write-up in the *New Yorker* ("Another Trudeau Makes Canada Cool") and a surprisingly steamy photo spread in *Vogue* ("Justin Trudeau Is the New Young Face of Canadian Politics") that included an image of the prime minister's hands resting on his wife's posterior. The *Daily Mirror*, a British tabloid, asked if he was the "sexiest politician in the world."

He was the cool new thing at an early series of international summits in the fall of 2015. At a meeting of Asia-Pacific leaders in Manila, he was mobbed by members of the public. "It was alarming, but he was not alarmed," says Roland Paris, the University of Ottawa professor who served as an advisor to Trudeau in 2015 and 2016. Paris recalls feeling physical relief when he himself escaped the crush of people that swarmed Trudeau at the hotel where the prime minister was giving a news conference. But Trudeau, surrounded by security, had slowed his pace as he made his way through the crowd. Afterwards Paris asked him why. "Because I know that if I'd walked faster, my guys would've knocked people over," Trudeau said.

Two months later, Trudeau was a hit at Davos. "This year, there is another kind of Davos man," a reporter with the *New York Times* explained. "He is a former snowboarder and schoolteacher who now runs that country just north of the United States." A young do-gooder attending the World Economic Forum's annual gathering of the elite gushed that Trudeau had "awakened, or reawakened rather, the spirit of an inclusive, welcoming, positive Canada."

GQ named him one of the most stylish men alive ("The Prime Minister of suave"). His tendency to wear quirky socks was widely documented. *Time* magazine put him on its list of the one hundred most influential people in the world. "There will be a few names globally that will become etched in our history books," Jacinda Ardern, the prime minister of New Zealand, wrote in the citation. "They will be the names that mark the shift in our political landscape, when younger politicians took the reins and heralded a different type of politics. Justin Trudeau will be one of them."

All the while, Trudeau kept going viral. There he was saying "Because it's 2015" to explain why his cabinet included an equal number of men and women. There he was dressed up for Halloween with his kids or welcoming Syrian refugees or explaining quantum computing or calling himself a feminist or cuddling with pandas or charming Ivanka Trump or planking on a table or hanging out with Barack Obama or marching in a Pride parade. In the summer of 2016, he was twice photographed shirtless. A photo of him wearing tight pants became a minor sensation. He was the internet's boyfriend and a shareable beacon of progressivism.

"Trudeau is the perfect prime minister for the social media age. He intuitively *gets* the kind of affirming identity politics that speaks to huge numbers of people on the internet," a writer for *Vox* explained.

In July 2017, the wave peaked with the image of the prime minister, jacket removed and white shirt sleeves rolled halfway up his forearms, staring out from the cover of *Rolling Stone* magazine: "Justin Trudeau: The North Star . . . Is he the free world's best hope?"

By then, Trudeau was flirting with the sort of overexposure that normally only actors and musicians need to worry about. There was at least little precedent in Canadian political history for this sort of thing. Perhaps only his father had ever reached a comparable level of international stature.

"All that has really mattered to most of us is that our prime ministers look good to outsiders," Richard Gwyn wrote in *The Northern Magus*, his majestic survey of Pierre Trudeau's first twelve years in power. "By casting a shadow when he goes abroad, Trudeau reinforces our self-esteem, which, in the manner of the Japanese, we measure by the way others esteem us."

By that measure, Justin Trudeau was also a success. And Canada basked in the reflected glow. In October 2016, the cover of the *Economist* declared "Liberty moves north," beside an image of the Statue of Liberty wearing a red maple leaf crown. "In this depressing company of wall-builders, door-slammers and drawbridge-raisers, Canada stands out as a heartening exception," the editors wrote, contrasting Canada with the populist and anti-immigrant sentiments in the United States, the United Kingdom, Germany and France. In a survey by Ipsos MORI in 2017, 81 percent of global respondents said Canada made a positive contribution to the world, the highest mark of any country tested.

Such was the appreciation for Trudeau and Canada from 2015 to 2018 that it spawned its own cottage industry of Canadian writers who scrambled to publish pieces explaining for international audiences that, in fact, the prime minister and this country were not perfect.

From up close, one can see the blemishes and wrinkles. But take a few steps back and it's not hard to see what the rest of the world saw in Trudeau: a young leader who championed diversity, gender equality and protecting the environment. In the Trump era, that had special appeal. And, as Gwyn suggested, Canadians appreciated the esteem—an Abacus poll in December 2018 gave Trudeau his highest approval rating for how he represented Canada internationally.

However much the Canadian public's own fascination with their prime minister has inevitably waned, he remains a point of interest abroad. On a visit to New York and the United Nations in the fall of 2018, he still turned heads, still attracted well-wishers and picture-seekers. Jesse Jackson, the American civil rights leader, turned up to see him speak at the Council on Foreign Relations. A woman at the United Nations headquarters, upon seeing Trudeau as he walked past her, grabbed the arm of her companion in excitement. At the conclusion of one panel discussion, Trudeau stopped to have a word with Bill Gates, specifically to thank the Microsoft founder for a book he'd recently mailed to him (Hans Rosling's *Factfulness*).

It was also not just the international press who took a liking to our prime minister.

"I have to say that there are few leaders around the world who I think combine vision and talent and values the way that Justin does," Barack Obama said in November 2016, sitting beside Trudeau ahead of a bilateral meeting during the Asia-Pacific Economic Cooperation summit in Lima, Peru—their last official meeting as president and prime minister. "And I am very much looking forward to his continued leadership in the years to come." This was just twelve days after Donald Trump was declared the winner of the U.S. presidential election. In private, after the photographers and cameramen had left, the president was more direct. "Justin, your voice is going to be needed more," he said. "You're going to have to speak out when certain values are threatened."

———

ON JANUARY 27, 2017, Donald Trump signed Executive Order 13769. The presidential memorandum halted the admission of refugees from Syria and banned entry to the United States of visitors from Iraq, Iran, Libya, Somalia, Sudan, Syria and Yemen.

During the presidential campaign in 2016, Trump had advocated for "a total and complete shutdown of Muslims entering the United States until our country's representatives can figure out what the hell is going on." This was justified, he said, because of the "hatred" that many Muslims had for Americans. Now in office, he was moving to close the United States to seven countries where Muslims represented a majority of the population.

The order was implemented almost immediately on the Friday it was signed, inciting a weekend of chaos and outrage. Protesters gathered around and inside airports. Lawyers scrambled to assist stranded and detained travellers, legal challenges were rushed before judges. All of it played out online, in images, news reports and anger.

Trudeau and his advisors faced two questions. Was this one of those moments when something needed to be said? And, if so, what to say? After the first was answered in the affirmative, there were conference calls to hash out the second. "We have said, from the very beginning, that we are not going to be afraid to project our values into the world and that now, in particular, is a time when people around the world are looking at Canada as a custodian of those values and we can't shy away from that," Gerry Butts says.

The result was a short message posted to Twitter and Facebook: "To those fleeing persecution, terror & war, Canadians will welcome you, regardless of your faith. Diversity is our strength #WelcomeToCanada" The hashtag had previously been used to mark the arrival of refugees from Syria. The rest of the message hewed closely to the UN's definition of a refugee: "someone who has been forced to flee his or her country because of persecution, war or violence." A photo was added of Trudeau crouching down to greet a young girl from Syria after her arrival at Toronto's Pearson International Airport in December 2015.

"His view is that if he's cowed into silence in moments like that, then what signal does that send to the country, first and foremost," Butts says of Trudeau. "And what licence does it give to politicians on the other side of the equation to push the opposite end of the issue?"

Trudeau was not the only foreign leader to speak out that weekend.

Angela Merkel said Trump's actions were "against the core idea of international aid for refugees and international cooperation." Boris Johnson, the British foreign minister, tweeted that it was "divisive and wrong to stigmatise because of nationality," and French foreign minister Jean-Marc Ayrault tweeted that "welcoming refugees is a duty of solidarity."

But Trudeau's eighteen words resonated far more than any of those comments. On Twitter, his message was shared more than 400,000 times. On Facebook, it was shared another 235,000 times.

The first criticism of Trudeau's tweet was that he hadn't gone far enough. In the House, Tom Mulcair challenged him to directly address Trump's policy. "The Prime Minister talks about the importance of standing up to intolerance and racism," Mulcair said. "Why is he refusing to denounce this policy that breaches fundamental human rights and that will inevitably have consequences for Canada?"

Trudeau responded that Mulcair's question and a previous question from Rona Ambrose about the government's response to Trump's protectionist trade policies demonstrated "the important double role that this government has."

"We need to make sure we are protecting Canadian jobs and growing the economy by having a constructive working relationship with our most important trade partner and ally," he explained. "We are also standing up for Canadian values and principles. This is what Canadians expect of us, and that is what we have demonstrated over the past days as we have stood loudly and clearly for the openness, for the welcoming, for the compassion, for the strength that Canadians expect of all of us."

Shortly thereafter, attention turned to Emerson, Manitoba, a small town situated flush against the Canadian-American border.

Through the first two months of 2017, the RCMP intercepted 183 people in the area who had walked across the border from North Dakota and Minnesota. Many of those who crossed had been in the United States after fleeing countries in Africa. Such crossings were not entirely unusual—410 people were known to have crossed between April and December 2016—but this was a notable increase. In the middle of winter, these long walks across the border could also be dangerous. In December, a man from Ghana suffered severe frostbite to his hands, and all his fingers had to be amputated. In April, hypothermia was blamed for the death of a woman whose body was found across the border in Minnesota.

The premier of Manitoba appealed for federal assistance. Kellie Leitch, in her quest to win the Conservative leadership as a miniature version of Donald Trump, went to Emerson to declare that she would immediately turn back anyone who tried to get in. The local Conservative MP, Ted Falk, blamed Trudeau's tweet.

"Is this an open invitation for folks that want to illegally cross into Canada to come here and take advantage of our generous immigration and refugee policy?" Falk asked.

No one would have been walking across the border if not for an agreement signed by Canada and the United States in 2002. The Safe Third Country Agreement sets out that anyone seeking to claim asylum in either Canada or the United States must do so within the country in which they first land—the premise being that the two countries are equally safe and just, and asylum seekers should be discouraged from shopping between the two. As a result, Canadian officials can turn back anyone who arrives at an official border crossing and attempts to make a claim.

At the same time, Canada is still obligated to afford due process to anyone who makes it onto Canadian soil. And it is the combination of that obligation and the Safe Third Country Agreement that leads to people walking into a place like Emerson. Or a place like Roxham Road, near the town of Saint-Bernard-de-Lacolle in southern Quebec. There, at the border between Quebec and the state of New York, people started to show up by the thousands.

The first significant increase in such crossings occurred in 2016, when approximately 2,400 people were intercepted (compared to a few hundred the year before). But in the month of August 2017, the RCMP intercepted 5,530 people who had crossed into Quebec. Like Falk, Conservative immigration critic Michelle Rempel blamed Trudeau's tweet.

Nationally, the RCMP reported 20,593 interceptions in 2017. Though the rate of arrivals declined after the fall of 2017, another 19,419 interceptions were made in 2018.

Of course, Trudeau's tweet was not the only potentially relevant development in January 2017: eight days earlier, Donald Trump had been sworn in as the forty-fifth president of the United States. As a candidate, Trump had demonized Muslims, vowed to build a wall along the border with Mexico (because, he said, criminals, drugs and "rapists" were getting into the United States) and called for the mass deportation of undocumented immigrants. Once in office, his administration empowered the Immigration and Customs Enforcement agency to be more aggressive, ended temporary protected status for hundreds of thousands of people from other countries and moved to end a program that protected undocumented immigrants who had come to the United States as children.

That some number of people residing in the United States decided to come to Canada in the first two years of the Trump presidency was thus probably not entirely, or even predominantly, because of a tweet. But Trudeau was eventually compelled to concede the obvious: that receiving asylum in Canada was not as easy as showing up—#WelcomeToCanada was not an open and unconditional invite. Then his government had to figure out how to both handle the influx and dissuade further arrivals.

An intergovernmental task force on irregular migration was established, with representation from the Quebec and Ontario governments. Two Liberal MPs—Emmanuel Dubourg and Pablo Rodriguez—were dispatched to the United States to warn certain diasporas against trying to cross the border. Public Safety Minister Ralph Goodale sought American assistance to deal with the fact that many of those arriving in Canada had entered the United States with visas issued by the American embassy in Riyadh, Saudi Arabia. Immigration Minister Ahmed Hussen, himself a former refugee from Somalia, went to Nigeria to meet with government officials: a large percentage of arrivals in Canada were Nigerians who had arrived in the United States on travel visas.

The 2018 budget included $173 million to provide additional border security and assist in processing claims. Another $13 million was set aside to cover legal aid for asylum seekers. The provinces of Ontario, Quebec and Manitoba were given $50 million to deal with housing costs in 2018, and another $114 million was set aside in 2019. An analysis by the parliamentary budget officer estimated that the total cost to the federal government, excluding provincial compensation, could reach $400 million in 2019–20, in large part because of the time required to process each case.

By no means did such an influx constitute a public crisis—even if news reports of Montreal's Olympic Stadium being used to house asylum seekers suggested otherwise, and even if provincial and municipal leaders complained that they needed federal assistance to house and care for so many newcomers. Canada is a large and prosperous country. It could accommodate an additional 40,000 people. By comparison, Germany took in more than a million refugees in 2015 at the height of the mass migration that was triggered by the civil war in Syria and the emergence of the Islamic State.

But populist politicians in both Europe and the United States have used the spectre of uncontrolled or dramatically increased immigration to stoke conflict and rally support. Geography has largely spared Canada from such forces: there is nothing here like the "illegal immigration" debate that bedevils American politics. But the arrivals at Emerson and Roxham Road were an excuse for similar politics.

The Conservatives insisted on referring to the asylum seekers as "illegal"—while it can be illegal to cross a national border, individuals are legally protected when crossing a national border to claim asylum—and worried aloud that Trudeau was endangering the public's general support for immigration. In July 2018, the Conservative Party retracted a graphic that showed a black man using Trudeau's tweet as a bridge to enter Canada through a broken fence. A few months later, the Conservatives came out against the UN's Global Compact for Migration, a non-binding statement of principles that Andrew Scheer said was a threat to Canada's sovereignty. In opposing the pact, Scheer's

Conservatives joined a handful of far-right parties and governments in Europe and the United States. Under Trudeau, Canada was one of 164 countries to sign the declaration.

Since the PMO began tracking correspondence by topic in the fall of 2016, no issue generated more mail to the prime minister than Trump's travel ban. But internal Liberal polling on Trudeau's response was split. In May 2018, 42 percent approved of it as a statement of Canadian values, while 47 percent said it was irresponsible and would encourage asylum claims.

More than a year after Trudeau's tweet, the new arrivals also became Ontario premier Doug Ford's latest excuse to criticize the Trudeau Liberals.

"The Federal Government encouraged illegal border crossers to come into our country, and the Federal Government continues to usher people across the U.S.-Quebec border into Ontario," Ford's office declared in a statement on July 5, 2018. "This has resulted in a housing crisis, and threats to the services that Ontario families depend on. This mess was 100 per cent the result of the Federal Government, and the Federal Government should foot 100 per cent of the bills."

The statement was issued just as Trudeau, Butts and Katie Telford were arriving at Queen's Park to meet with Ford and his top advisors. The federal delegation saw it only after they came out of the meeting. Trudeau proceeded to his scheduled news conference and returned the favour, not so subtly implying that the premier didn't understand international law.

"It didn't seem to me that the premier was quite as aware of our international obligations to the UN convention on refugees as he might have been," Trudeau said. "So I spent a little time explaining how the asylum-seeking system works and how our system is supposed to operate."

Ford reportedly fumed at Trudeau's explanations. "That son of a bitch got up and said, 'Do you know about the Geneva Convention?'" he apparently groused. "That son of a bitch lecturing me?"

The next day, in a radio interview, the prime minister said "conservative politicians, here and around the world" were playing a "very dangerous game" with the issue of immigration.

In Ford's defence, his government was rather indiscriminate in its attacks on the Trudeau government. Complaints about the federal carbon tax and asylum seekers were followed by criticisms of marijuana legalization and Statistics Canada's interest in acquiring financial data and the new trade deal with the United States and Mexico and the possible return of foreign fighters associated with the Islamic State and the federal-provincial equalization formula and the federal government's fall economic update and the use of retaliatory tariffs to respond to the Trump administration's tariffs on steel and aluminum. Rarely a week passed without the government of Ontario registering some kind of grievance.

But less than two weeks after his meeting with Ford, Trudeau made a move: Bill Blair, a parliamentary secretary, was promoted to cabinet as a minister responsible for border security and reducing organized crime. Blair, the former chief of the Toronto Police Service, was already serving as the government's point man on the legalization of marijuana.

As luck would have it, Blair's time as police chief in Toronto had coincided with the ignominious spectacle of Rob Ford's mayoralty. It was Blair who confirmed that police had come into possession of a videotape that showed the mayor smoking crack cocaine, thus proving that such a videotape existed. Doug Ford, a city councillor at the time, publicly admonished Blair and later accused the chief of leaking information to the *Toronto Star*. Blair threatened to sue and backed off only after Ford formally apologized in writing.

If the Ford government now insisted on pressing the issue of asylum seekers, Premier Ford and Bill Blair could get reacquainted.

Regardless, Blair had the advantage of looking and sounding like a former police chief: big, grizzled and a little gruff. Beyond what he brought to the job in terms of management and administrative experience, it was handy to have him around. Worried about legal weed? Here was a former police chief to tell you everything will be fine. Worried about people crossing the border? Here now would be Bill Blair to tell you everything was under control.

But that everything was under control would not be an easy

impression to maintain. The Liberals could discourage people from coming. They could spend extra funds to deal with those who nonetheless came (though whether they spent enough to expand and accelerate the processing of claimants could be debated). But there were no great options for addressing the basic problem.

The New Democrats called on the government to fully renounce the Safe Third Country Agreement. That would have been a provocative move—effectively declaring that the United States was no longer to be trusted in its treatment of asylum seekers—and it might have only resulted in even more people claiming asylum at official ports of entry. The Conservatives countered that the Liberals should instead close the "loophole" in the agreement so that everywhere along the border would be considered an official point of entry. That, though, would present a significant logistical challenge—the Canada-U.S. border is approximately 9,000 kilometres long—and it might only motivate asylum seekers to find more remote entry points. It would also require renegotiating the agreement with the United States. And Canadians might not appreciate their government working with the Trump administration on immigration policy.

Ahmed Hussen suggested Conservatives were proposing to "militarize" the border. But Canadian ministers did engage with American officials about changing the agreement, and by March 2019 the Liberals seemed willing to concede that the Safe Third Country Agreement wasn't working. The Trudeau government's reported proposal was that Canadian border officials be empowered to transport irregular crossers to official ports of entry, where the asylum seekers could be turned away.

In the meantime, the Liberals took a smaller step, tabling a law that would make it harder to apply for asylum in Canada if you had previously sought asylum in the United States. Jean-Nicolas Beuze, the United Nations High Commissioner for Refugees' representative in Canada, told the *Globe and Mail* that the change was in line with international law. But the government had to fight the impression that it was betraying its tweeted principles.

Both changes could be challenged politically and legally. Either could be contrasted with Trudeau's tweet to suggest hypocrisy. But the Liberals had seemingly decided that the spectre of unplanned immigration was so powerful that it necessitated action.

"It's legitimate that the government wants to reassure its population that it has a functioning asylum system," Beuze told the *Globe*. "All governments would want to make sure that people trust public institutions."

Here was the basic crux of the balancing act that was immigration policy and national identity in Canada in 2019. Maintaining the ideals of openness and compassion and diversity meant not saying yes to everyone who wanted to come.

IN JUNE 2018, the world took note of another American horror: the Trump administration was enforcing a policy that separated migrant children from their parents after families crossed the U.S. border with Mexico. The U.S. government apparently hoped this cruelty would discourage asylum seekers. Heart-rending images and stories began to emerge. Children were being kept in large cages. An audio recording of children crying for their mothers circulated online.

Once again, the furor played out over a weekend. On the following Monday, Trudeau's ministers seemed to struggle for a response. There were official assurances about the Safe Third Country Agreement and Canadian policy toward minors seeking asylum and the importance of upholding Canadian values toward refugees.

It was not entirely clear what was occurring in the United States: Trump's secretary for homeland security went so far as to claim there was no policy of separating families. But not until a reporter asked Ralph Goodale for his personal reaction did anyone offer the sort of answer the moment seemed to require. "Obviously, anyone looking at the human images would be very, very concerned," he said. "Children are very precious creatures and we all, I'm sure, need to have their safety, their security, their wellbeing, first and foremost in our minds, and that is what lies at the very basis of Canadian policy." The next day, other ministers were repeating Goodale's response almost word for word.

The Trudeau cabinet met on Tuesday morning and the Trump policy was raised for discussion. Patty Hajdu couldn't be there—she was away from Ottawa for a funeral—so she texted some of her colleagues to tell them how she was feeling and what she felt needed to be said. "I actually never do that," she says. "But I was so upset about it."

Hajdu was four when she was separated from her mother, who struggled with mental health issues, and went to live with an aunt in Minnesota. "I felt personally, I could feel that feeling, if that makes sense. I could feel that feeling," Hajdu says. "I have seen [my mother] struggle her whole life as a result of that decision, right or wrong. And I have paid an emotional price for that separation. And it's irrevocable, those things—when we're talking about months and years and the trauma that goes with that."

Hajdu believed the government needed to speak up. "I felt we had to say something . . . I felt Canadians wanted that. Everywhere I went, people were saying to me, like, 'Somebody's got to do something. Somebody's got to say something.'"

There were tears, she says, when she returned to Ottawa and had a chance to speak with Trudeau directly.

Hajdu was not the only person in Trudeau's government who wanted to say something. And when he stopped to speak with reporters before a meeting of the Liberal caucus on Wednesday morning, Trudeau was unqualified in his comments. "What's going on in the United States is wrong," he said. "I can't imagine what the families living through this are enduring. Obviously, this is not the way we do things in Canada."

This was further than Trudeau had gone previously. The tweet of January 2017 had avoided direct criticism. Trudeau and Chrystia Freeland had criticized Trump's imposition of steel and aluminum tariffs, but in that case there was an impact on Canadians. This was a direct comment on a domestic American policy.

According to a source, the Trump administration noticed Trudeau's criticism and didn't appreciate it. But the administration could hardly quibble with Trudeau's assessment: hours after the prime minister said it was wrong, Trump signed an executive order to end the policy of family separation.

Officially, more than 2,600 children were separated from their families after crossing the border into the United States. Reuniting them took months. As of November 2018, 140 of those children were still in custody.

========

ON JANUARY 22, 2018, a memo went out from Telford and Butts to announce a series of changes within the Prime Minister's Office. Chief among those moves was a promotion for Kate Purchase, the director of communications. When she returned from a planned maternity leave, Purchase would serve as the executive director of communications and planning, a new role that would oversee both the communications and tour departments within the PMO.

"This decision reflects the obvious reality that our communications and visual identity as a government are one and the same, and should be **properly consolidated under one leader, reporting directly to us,**" Telford and Butts wrote, putting that sentence in bold for emphasis. "To put it a different way, as Dan Arnold might say, 'pics or it didn't happen.'"

Three weeks later, Trudeau departed for a seven-day tour of India.

On a certain practical level, the biggest problem with that trip was the fact Jaspal Atwal, a man convicted of attempting to murder an Indian cabinet minister in 1986, was able to attend an official reception in Mumbai and get his picture taken with Sophie Grégoire Trudeau and a pair of cabinet ministers. When those photos surfaced in the media, Trudeau's national security advisor, Daniel Jean, briefed reporters off the record to allege, obliquely, that unfriendly elements in the Indian government had somehow been involved in embarrassing the Liberal government. Rather than limit the damage, Jean's involvement only extended the life of the story, culminating in his appearance before the public safety committee in April and then a full review by the new national security committee.

But the real problem was the pics of Trudeau, ostentatiously dressed in traditional Indian attire, his hands together in the reverential pose and his family in tow. There were multiple outfits, worn to several events. It was all a bit much. In one particularly painful photo, the lavishly attired Trudeau family posed beside a Bollywood actor, Shah Rukh Khan, who had chosen to wear a comparatively simple black suit. Eyebrows were raised in India. The Canadian and international press delighted in the awkward spectacle. Late-night comedians piled on.

Shareable photos and moments had fed Trudeau's global fame, but now the forces that made him a phenomenon were turned against him. The pics were undeniable. Worse, for a Canadian audience, the images seemed to confirm the worst idea of Trudeau: that he was flighty and unserious, vain and out of his depth.

There had been other rocky moments on the world stage. In November 2017, Trudeau upset Japan and Australia when he declined to give final approval to the Trans-Pacific Partnership (the deal was instead completed two months later). Then, in December 2017, Trudeau returned from a trip to China without an agreement to start free trade talks, purportedly because of Trudeau's insistence on a deal that included "progressive" elements on labour standards, the environment and gender equality. (That the Trudeau government had even made the effort of trying to start talks with China is said to have angered U.S. trade representative Robert Lighthizer.)

But neither of those events seemed to wound Trudeau like India. Internal polling on whether the government was on the right track slumped through the spring, with those who felt the government was on the wrong track surpassing the right track for the first time in May 2018. Awareness of the trip was high and it was blamed for a significant drop in the number of Canadians describing Trudeau as "strong."

The government's numbers improved again in June, in part because Trudeau, wearing a suit, was seen standing up to Donald Trump. The same guy who looked silly in India then presided over a successful summit of the G7 and kept his cool while waging a tariff battle with the president of the United States.

Trump's presence made a lot of things more difficult. But then sometimes it provided a chance for Trudeau to show himself as something
other than the worst caricature his critics could draw.

<hr>

LESS THAN TWENTY-FOUR HOURS after the Liberal victory in October 2015, Justin Trudeau stood on a stage in Ottawa and declared that
Canada was "back."

"I want to say this to this country's friends around the world: Many
of you have worried that Canada has lost its compassionate and constructive voice in the world over the past 10 years," he said. "Well,
I have a simple message for you on behalf of 35 million Canadians.
We're back."

Six weeks later he went to Paris, for the UN's twenty-first conference
on climate change, and repeated the declaration. "Canada is back, my
good friends," he said.

Canada had not entirely disappeared in the previous decade. If it
hadn't been Trudeau in Paris, for instance, it presumably would have
been some cabinet minister from Stephen Harper's government. But
that Conservative might have been rather less excited to be there.

Oddly enough, Harper had made a similar declaration nine years
earlier, telling an audience in New York that "Canada intends to be a
player . . . Canada's back." But what Trudeau seemed to have in mind
was getting back to what Canada was before Harper. Back to a certain
idea of Canada: a nice, co-operative, helpful and progressive country
that was eager to work with the other nations of the world. As Trudeau
put it in a speech to the United Nations in September 2016, "We're
Canada and we're here to help."

That was not quite the way John Baird, Harper's loudest foreign affairs
minister, had put it when he addressed the general assembly in 2011.
"Canada does not just go along in order to get along," Baird proudly
said. A year earlier, Canada had failed to win a seat on the UN Security
Council. Not going along to get along was a tidy way of explaining that

defeat. But, for both critics and supporters, it also became the defining mantra of foreign policy in the Harper era.

"Rather than maintaining the virtuous circle of effective bilateral and multilateral diplomacy, Canada has been marginalizing itself," Roland Paris wrote in an essay published in March 2015. "It is one thing to excoriate our adversaries, as we have recently taken to doing, but carelessly alienating our friends and disconnecting ourselves from international discussions is simply self-defeating. Canada is not powerful enough to dictate to others, even if we wished to do so. We have succeeded in international affairs by building bridges, not burning them." Shortly thereafter, Paris began advising Trudeau on foreign affairs.

At that first speech to the UN in September 2016, Trudeau struck a similar note: "We need to focus on what brings us together, not what divides us. For Canada, that means re-engaging in global affairs through institutions like the United Nations."

Re-engaging meant the prime minister, not just the environment minister, went to Paris, and Canada committed $2.65 billion to an international fund to help developing countries adapt to climate change and reduce emissions. "I'm here today not just to say Canada's back, but to show it," Trudeau said in announcing the funds. The Conservatives howled that he was throwing money at countries other than Canada.

Showing it would get harder from there.

A promised return to peacekeeping took a while to materialize. The government first announced that up to 600 personnel and 150 police officers could be made available for a UN mission, but then committed 250 personnel and six helicopters to Mali—less than some had expected and into a situation that was thought to be highly dangerous.

In June 2017, the government announced that, under a new feminist international assistance policy, the foreign aid budget would be directed toward women and girls and the promotion of gender equality. But the new policy did not come with a significant influx of new funding and, a year later, the Organisation for Economic Co-operation and Development scolded Canada for a declining rate of aid spending.

The world that Canada came back to in the fall of 2015 was also very different than the world that Canada faced by the fall of 2016. For one thing, the first and predominant task for Trudeau's second foreign minister, Chrystia Freeland, would be the renegotiation of NAFTA. It wouldn't be the only thing she and the rest of the government thought about, but it would take up a great amount of time and attention. It necessarily had to.

"I would cut Trudeau a lot of slack because there is a four-alarm fire taking place in the neighbour's house," says Paris. "So, so much of the foreign policy apparatus of the country, especially the time and attention of the politicians, is focused on dealing with that immediate threat. And there's nothing in our foreign policy that comes close to the importance of our relationship with the United States. It's like first, second, third, fourth, fifth in terms of priorities."

But in 2017, after having left Trudeau's office in June 2016, Paris wrote another essay, this one taking stock of the Liberal government's accomplishments.

"There is a real risk that the Trudeau government will be so consumed by its relations with the United States that it will fail to make real breakthroughs in other areas of its foreign policy," he wrote. "Trudeau's success or failure to protect Canada's interests with the Trump Administration will almost certainly be a defining element of his foreign-policy record as prime minister. On the other hand, focusing too narrowly on relations with the United States would also be risky. Canada's interests extend well beyond North America, and current conditions are unusually promising for Trudeau to pursue an ambitious and effective foreign policy. Failing to capitalize on this moment—due to a lack of attention, strategic clarity, or ambition—would also figure in Trudeau's eventual foreign-policy legacy: as a missed opportunity of historic significance."

Trudeau's "international profile and positive global reputation" positioned him well, Paris suggested, to marshal nations and agencies around a signature cause—perhaps, to address the global refugee crisis, "an international campaign aimed at providing 100 per cent of refugee youth with quality primary education and older youths with skills training."

The Trudeau government would not find anything that tidy (though Trudeau was part of the initial push that eventually became the UN's Global Compact for Migration). Instead, Liberal foreign policy would be framed around contending with that new Trumpian world.

"Here is a question," Freeland offered in a speech to the House of Commons in June 2017. "Is Canada an essential country, at this time in the life of our planet?"

Freeland contended that it was.

"But if we assert this, we are called to explain why," she said. "And we are called to consider the specifics of what we must do as a consequence."

It is perhaps a consequence of living beside the United States—the most essential country—that we dare to think of ourselves in such terms (do they have these discussions in Finland or Peru?). Though it is probably better to imagine that we should matter than to presume that we can't.

The United States had become uncomfortable with having to carry the mantle of global leadership, Freeland explained, and now the international order and the idea of common cause needed defending. Canada's priorities would be supporting and strengthening multilateral institutions, increasing funding for the Canadian Forces and expanding and improving international trade.

In the meantime, Freeland and her colleagues set about trying to be helpful.

In January 2018, at the height of tensions between the United States and North Korea, Freeland convened a meeting in Vancouver of foreign ministers from twenty countries to discuss hopes for a "negotiated, diplomatic solution." After the United States pulled out of the Paris Agreement, Catherine McKenna joined her counterparts from China and the European Union to form a trilateral working group on climate policy. Jim Carr, as trade minister, hosted a meeting of thirteen countries to discuss reforming the World Trade Organization. Freeland was then front and centre in an attempt to contain the crisis in Venezuela, condemning the illegitimate re-election of President Nicolás Maduro, endorsing opposition leader Juan Guaidó and then gathering the fourteen members of the Lima Group in Ottawa to discuss further steps.

The Liberals also followed the settlement of 40,000 Syrian refugees with a series of high-profile asylum efforts. When security forces in the Russian republic of Chechnya began arresting and torturing gay men, Freeland helped organize a clandestine operation to bring twenty-two men to Canada. Freeland later took a leadership role in an international effort to help ninety-eight rescue workers—the famous "White Helmets"—and their families escape Syria. In response to an open call by the United Nations, Canada was one of only a few countries to agree to resettle former slaves from Libya. And when the case of Rahaf Mohammed, an eighteen-year-old woman who was detained in Thailand while claiming to flee abuse and oppression by her family in Saudi Arabia, became an international concern, Canadian authorities offered immediate asylum.

Freeland's decision to show up at Pearson International Airport in Toronto to welcome Mohammed to Canada came close to undermining the basic virtue of the act. But then there was something to be said in 2019 for being loudly hospitable toward people from foreign lands. There was also something to be said for standing up to Saudi Arabia.

The Liberals had found themselves in a fight with the Saudi government just as the NAFTA renegotiations were nearing a dramatic conclusion. In August 2018, Freeland tweeted her concern for Samar Badawi, a human rights activist who had been imprisoned by Saudi authorities—Samar's brother, Raif Badawi, has been held since 2012 and his wife, Ensaf Haidar, now lives in Canada. The Canadian embassy in Riyadh then translated Freeland's message into Arabic and posted it online. That set off the Saudi government, which expelled the Canadian ambassador and launched a series of economic reprisals: recalling Saudi students from Canadian universities, suspending air travel and freezing trade.

That could be dismissed as the posturing of the newly elevated, thirty-three-year-old ruler, Crown Prince Mohammed bin Salman. But then the Trump administration did not come to Canada's defence. "Canada and Saudi Arabia are both close allies of the United States," a State Department official said.

Four months later, in response to an extradition request filed by the United States, Canadian officials agreed to detain Meng Wanzhou—the chief financial officer of Huawei, a Chinese telecommunications giant—when she arrived in Vancouver. The Chinese government threatened there would be "consequences" if Meng was not released. She was not and matters escalated quickly from there. Michael Kovrig, a former Canadian diplomat working in China, was detained by authorities, apparently in retaliation. In an interview with Reuters, Donald Trump suggested he could intervene in the Meng case if he thought it would help him in his trade negotiations with the Chinese: "if I think it's good for what will be certainly the largest trade deal ever made . . . I would certainly intervene if I thought it was necessary." Then came word that a second Canadian, Michael Spavor, had been detained. A month later, a Canadian citizen previously arrested in China on drug charges and sentenced to fifteen years in prison was retried and sentenced to death.

In an echo of the wider outreach that the Trudeau government did around Trump and NAFTA, Trudeau and Freeland set about soliciting help from other countries. By mid-January, the leaders of Australia, France, Germany, the United Kingdom, the Netherlands, Latvia, Lithuania, Estonia, Spain and the European Union had all publicly expressed concern about the detention of the two Canadians.

But while Trudeau's ambassador in Washington had counselled discipline when publicly discussing American politics, Trudeau's emissary to China could not stop himself from offering his own legal analysis. At a news conference with Chinese-language media in Markham, Ontario, John McCallum remarked that Meng had "quite good arguments on her side" in her fight against extradition. Trudeau initially resisted calls to fire his ambassador over those comments. But two days later the former immigration minister did it again, this time telling a reporter in Vancouver that it "would be great for Canada" if the United States dropped its extradition request.

After Trump's comments about using Meng as a bargaining chip, Trudeau and Freeland insisted that Canada was a country where the rule of law was paramount and that it was the rule of law, not politics, that would determine whether the Huawei executive was extradited. "Different countries do things differently, but in Canada politicians don't get to weigh in on court proceedings," he told a town hall in Milton, Ontario, on January 9. But McCallum had now walked all over the prime minister's line, twice. After the second comment, Trudeau called McCallum and told him to tender his resignation.

McCallum's willingness to ruminate aloud had caused trouble once before—in 2018, he suggested that Canadian foreign policy now had more in common with China than the United States—but his appointment in 2017 had been meant to show the seriousness with which the Trudeau government regarded Canada's relationship with China. Like David MacNaughton, Trudeau's man in Washington, McCallum was someone who had a connection to Trudeau and his inner circle—he had been dean of arts at McGill when both Trudeau and Butts were students. His unravelling, at the worst moment, was likely the real low point for Canadian foreign policy between 2015 and 2019.

It would be argued, particularly of his second comment, that McCallum was merely telling the truth. In a way, he probably was. It *would* have been great for the Trudeau government if the whole mess just went away. Similarly, some commentators suggested Canadian officials should have found a way to avoid getting involved in the Meng case, perhaps by getting a warning to her that she should avoid setting foot in Canada.

But helping an individual avoid the Canadian and American justice systems for the sake of not angering an authoritarian regime does not seem like the sort of thing a liberal democracy should be doing. And this was now something much more than an awkward situation.

"With the arbitrary arrests of NGO employees Michael Kovrig and Michael Spavor, Beijing has introduced hostage-taking of Western citizens as an instrument of its power projection. By bullying Canada, Beijing wants to set an example: Every country that stands in China's way will be hit with full force," wrote Thorsten Benner, a German analyst and one of more than a hundred scholars who wrote an open letter calling on China to release the two Canadians. "Beijing's calculus is simple. It expects Canada's allies to put their own good relations and economic interests with China above solidarity with Ottawa over Beijing's unprecedented aggression, allowing China to get away with it."

Freeland had foreshadowed something like this in that speech of June 2017, even if she was looking south, not west, at the time.

"Whatever their politics, Canadians understand that, as a middle power living next to the world's only superpower, Canada has a huge interest in an international order based on rules," she said. "One in which might is not always right. One in which more powerful countries are constrained in their treatment of smaller ones by standards that are internationally respected, enforced and upheld."

In June 2017, it was the United States that Canada seemed to need to fear, and China that offered an important opportunity to diversify Canada's trade and economic relationships. In January 2019, Canada had a trade deal with the United States, but China was holding Canadian citizens hostage.

"Like many of its peers, Ottawa is struggling to find its place between the moral high ground and a fast-changing geopolitical environment," observed the organizers of the Munich Security Conference in 2019.

Being a city upon a hill is apparently not easy.

In late January 2019, Trudeau is asked whether the issues with China and Saudi Arabia can be traced back to the fact that the United States is not the global leader it used to be.

"Obviously that's a reflection of part of it," he says. "But having the Americans there to enforce Pax Americana around the globe over the past decades made it a little bit easier for all of us who have our lot in with the Americans. And I think what we've seen was that if the stability and the rules-based order we've built as a world relies entirely on one country continuing to behave in a very specific, particular way, then maybe the world's not as resiliently rules-based as we think it is. And had it not been the particular circumstance we have right now, maybe it would've been something else.

"At one point you've got to decide—well, are you a world, are you countries, are you an international community that believes in those rules or not? And it shouldn't be fear of punishment or consequences that keeps you behaving right. I mean, the reason you and I don't go murdering people is not because, 'Well, it's against the law.' It's because that's where our values and where our beliefs are. So if we're going to actually build a better world that is rules-based and solid and predictable, I think there was always going to be a moment where people have to sort of put up or shut up: either you're standing for the rules even as it gets awkward and difficult and people are unhappy with you because you're applying the rules. Or you don't.

"And I think this is something that we're obviously going through as a world right now, and people are deciding how they want to position themselves. But I am very, very serene about Canada's positioning in this and our history that leads us to this. But also our vision for the future that says, if we don't follow rules and we accept that might is right in the international rules-based order, then nobody's going to do very well in the coming decades. As the Americans make different political decisions over the cycles, and even if the Americans do re-engage in a way, I think the lesson is that all of us need to be a little more rigorous in the way we stand for and expect and push back on others who are not following the rules that we abide by and accept. I think this is probably a moment that, again, in hindsight, fifty, a hundred years from now, we'll say, 'Yeah, this was a moment where people had to decide whether we do believe in an international rules-based order or not.'"

Very soon after saying this, his own commitment to the rule of law would be loudly questioned.

CHAPTER 11

REAL CHANGE

That things are different now than would have been the case if Stephen Harper were still prime minister is indisputable. But Justin Trudeau didn't just promise different. He promised that things would be *really* different. And to him were attached a number of high principles: sunny ways, openness, transparency, diversity, feminism, reconciliation. The result was an ongoing exercise in measuring Trudeau against both the change he promised and the ideals of which he spoke. For everything that did change, there was always something that hadn't.

There is at least one quantifiable example of profound change: the 40,081 people from Syria who came to Canada between November 2015 and January 2017.

During the 2015 campaign, Justin Trudeau promised that a Liberal government would bring 25,000 refugees from Syria by the end of the year. He had first suggested that number in March 2015, back when it might've been a bit easier to do. By the time the new cabinet was sworn in, there was relatively little time left to fulfill the commitment—just seven weeks, in theory, to screen, select and transport the equivalent of a mid-sized town.

"The public service came back and said that they couldn't do it," Trudeau says of the first meeting after the election to discuss that promise.

In fairness, it was a tall order. And, in the end, it didn't happen, at least not on Trudeau's proposed timeline.

But Trudeau didn't like the first answer, so he pushed back. "I didn't want to get off of the Christmas deadline too quickly," Trudeau says, "because we needed to light the fire under people."

"Every stone had to be turned," says Jane Philpott, who chaired the cabinet subcommittee that was set up to oversee the resettlement. "We were exploring options that never became public because we never followed through on them, but we really did push a whole range of what-if scenarios so that we could actually deliver on the outcome. And by doing that it really started to stretch people's imagination."

Not until late November did the government publicly concede it would not meet its original timeline.

"We got them to the place where the capacity was there and then I was comfortable in saying, 'Okay, I think people will understand,'" Trudeau says. "I wanted to know that they would be able to actually get the machines rolling in time to start having people come here."

"There's a bit of me that felt really guilty about the fact that public servants worked solidly right through that holiday season because we had to get those planes moving," Philpott says.

In the end, the 25,000th refugee arrived on February 29, 2016. "I think history will look back on that initiative as changing the face of our country in a positive way," Philpott says.

By no means was it a seamless endeavour. For any number of new arrivals, the transition has been, and will continue to be, difficult. Studies in both the House and Senate raised a number of questions about the infrastructure that exists to support people once they arrive. An auditor general's investigation found the government was broadly assessing the needs of Syrian refugees, but not doing enough to track their progress.

But if you wanted to measure change in Justin Trudeau's time as prime minister, you would start with those 40,081 people and the thousands of ways, great and small, that they will have an impact on this country.

The first official change was that gender-balanced cabinet. The second came on the day after the cabinet was sworn in, when two ministers were dispatched to announce that the long-form census would be restored, thus reversing the Harper government's widely derided attempt to limit the capacity of the federal government. This was what the new government wanted to be its first announcement. "We know the history of the past government and they very much focused on ideology," Innovation Minister Navdeep Bains explained. "We want to make sure we're driving good policies based on good evidence and quality data."

Canadians duly embraced their responsibility to fill out the compulsory paperwork with new zeal—the 97.8 percent response rate for the long-form census in 2016 was the highest ever. And after restoring the census, the Liberals set about doing various other things that the Conservatives wouldn't have done.

Marijuana, for instance, is legal now, though the Liberals never allowed themselves to be seen celebrating that fact. (Ralph Goodale's presence at official announcements on the issue were a recurring buzz-kill.) Meanwhile, the words to "O Canada" now officially read "in all of us command" rather than "in all thy sons command"—a gender-conscious change made after the government threw its full support behind a private member's bill introduced by Mauril Bélanger, the Liberal MP who succumbed to amyotrophic lateral sclerosis in 2016. As of this writing, there is a proposal to change the citizenship oath to include an acknowledgement of Indigenous treaty rights.

Gender identity was made a prohibited reason for discrimination in the Canadian Human Rights Act and added to the list of characteristics of identifiable groups protected against hate speech under the Criminal Code. The Court Challenges Program, which provides financial support to individuals and groups who wish to raise legal cases related to human rights and official languages, was revived after being cancelled by the Harper Conservatives.

The Liberals restored the federal program that provided health care services for asylum claimants. They repealed Conservative changes to the Citizenship Act that allowed the federal government to strip citizenship from dual nationals convicted of treason, espionage or terrorism, following from Trudeau's campaign declaration that "a Canadian is a Canadian is a Canadian." And they abandoned the former government's attempt to ban the niqab from being worn during the swearing of the citizenship oath. In the spring of 2017, the government then put its support behind a motion that condemned Islamophobia and called for a study of such bigotry.

On November 4, 2015, there was one supervised drug consumption site operating in Canada, and that facility, Vancouver's Insite, was only open because the Supreme Court had ordered the Harper government to leave it alone. Three years later, twenty-seven sites were operating with Health Canada's approval—spurred by both a widening epidemic of opioid addiction and a federal government that was willing to use all options to deal with it. As health minister, Philpott also reversed a Conservative ban on the use of pharmaceutical-grade heroin to treat addicts who did not respond to other treatments.

A chief science officer was appointed with a mandate to advise the prime minister and report annually on "the state of federal government science in Canada." Annual funding for the CBC was increased by $150 million. The parliamentary budget officer was made a fully independent officer of Parliament, provided with more funding and empowered to analyze political campaign promises. A new commissioner was appointed to organize election debates. New rules were introduced to limit pre-election spending by political parties. And a new committee of parliamentarians was created with the clearance to review classified information and report on national security operations.

Nine Veterans Affairs offices were reopened after being closed by the Conservatives. Gender-based analysis was incorporated into the evaluation of federal policy. Parliamentary secretaries—MPs assigned to assist cabinet ministers—are no longer allowed to vote on business before House of Commons committees. Conservative changes to elections laws, the national security regime and the assessment of major resource projects were rewritten. The federal government's advertising budget has not been used to blanket the nation's television airwaves with the sort of self-serving advertisements that the Harper

Conservatives made enthusiastic use of. The Liberal Party has not spent millions to frame Andrew Scheer with negative ads in the way that the Conservative Party successfully framed Stéphane Dion and Michael Ignatieff.

The face of government changed too. There is the gender-balanced cabinet, of course, but the federal cabinet is also empowered to fill more than 1,500 positions across the government, including appointments to public agencies, boards, tribunals and Crown corporations, officers of Parliament, deputy ministers and judges. And when the Liberals implemented a new appointment process, they put an emphasis on diversifying the roster.

On the day the new government was sworn in, 34 percent of governor-in-council appointees were women, 4.5 percent were visible minorities and 3.9 percent were Indigenous. As of December 2018, those numbers were 47.8 percent, 7.4 percent and 6.3 percent.

There are, as well, the various ways in which Justin Trudeau is rather unlike his immediate predecessor.

For one thing, the prime minister marches in Pride parades now—Trudeau being the first to do so. The prime minister also proudly calls himself a feminist. Trudeau convened four first ministers' conferences with the premiers in his first three years, whereas Harper held just two in his ten years as prime minister. Trudeau chose an astronaut, Julie Payette, to be governor general; Harper chose a university administrator, David Johnston. Trudeau has been photographed wearing Halloween costumes with his children. He has allowed himself to be seen crying in public.

Trudeau is, as noted, much more present and talkative. Most Wednesdays, Trudeau takes all questions in Question Period, an ad hoc attempt to create something like the Prime Minister's Questions that exists in the United Kingdom. But for all that talking, Trudeau and his ministers don't always say very much. They are happy to speak about their values and guiding principles. They like to remind you of their good works. They are less ready with details and explanation. They are somewhat nicer in Question Period, but not always much more informative. The Liberals could blame that on the realities of modern media and the public's relative inattention to politics: message discipline exists because it limits controversy and increases the odds that your preferred message will be heard by inattentive voters.

Indeed, Trudeau himself is sometimes an example of what can happen when a politician dares to stray from his talking points. There was, for instance, a brief tempest in December 2018 when Trudeau, participating in a panel on gender equality, remarked upon the "gender impacts when you bring construction workers into a rural area." "There are social impacts because they're mostly male construction workers," he said. His political opponents, particularly in Alberta, cast this as an attack on workers. In fact, there is evidence that a sudden influx of mostly male workers into an area can have an impact on the surrounding community, even negative consequences. But, put on the defensive, Trudeau's office subsequently backed away from that discussion.

Nonetheless, Trudeau cannot be said to have changed the modern approach to political discourse. To that end, a separate list could be drawn up of all the things that haven't changed, or at least not changed enough. The government's justice reforms have fallen short of a clear break from the Harper approach. For all the talk of openness and transparency, the access-to-information system still produces more redaction than disclosure, and the Liberals retreated from a promise to extend the system to ministers' offices. Though a new rule was created to deal with omnibus legislation, large budget bills are still being tabled in the House to advance the government's agenda. Veterans groups have complained that the government's actions on pensions and benefits did not match the Liberal campaign commitments. A promise to end the ban on blood donation for gay and bisexual men has not been fulfilled. And, of course, the federal electoral system remains resolutely unreformed.

If not for that failure of electoral reform, Trudeau would at least have more latitude to boast about initiating one of the more interesting changes in the history of the Canadian Parliament: the move toward an independent and non-partisan Senate.

"I DON'T THINK THE Senate should ever judge its success on the degree of affection Canadians have for the institution, but I don't sense the hostility," says Peter Harder, sitting in the corner office of Centre Block that now belongs to the government's "representative" in the upper chamber.

Not being passionately despised by the general public is perhaps as good as the Senate—an unelected anachronism that primarily still exists because it is too much trouble to get rid of—can ever really hope for. And, by that measure, the last few years have probably been an improvement; it has at least been harder to regard the Senate as a complete embarrassment.

Harder was an assistant to Progressive Conservative leader Joe Clark during the final years of Pierre Trudeau's government and then chief of staff to Erik Nielsen, the deputy prime minister, after Brian Mulroney came to power. From there, he moved into the public service, where, over the next two decades, he served as the first executive director of the Immigration and Refugee Board and then deputy minister at five departments.

He was working as a consultant in the private sector in April 2015 when Trudeau's office called to ask if he might meet with the Liberal leader to discuss matters related to foreign policy and the public service. They had a good chat and, a few weeks later, Trudeau's office called back. This time, Harder was asked if he was interested in a senior role on the Liberal transition team. On the morning after the Liberal victory in October, Harder and Trudeau met to begin what Harder describes as the "most fascinating two weeks of public service."

During his own preparations, Harder had given some thought to the implications of Trudeau's promise of Senate reform. But it was not a major topic during the two-week rush to put a government together. "I think that their political experience of the divorce of the caucus left them less than enthusiastic about putting their mind to the Senate," Harder says, "and there was so much priority on just getting the place organized and that could wait. And it did, for some time."

It was with dramatic suddenness, one morning in January 2014, that Trudeau announced he had expelled all senators from the Liberal parliamentary caucus. It was a particular surprise for those thirty-two senators, some of whom had spent years working in and around the Liberal Party. And not everyone appreciated what Trudeau was trying to do. There were also guffaws from Conservatives and New Democrats when the Liberals in the Senate turned around and branded themselves as "Senate Liberals."

In the short term, the move put some distance between Trudeau and the unfolding expense scandal that was dragging the unelected upper chamber to new depths of disrepute. But the excommunication was also part of a larger proposal for Senate reform. As prime minister, Trudeau explained, he would rely on an independent and "non-partisan" appointment process that would recommend nominees for the Senate. Once appointed, those senators would sit as independents.

"The Senate, through extreme patronage and partisanship, has become an institution that poorly serves the interests of Canadians," Trudeau said.

The result of his reform would, in theory, be an appointed chamber that was less dominated by such things and thus, hopefully, more useful.

Three months after Trudeau's move, the Supreme Court came back with answers to a series of questions the Harper government had belatedly asked about Parliament's power to unilaterally reform the Senate. In the court's opinion, moving to an elected upper chamber, as the Conservatives favoured, would require the agreement of at least seven provinces representing more than 50 percent of the population. Abolishing the chamber outright, as the NDP preferred, would require the unanimous agreement of all ten provinces.

With that, Trudeau was suddenly the only federal leader with a plan for reforming the Senate that did not require amending the constitution. For that matter, he seemed to have a plan that was in keeping with the Senate's stated purpose. Much of the court's decision in the Senate reference rested on the notion of "sober second thought"—a defining phrase uttered by John A. Macdonald in 1865. "As this Court wrote in the Upper House Reference," the justices recalled, "'[i]n creating the

Senate in the manner provided in the Act, it is clear that the intention was to make the Senate a thoroughly independent body which could canvass dispassionately the measures of the House of Commons.'"

Partisans have many admirable qualities, but dispassionate they are not.

Trudeau's office came calling on Harder again in March 2016. This time, the prime minister wanted to talk to Harder about an appointment to the Senate, as the government's chief emissary to the upper chamber. (Harder's name had been submitted for consideration by the Institute for Research on Public Policy.) "I think any more-than-casual observer of politics at the time knew that I was buying low," Harder says of joining the Senate at that moment, though, he adds, "I've known enough senators to have huge respect for the institution and the individuals and what it can do."

Typically, the government of the day would appoint a "leader" in the Senate. But now there would be no government caucus in the Senate to lead, so Harder was styled the government's "representative." He was also not appointed to cabinet, though he was sworn in as a member of the Privy Council—giving him the clearance to review cabinet documents—and he does attend cabinet committee meetings. Harder eventually named two deputies: Grant Mitchell (nominated to the Senate by Paul Martin in 2005) and Diane Bellemare (nominated by Stephen Harper in 2012). Most of the rest of those nominated by Trudeau eventually gravitated to a loose collective that styled itself the "independent senators group."

Joining Harder in the first cohort of nominees were a revered jurist and Indigenous leader (Murray Sinclair), a highly regarded journalist (André Pratte), a former NDP cabinet minister in Ontario (Frances Lankin), a former university president (Raymonde Gagné), an expert in diversity and immigration policy (Ratna Omidvar) and a decorated paralympian (Chantal Petitclerc). With the exception of Harder, all would sit as independents. With the exception of Lankin, none had a long history in partisan politics. Most important, there was nary a party bagman or organizer among them.

"Without in any way casting aspersions on anybody who got to the Senate in the other way, I don't think you would have attracted to the

Senate a number of the people that are in the Senate today by the old method," Harder says.

In the waning days of his Conservative government, Harper had stopped filling vacancies in the upper chamber. Given all the problems his previous nominees had caused, this made a certain amount of political sense. But it also left Trudeau with a sizeable opening to implement his reform. By the time Trudeau started making nominations, he had twenty-six vacancies to work with.

With further retirements, Trudeau was able to nominate forty-nine senators for the red chamber in his first three years. Those appointees were joined by a handful of partisan senators who decided they would rather sit as independents too. The result was a complete reversal of the Senate standings. Trudeau inherited a Senate that had forty-seven Conservatives, twenty-nine Liberals and six independents. As of April 2019, the Senate had sixty-five independents, thirty-one Conservatives and nine Liberals.

The remaining Conservatives regularly carped that the independents were not independent enough: that those appointed by Trudeau hadn't opposed the government's legislation as loudly or as often as they should. Many of those appointed might have been Liberal voters in their pre-Senate lives, and a discussion might be had about whether they represented a sufficient diversity of perspectives. But what is indisputable is that the Senate has shown a friskiness that was not evident between 2011 and 2015, when the Conservatives had a majority in both chambers.

In those four years, the Senate sent just a single government bill back to the House with an amendment attached. Between the fall of 2015 and the spring of 2019, the Senate amended seventeen government bills that originated in the House, on par with some of the most active periods in the chamber's recent history. The landmark bills that legalized both medical assistance in dying and the recreational use of marijuana were passed with Senate amendments. In 2016, opposition in the Senate, led by Pratte, helped convince the government to amend its own budget bill to remove changes to the Bank Act. In 2017, the Senate very nearly forced the splitting of another budget bill: an amendment, sponsored by Pratte, to remove a section related to the infrastructure bank was defeated on a tie vote, forty-nine to forty-nine.

There is some acknowledgement that the Trudeau government was slow to appreciate the ramifications of what it had created. "Particularly," Harder says, "ministers who had been around longer and had seen it in a different model." A more independent Senate has added a degree of difficulty to getting legislation passed, and perhaps some delay. But at least one member of cabinet is said to be quite at peace with the new situation. "I must say, the most serene person about this change of a more independent Senate, that amends legislation, is the prime minister," Harder says.

In several ways, Trudeau's promise of Senate reform was the precise opposite of his commitment to electoral reform: clear and decisive. And only after implementing it did Trudeau step back to let the democratic system run its course.

Trudeau's changes are not irreversible though. Barring a rush of early retirements, independents will retain a majority in the Senate for several more years, but Andrew Scheer has said a Conservative government would return to partisan appointments. That, at the very least, would test whether Trudeau's appointees act any differently when reviewing the legislation of a Conservative government. "What I've said to my Conservative friends in the Senate is, if that happens, I'm not going to change what I say, but I can guarantee you're going to change what you've been saying," Harder says.

If Trudeau's Liberals win in 2019, the independents could gain an overwhelming and enduring advantage. Between August 2019 and the spring of 2023, another fifteen Conservative or Liberal senators are due to retire. By the time of the 2023 election, seventy-nine or more of the Senate's 105 seats could be filled by independents.

Beside Conservative complaints that Trudeau's reforms don't amount to anything, there has been fretting that the changes will amount to too much: that a Senate of free-spirited independents will be too willing to stand in the way of the House, leading to legislative gridlock or some kind of constitutional crisis. But such showdowns have so far failed to materialize. If the new Senate has been more assertive over the last four years, it also hasn't been obstinate. On only one occasion did the Senate send a bill back to the House more than once. In that case— on transport legislation—senators stood down after a second round of bicameral Ping-Pong.

In lieu of the partisan power structures that helped restrain the Senate in previous eras, Harder has tried to assert a set of foundational principles: That the Senate is a complementary body, not a rival to the elected chamber. That it should offer advice, but almost always defer to the House. That it should adhere to the Salisbury doctrine, a British convention that says the appointed House of Lords will not reject legislation that implements a commitment made in the governing party's election platform.

Such ideas go some way toward getting at the eternal riddle of an appointed upper chamber. For a certain brand of democrat, the only thing worse than a Senate that does nothing is a Senate that does things. At some point, the Senate no doubt risks overstepping its mandate and incurring the public's wrath. But in making the case for "complementarity," Harder has suggested a very contemporary reason for maintaining a credible Senate. "It is crucial, in this time of change in the Senate, to recognize the subtlety of the role that the Founders of Confederation envisioned for the Senate," he wrote in a fifty-one-page discussion paper on the topic in April 2018. "They sought an upper house with enough power to act as a legally effective safety valve against the tyranny of the majority . . . a complementary 'check' on the excesses of a winner-take-all majority rule. In doing so, Senators appropriately assign particular importance to the impact of legislation on their region, minorities and fundamental rights and freedoms. This role remains highly relevant today given the significant power that majority governments wield in Canada and the wave of populism that has hit some corners of the world."

Which is to suggest the Senate, an unelected curiosity and so often a den of disrepute, might one day stand as the safeguard of liberal democracy in Canada. That anyone would dare put forward such an idea, just a few years removed from the criminal trial of Mike Duffy, is likely a measure of some progress.

—————

THAT JUSTIN TRUDEAU IS a feminist is by now rather well known. "I'm going to keep saying loud and clearly that I am a feminist until it is met with a shrug," he once said.

Patty Hajdu, Trudeau's first minister for the status of women, contends that Trudeau's calling himself by the f-word is a good thing. The term, she says, had become a "dirty word," associated with radical activists. "It was actively portrayed as a dirty word because it demeaned the movement," she says. In calling himself a feminist, Trudeau is "essentially reclaiming it," she argues. "He's saying, 'No, there's absolutely nothing wrong with fighting for women's equal rights. Women in this country deserve a fair chance. When we actually include women, we will be more prosperous. There are amazing women and I'm going to make sure I find them and support them, whether it's through policy, whether it's through the direct powers that I have in terms of cabinet.'"

In *Common Ground*, Trudeau recalls arguing with female members of the McGill debating team over whether a man could use the term. "I remember going toe to toe over beers with a few of them on the issue of whether a man could be a feminist. Some argued that by definition alone, feminism demanded a female perspective, while I suggested that the exclusion of men was antithetical to the egalitarian principle at the core of feminist thought."

This was a singular moment to be a young person in Montreal. In December 1989, fourteen young women had been murdered at École Polytechnique. "Women's issues had come to the fore for me with the horrific massacre at the University of Montreal's École Polytechnique a few years before, which happened a stone's throw from my high school," Trudeau wrote in *Common Ground*.

Trudeau credits Mary-Margaret Jones, a member of the debate team at McGill and a co-founder of the sexual assault centre of the students society, with encouraging him to get involved as a facilitator—an experience he has invoked on several occasions since becoming prime minister. Jones remembers Trudeau as shy. But she says he walked into the centre of his own volition. "He was different than a lot of guys. Of course, everyone knew who he was. But he was this tall, fit, good-looking guy who was also really emotionally available," Jones says. "And that was a lot different than a lot of other guys, who were sort of still uncomfortable with talking about consent and sexual assault and rape culture and a lot of things that needed to be discussed and handling the questions. He wasn't a great debater, but he was good on his feet in that regard."

He was a committed volunteer and "definitely showing what it meant to be an ally to women, to feminism." In the next breath, though, Jones adds a caveat: "I am really hesitant to call any man a feminist, and it's partly to protect any guy because you set yourself up for failure." In fact, Jones thinks the prime minister calling himself a feminist was "the stupidest thing he could have done."

Feminism is an ideal. And no man is perfect. Least of all a man who is in charge of a government.

Trudeau could point to ways his government has lived up to his own billing.

As noted, women are better represented in cabinet and the public service—the proportion of women in the Senate has also risen from 37 percent to 47 percent. Pay equity legislation was passed for federally regulated workers, and new legislation was introduced to deal with sexual harassment in Parliament and other federal workplaces. Publicly traded companies are now required to report on the number of women on their boards. Status of Women Canada, created as a federal agency in 1976, was made a full department of the federal government and renamed the Department for Women and Gender Equality. That gender-focused budget in 2018 included $1.7 billion in financing for women entrepreneurs and a new parental leave option designed to encourage men to be more involved in taking care of children. A hundred million dollars over five years has been set aside to support a national strategy to address gender-based violence.

All this seemed to speak to the spirit of the times, of #MeToo and the Women's March. But this is also one area in which most Canadians can agree the prime minister has done well. In December 2018, 72 percent of respondents to an Abacus Data survey said Trudeau has done a "good" or "acceptable" job on "gender" issues.

In fairness, Trudeau might have owed the women of Canada that much: it was the generally overwhelming support of women that allowed the Liberals to maintain a polling advantage throughout the first three years of the Trudeau government. Among men, according to weekly tracking by Nanos Research, the Liberals and Conservatives actually traded the lead throughout 2017, 2018 and 2019. But among women it was rarely even close. Through the government's first three and a half years, the Liberal lead with women was generally more than 10 percentage points, and sometimes more than 20 points. Even at the government's lowest moments, it never completely lost its lead among women.

That Canadian women, their concerns and their support would be so integral to a federal government was perhaps its own kind of progress. Indeed, even when challenged on his feminist bona fides in the spring of 2019, Trudeau found a silver lining. "I am proud that there is now a contest among party leaders to see who can be the better feminist," he said during a heated Question Period. "I think that is a great thing for this country."

But a prime minister who describes himself as a feminist invites people to measure him against that ideal. And, in that respect, there were regular and significant challenges.

Would a feminist sell light armoured vehicles to Saudi Arabia? Would a feminist not move faster to protect sex workers by repealing Conservative changes to Canada's prostitution laws? Wouldn't a feminist put more funding toward Canada's relatively modest foreign aid budget? Had the feminist prime minister set up one of his young, female ministers—Maryam Monsef—for failure when he gave the impossible task of electoral reform to an inexperienced politician? (Jones is among those who would ask some of these questions.)

Then, in that spring of 2019, a profound symbolic challenge: Would a truly feminist prime minister run afoul of two strong women like Jody

Wilson-Raybould and Jane Philpott? And would he then kick them out of his caucus?

These are the sorts of questions that can get a government accused of being more style than substance.

Still, the hardest question for the feminist prime minister to answer was about what happened in Creston, British Columbia, in August 2000. A copy of an unsigned editorial in the *Creston Valley Advance* from that time began to circulate in the spring of 2018. Without quite detailing what had happened, the editorial accused Trudeau, then twenty-eight, of "inappropriately handling" and "groping" a female reporter for the paper. Trudeau had apparently apologized with the awkward explanation that "if I had known you were reporting for a national paper I would never have been so forward."

When the prime minister was asked about it, on Canada Day, he responded that he did not remember any "negative interactions" during that day in Creston. This was a politician's answer, the sort of antiseptic statement a lawyer would draft. But, amidst the #MeToo reckoning, Trudeau himself had said that women deserved to be believed. His own minister for sport and disabilities, Kent Hehr, had been removed from cabinet because of allegations from his past. This was not a simple situation—the woman herself did not want to say anything more—but not remembering any "negative interactions" was not going to suffice as a response.

A few days later, he had another opportunity to explain himself. He repeated that he did not recall doing anything inappropriate. "But part of the lesson that we all have to learn through this," he said, "is respecting that the same interactions can be felt very differently by different people going through them."

This was not a perfect answer either. But, without further revelations, the moment passed.

There was also the trouble that came when Trudeau's Liberals attempted to impose their standard on others.

It had emerged in 2017 that a Liberal MP, Iqra Khalid, had signed off the year before on a Canada Summer Jobs grant for the Canadian

Centre for Bio-Ethical Reform, which, despite its vague name, is an anti-abortion activist organization. The grant was reported as a contradiction of Trudeau's categorically pro-choice stance. But the Abortion Rights Coalition of Canada also pointed to a more wide-spread and long-standing issue of summer jobs grants going to anti-choice organizations.

Funding from the Canada Summer Jobs program is ultimately directed by MPs, but Employment and Social Development Canada exercises some oversight over which applications are deemed eligible. So Hajdu, as labour minister, added a new requirement to the application form: groups seeking funds would have to sign an attestation stating that "both the job and the organization's core mandate respect individual human rights in Canada," including "reproductive rights," which were defined as "the right to access safe and legal abortions."

This had the potential to be good politics for the Liberals—showcasing their pro-choice position and maybe baiting the Conservatives into a fight. But it was an awkward policy. And that awkwardness caused it to backfire.

Hajdu argued that the new language did not prevent churches and other faith-based groups from receiving funding. Various churches and faith-based groups felt otherwise. The phrase "core mandate" seemed to be the root of the problem. A church's core mandate, Hajdu suggested, might be "administering the word of God, or administering spiritual guidance for people." But in doing such administering, of course, any number of churches would no doubt counsel that abortion is wrong and sinful. And therein lay makings of a great tempest.

The government followed up to say that "core mandate" should be understood as the "primary activities undertaken by the organization." "It is not the beliefs of the organization, and it is not the values of the organization," the department explained in a supplementary document issued in response to complaints.

If the government wanted to focus on the "activities" involved, it might have just said so. With "core mandate" still invoked, religious organizations remained aggrieved. "There is still a requirement to check an attestation box that endorses values . . . that would run counter to the conscience and beliefs of countless religious organizations and many other Canadians," said a spokesman for the Archdiocese of Toronto.

The controversy recalled Trudeau's edict in 2014 that, under his leadership, all Liberal MPs would be expected to take a pro-choice position in the House of Commons when voting on matters related to abortion. That produced a good deal of consternation over such vague notions as the individual conscience and freedom of elected representatives. But ultimately the only people impacted were current and prospective Liberal MPs. That a leader might whip a vote is a concept as old as parliamentary democracy, and anyone who couldn't accept Trudeau's line was free to join a different party.

To some degree, the same logic might have applied to summer jobs grants. Surely no one is entitled to such funding. And governments are broadly empowered to decide how public funds are dispersed—the Harper government, for instance, had previously decided that aid for maternal and newborn health assistance overseas would not go toward abortion services.

But in this case the complaints about conscience and religious freedom were coming from churches, many of which were likely only looking to hire students for a few months of perfectly innocuous, or even admirable, work. "This change in policy directly impacts 27 charitable organizations," the Archdiocese of Toronto reported of its own operations. "These groups applied for more than $1.1 million in funding to hire 150 summer students at camps and other charities, serving children with special needs, at-risk youth and refugee families."

In 2017, just 126 applications for funding were rejected. In 2018, there were more than 1,500 rejections, with likely many of those resulting from a refusal to sign the attestation.

When it came time to open applications for 2019, the government announced a change. In the new attestation, applicants had to only swear that funding "will not be used to undermine or restrict the exercise of rights legally protected in Canada." Within the eligibility criteria was a specific reference disqualifying anything that would "actively work to undermine or restrict a woman's access to sexual and reproductive health services."

"I think the criticism that the language was confusing, I think we'll take that. That, absolutely, I'll take that on the chin," Hajdu says. "I hope that we've managed to land in a place where we are essentially upholding Canada's laws around people's rights, but also making sure that people feel that there's no judgment around values."

Whether the Liberals were too righteous in insisting upon their own values would emerge as a theme, at least among those who felt they were being insulted.

When Conservative MP Lisa Raitt questioned the Liberal commitment to gender equality during a meeting of the House finance committee in March 2018, Bill Morneau responded that the government would "drag along the neanderthals" who did not agree with the promotion of women into leadership roles. The Conservatives demanded an apology.

A few months later, Immigration Minister Ahmed Hussen responded to the Doug Ford government's complaints about "illegal border crossers" by saying such rhetoric was not only "divisive" but "not Canadian." Lisa MacLeod, Hussen's counterpart in Ontario, demanded that he apologize.

Then, in August 2018, Trudeau engaged with a heckler at an event in Sabrevois, Quebec. After she shouted something about "your illegal immigrants," Trudeau said her "intolerance" had no place in Canada. Then she asked him if he was tolerant of "*Québécois de souche*," a loaded phrase that refers to "old-stock" Quebecers or those who can trace their ancestry to the original French settlers. Trudeau responded by saying her "racism" had no place in Canada.

Andrew Scheer leapt at video of the exchange. "By sweeping away legitimate questions on his failed border policy with vile personal insults, it is Trudeau himself who is guilty of polarizing the debate. No one has done more to divide Canadians than he has," he tweeted.

"This is how you can tell when Liberals are losing. Concerned about illegal border crossers? You're a racist. Worried about the cost? You're un-Canadian. Don't like the carbon tax? You're a denier. Canadians are sick and tired of this."

As it turned out, the woman was linked to the "ultranationalist" Storm Alliance, a far-right group in Quebec. Any argument that Trudeau had been mean to her seemed to fade away.

The prime minister could also show restraint. Just three weeks after the exchange in Sabrevois, a young man at a town hall in Saskatoon asked Trudeau how he could "justify spending millions of dollars on refugees whose ideologies don't at all align with ours while veterans are denied money they need to support their families, many of whom were seriously wounded fighting these same extremist ideologies you're welcoming?" Many in the crowd applauded.

"Okay," Trudeau said, "let's unpack that question for a bit."

Several days later, Trudeau described his thinking this way: "I was just like—okay, let's see if I can't answer this question in a way that doesn't divide this room, because I'm trying to demonstrate that there is room for these discussions in a way that isn't intolerant. And, quite frankly, I am also aware that, given the [Sabrevois] incident or exchange, people are ready to jump on me accusing anyone else of intolerance if they're just asking questions."

In Saskatoon, he reminded his audience that those seeking refuge in Canada were likely fleeing the extremism and violence in other places, that the story of Canada is one of people coming here from elsewhere and that every single non-Indigenous person in that room had ancestors who came in hopes of building a better life. Behind him a woman in a hijab nodded and smiled.

Five months later, at a town hall in Regina, a man said he was worried that Canada's "open border" was allowing "this stuff to come in freely" and "these two cultures will not mix." Trudeau asked him which two cultures and the man said "Islam and Christianity."

People in the crowd booed, but Trudeau admonished them. "No, no, no, hang on, sorry. Democracy only works in a country like Canada if people are free to express their fears, their concerns, their opinions. And we get an opportunity to respond to them. So I'm going to ask you all to be respectful of the speaker's question. And thank you for sharing your concerns, sir."

The man spoke again to say that "they" had "openly stated that they want to kill us."

After hesitating for a second—"Hmm, how am I going to go at this one," he said, with a slight smile—Trudeau launched into similar remarks about Canada as a country built by immigration.

In such moments, Trudeau was less an agent of change than a manager of it.

———

NOT LONG AFTER THE new cabinet was appointed in 2015, Justin Trudeau's ministers were introduced to a bookish fellow named Sir Michael Barber, a former advisor to Tony Blair's Labour government in the United Kingdom.

From 2001 to 2005, Barber was the leader of Blair's "delivery unit," a special team created to ensure that the government implemented its priorities and achieved its desired outcomes. The result of Barber's work was a system of setting goals, tracking progress and measuring performance that came to be known as "deliverology." It had worked well enough with Blair's government that Barber was brought in to advise Dalton McGuinty's Liberal government in Ontario. Gerry Butts and Katie Telford, two senior officials in McGuinty's administration, then called on Barber when they ended up at the top of Justin Trudeau's office.

The Trudeau government needed to think about delivery because it had come to office with so many things to deliver. A team of researchers at Laval University counted 353 promises in the Liberal Party's 2015 platform. Later, when the Trudeau government made its own tally of the assignments that were included in the mandate letters sent to each minister, it counted 364 commitments.

That is a significant number of things to do in the space of four years. In fact, it is, by a wide margin, a larger number of promises than any recent government has found itself committed to. The platform for Stephen Harper's Conservative Party in 2006, according to the same researchers at Laval, contained 192 promises. Jean Chrétien's Liberals came to office in 1993 with 164 promises. Trudeau's Liberals had somehow managed to make as many commitments as those two governments combined.

The promise of deliverology was that it would not only assist in getting all those things done, but that it would also broaden the conversation about what a government can do. Focusing on results and outcomes could clarify how government policies actually impact individuals and society. "How we actually figure out whether what we're doing is having a positive impact on the lives of Canadians isn't something that governments have spent a tremendous amount of time worrying about in the past," Trudeau explained at one point. "A lot of energy is placed on announcements—oh, we're investing $20 million in this project. And the follow-up a year later or two years later—to say, well, X number of people have had their lives affected positively by that investment—isn't always part of the operations or philosophies of government."

As part of the process, Matthew Mendelsohn, a former deputy minister in Ontario, was recruited to serve in a Barber-like role as the deputy secretary to cabinet with responsibility for results and delivery. Results and delivery officers were then appointed in each department. The prime minister has convened a regular series of rotating "stocktakes," meetings in which ministers, deputy ministers, government officials and outside experts sit down to discuss progress in a particular area of concern. Those meetings were at first broadly focused on four major priorities: the middle class, reconciliation, diversity and international engagement. In time, international engagement was dealt with separately, leaving more focus on the first three. Meanwhile, in hopes of better measuring trends in society and the impact of policy, tens of millions of dollars has been committed to collecting more data: on health care, housing, clean technology, infrastructure, child care, tourism and other matters.

The actual success of deliverology is hard to measure. It does not yet seem to have revolutionized the work of government or the way that work is publicly discussed. It is broadly credited with nurturing a greater focus on implementation and results within the government. The regular stock-takes, in particular, are said to be useful for bringing the attention of the prime minister to bear on an issue. That the prime minister will be asking about something helps to ensure that thing gets done, and the prime minister's involvement helps to sort through issues that cut across different departments.

The first attempt to bring deliverology into the public discussion was a "mandate tracker" released in November 2017. At canada.ca/results, the public was presented with a tally of the 364 items listed across the mandate letters issued to each minister. Those items were grouped into a dozen broad policy areas and then categorized according to the government's success in fulfilling the commitment: "completed fully," "completed with modifications," "underway and on track," "underway with challenges," or "not being pursued." In the initial tally, 67 commitments were marked as completed and another 231 were underway.

The effort was roundly mocked, in some cases for justifiable reasons. The promise of electoral reform was listed as "not being pursued," which seemed a rather genteel way of describing what had actually occurred there. The commitment to return the budget to balance by 2019 was grouped under the heading of "underway with challenges," the "challenge" presumably being that the government was no longer particularly interested in making sure it happened. To some observers it was simply ridiculous that a government would attempt to write its own report card.

A second phase, focused on measuring the impact of the government's policies, was supposed to follow soon thereafter. But, though more information on results was added to the website over time, a full follow-up never materialized. Instead, there have been isolated efforts at publicly tracking change, most notably a well-publicized and regularly updated tally of how many long-term drinking water advisories have been eliminated for Indigenous communities and how many remain to be dealt with.

This was at least rather more involved and transparent than anything the Harper government had attempted. Indeed, Stephen Harper's first government had taken something like the opposite approach.

However many promises the Conservative Party made in 2006, Stephen Harper put the focus on "five priorities": passing new ethics legislation, cutting the GST, strengthening the justice system, introducing a new child benefit and establishing a wait-times guarantee for health services with the provinces. These were not small things, but most were relatively easy to accomplish. Except for that last one, which Harper soon forgot about anyway. Within a year, Harper had completed the first four.

The Trudeau Liberals could have framed a similar list of priorities: say, implementing their own child benefit, enhancing the Canada Pension Plan, increasing investments in infrastructure, introducing a national price on carbon emissions, and reforming the Senate. All those were more or less complete by the end of 2018.

But the Trudeau era would not be so easily framed. As of March 22, 2019, with new goals and initiatives added over time, the mandate tracker listed 432 commitments: 161 completed, 267 in progress and four not being pursued (including, belatedly, that promise about balancing the budget). This was, perhaps, a more accurate picture of all a government might hope do. But it was not a tidy or tweetable summary.

Those researchers at Laval offered a slightly simpler tally. Through April 2019, they had categorized 178 of 353 commitments—50.4 percent—as "promises kept." Another 140—39.7 percent—were rated as "promises kept in part or in the works." Nineteen promises were deemed to have been "broken," including electoral reform and the budget deficit, but also commitments related to veterans, gun-marking regulations and the purchase of new fighter jets.

Assessing those numbers is somewhat subjective—if you were particularly invested in electoral reform, you might not be swayed by the fact that the government has made good on 178 other commitments. But the Laval researchers have performed similar analyses going back to 1993, and those findings provide a few points of broad comparison.

In 2011, for instance, Stephen Harper Conservatives' made 143 promises. Of those, 77 percent were fully implemented and another 7 percent were partially completed. That, though, was a government that had already been in office for five years. Going back to 2006, 60 percent of the Conservative Party's promises at that time were fully kept, and 8 percent were partially implemented. But that was a minority government that was only in office for two and a half years.

The last example of a new majority government was Jean Chrétien's Liberals in 1993. That government fully kept just 37 percent of its promises, while another 16 percent were partially implemented. But that, of course, was a government that had to confront a debt crisis halfway through its first four years.

Cumulatively, between 1993 and 2015—a period that covered seven federal elections—the Laval researchers determined that 59 percent of promises were fully kept and 10 percent were partially fulfilled. By those standards, the current Liberals have at least held their own: perhaps less completely along, but more broadly successful.

But, of course, politics is not simple math. Except when it comes time to count the ballots.

CHAPTER 12

A Falling Out with the Minister Who Couldn't Fail

Jody Wilson-Raybould was the fifty-first minister of justice and attorney general of Canada. She was just the third woman to serve in those offices, and the first Indigenous person.

Two months after she was sworn in as a member of Justin Trudeau's first cabinet, Wilson-Raybould went to Simon Fraser University (SFU) in British Columbia to deliver her first official speech as a minister of the crown. She used the opportunity to reflect on the significance of her new-found status. It was, she said, "an appointment that I see speaks volumes for how far our country has come and also the important work that lies ahead."

Wilson-Raybould had been a star candidate for the Liberals in 2015 after being personally recruited by Trudeau. A member of the We Wai Kai Nation, she was a former Crown prosecutor in British Columbia, an advisor to that province's treaty commission and a regional chief of the Assembly of First Nations from 2009 to 2015. Her father, Bill Wilson, had been a prominent First Nations leader himself. In fact, he had sparred with Pierre Trudeau during a constitutional conference in 1983 (video of Wilson telling Trudeau that two of his daughters wanted to be prime minister one day would circulate widely after Wilson-Raybould's appointment).

She was given a standing ovation when she arrived onstage at SFU. She recalled then that there had been an audible gasp and then applause from the audience inside Rideau Hall when her title was announced. This, she said, was not so much reflective of her, but of "the symbolism that I believe my appointment represents.

"That in a nation where someone who not so long ago would not have been able to vote, let alone run for office, nor be recognized legally as an Indian and a lawyer, someone against whom the law discriminated and in some cases still does, and who fought against the law for many years, is now the principal lawyer in charge of administering that very law on behalf of that very nation and advising its government."

There was a "woo!" from someone in the crowd and the audience at SFU broke into applause. Wilson-Raybould beamed.

"It takes a moment to sink in," she said.

As she continued, Wilson-Raybould sketched out a history of Indigenous governance and rights and a frame for moving forward. "Our collective challenge now, for both Indigenous peoples and the Crown—me—is to get back to the spirit and intent of the Two Row Wampum, while recognizing that the nature of the relationship within the modern state of Canada has changed," she said, referring to a treaty relationship that cast Indigenous peoples and European settlers as travellers moving along parallel rivers. "The laws of the nations and tribes of Indians and the Crown are not simply in their own canoe or boat, side by side. But today they co-exist together within the modern and advanced nation state of Canada, under a dynamic system that supports pluralism through multi-level governance." The goal now, she said, was to restore balance to the relationship.

Almost exactly three years later, Wilson-Raybould was back at Rideau Hall, this time to be sworn in as the minister of veterans affairs. David Lametti, a former law professor from Montreal, was now to be the justice minister. Wilson-Raybould barely smiled as she posed for the cameras with Trudeau and Governor General Julie Payette.

Speaking to reporters immediately afterward, she dismissed the suggestion that she had been demoted. "I can think of no world in which I would consider working for our veterans in Canada as a demotion," she said. But several hours later she nonetheless released a thousand-word statement detailing the highlights of her time as justice minister.

Within that retrospective, she also suggested a certain frustration with the government's approach to Indigenous issues. "While our government has taken some very important steps, and hard work is being done, the necessary shifts have not yet been fully achieved," she wrote. "Rather, a number of the proposals that our government has been pursuing so far require substantial work in co-operation and collaboration with Indigenous peoples to reset the new foundations for this most important relationship."

As reporters quickly came to realize, Wilson-Raybould had been leaving hints of dissatisfaction in speeches through the fall of 2018.

"While I have been thrilled in recent years to see how Canadians—and governments—have begun to talk the talk of reconciliation, I remain constantly, incessantly, vigilant in demanding that we honour the meaning of these important words, and that words translate into real, transformative action," she said in Saskatoon in September.

Two weeks later, she was in Comox, British Columbia, for another speech. "Part of what I want to reflect on tonight is how after three years as a Minister of the Crown I still have to contend—both personally and professionally—with a colonial legacy that remains pervasive despite best intentions and which is exacerbated by the trials and tribulations of partisan politics," she said.

After the shuffle, sources from within the government also began to talk. If Wilson-Raybould was feeling dissatisfied, she apparently wasn't alone. Wilson-Raybould, it was said, had been difficult to work with. "Some who spoke on background said she could be dismissive and quick to leap to confrontation when a more constructive approach to policy differences might have been employed," the CBC reported. The *Toronto Star*'s Chantal Hébert suggested that within the Trudeau government it was believed Wilson-Raybould had been a disappointment as justice minister. Much later, in a conversation for this book, Trudeau would acknowledge his own desire for a better relationship with his justice minister.

The *Star* later published an op-ed from two criminal defence lawyers that described "Wilson-Raybould's regrettable legacy as justice minister." She failed, they wrote, to reverse the Harper government's mandatory minimums, to fix the pardon system, to expand the use of restorative justice, and to eliminate the victim surcharge, and instead introduced problematic reforms of her own, such as the elimination of jury challenges and preliminary inquiries for some offences.

That same day, however, the *Globe and Mail* published a commentary written by six prominent Indigenous lawyers. "Looking back over the past three years, one can find little reason why Ms. Wilson-Raybould would be part of a 12th-hour shuffle ahead of the election," they wrote. "So why move her?"

The writers took issue with the post-shuffle criticism of Wilson-Raybould. "Her demotion from the vital portfolio has been accompanied by insider whispers, based on poisonous stereotypes that Indigenous peoples, and women in particular, face every day: that she was angry, difficult and uncompromising."

In such whispers, they wrote, "one finds reflections of many ugly notions that we're still confronting today: that Indigenous peoples are not as capable, or not as responsible for the achievements and success that they have. That somehow the marginalization of Indigenous peoples, and in particular women, can be justified. And that Indigenous peoples somehow are not ready to lead and govern in today's world." For that matter, they added, they had worked with Wilson-Raybould when she was an Indigenous leader in British Columbia and found her to be "determined, collaborative and hard-working."

"The cabinet shuffle doesn't say much about Ms. Wilson-Raybould—it speaks to the state of the government, its priorities, and how it functions," the six lawyers concluded. "Mr. Trudeau's professed most important relationship remains one grounded in oppression, colonialism and paternalism—and the events of the past few days demonstrate that."

Several days later, the Indigenous Bar Association added its concerns. "With the federal election looming, relieving a strong Indigenous advocate from her duties as the Justice Minister is a monumental symbol of the Liberal government's lack of commitment to the meaningful recognition of Indigenous rights and interests," the association concluded.

Complicating this narrative was the fact, leaked to some media outlets, that Wilson-Raybould had been given the opportunity to move to Indigenous Services, but had declined the offer. That much would later be aired publicly, during the justice committee's hearings into the SNC-Lavalin affair.

"Indigenous people have been sent precisely the opposite message from the one the Prime Minister intended," Gerry Butts, Trudeau's former principal secretary, told the justice committee in March, explaining the prime minister's thought process at the time of the shuffle. "He was preoccupied with the fact that we had the child and family services legislation coming up. He thought it would be one of the most important bills the government would pass. He wanted a person in Indigenous Services who would send a strong signal that the work would keep going at the same pace and that the file would have the same personal prominence for him."

But that offer would also become a point of dispute.

In response to Butts's testimony, Wilson-Raybould explained that she was "shocked" Trudeau and Butts had ever suggested such a move. "Since prior to being appointed to Cabinet I made it clear to the transition team and others that I could not and would not in good conscience ever be able to take on the Ministerial role of delivering services to 'Indians' and Indian Act bands under the Indian Act," she explained in a written submission to the justice committee. "In the language of many First Nations people, this role is understood as that of the 'Indian Agent' (for those who may be wondering, that term typically is used in a derogatory fashion). While the work is very important, and certainly I respect other Indigenous people who may wish to assume such a role, I would not and could not ever assume it myself."

In his own testimony, Butts acknowledged that he "should have known that, and that, had we had more time to think of the cabinet shuffle, I probably would have realized it."

Following through on a recommendation from the Royal Commission on Aboriginal Peoples in 1996, the former Department of Indigenous Affairs was split to create two departments in 2017: one focused on Crown-Indigenous relations, the other dedicated to delivering and supporting services in Indigenous communities. In a conversation for this book in April 2019, Trudeau says he thought the dissolution had addressed Wilson-Raybould's original concern.

"I totally understood that," he says of her objections in 2015. "But there was not a minister of Indigenous services at transition. It was minister of Indigenous affairs. Which was the government representative, 'the Indian Agent,' in dealing with Indigenous peoples. And what we did when we hived out those two things was Indigenous Services was all about delivering and empowering individuals and communities. So for my mind, the job she didn't feel comfortable with was Carolyn [Bennett]'s job. The Crown-Indigenous relationship. I was a little worried that she might see it as a bit of a demotion because it's not as prestigious a job as justice minister . . . But I genuinely thought that Indigenous Services would be okay for her."

Wilson-Raybould's rejection of Trudeau's offer of a move to Indigenous Services left the prime minister with a choice of how to respond. Butts later testified that he had never known anyone to refuse a cabinet appointment, and that he told the prime minister that it would be dangerous to set a precedent in this case. "If you allow a minister to veto a cabinet shuffle by refusing to move, you soon won't be able to manage cabinet," he explained. "My advice was that the Prime Minister should not set the precedent that a cabinet minister could refuse a new position and therefore remain in one position for the life of the government."

At least the initial narrative about the end of her time at Justice might have been different had she accepted that offer. But the hope that greeted Wilson-Raybould's original appointment and the frustration that came after her move seemed to underline the weight of the challenge Trudeau took on when he spoke about the "unfinished work of Confederation" and the need for a "a renewed, nation-to-nation relationship."

"I totally understand that when you have powerful, positive symbols it's also possible to have that snap back on you when you make other decisions," Trudeau says, in a conversation in late January 2019, before the SNC-Lavalin affair emerged and before Wilson-Raybould resigned from cabinet. "We didn't appoint Jody to be a symbol—we appointed her to be a great minister of justice and attorney general. And she was . . . I respect and understand symbolism as much as anyone else. But I'm also focused on making sure the team is doing all the right things in the right places. And Jody will continue to be, as everyone will be around the table, extremely involved in reconciliation."

Ask people who know him what Trudeau cares about most, what gets him out of bed in the morning, and reconciliation will inevitably come up. Testifying before the justice committee, Butts measured Trudeau's commitment in time. "The most valuable thing in any government is the first minister's time," Butts said. "The prime minister spends a lot of his time on Indigenous issues—a lot. He cares about the relationship deeply."

In Trudeau's telling, he was originally cautioned against focusing on Indigenous issues. "Around Christmas of 2006, I was trying to make the decision on whether or not to step up as an MP in the beginning. And I remember talking with Gerry and some others about what were the big issues that Canada still needed to [deal with]. And Indigenous was at the very top of my list. This is something where—because we just had [the] Kelowna [Accord], we just moved away from it—Canadians aren't actually living in the country we like to pretend we're living in. This needs to be addressed.

"And the expert advice from some of the éminences grises around me at that time was, absolutely right, it's a big thing. But there'll never be any political wins in their view. There's no votes for you on this one. And we proved that wrong in the 2015 election where non-Indigenous Canadians said, 'You know what? No. We have to do this big thing and do it right.'"

Reconciliation does seem to have come to the fore in the last four years, both as a public concern (the Toronto Public Library reported "increased, sustained interest" for Indigenous-related texts in 2018) and as a government priority (each of the Trudeau government's four budgets has included a section focused on Indigenous peoples). But the éminences grises might nonetheless argue that some of their concerns have been borne out by the last four years. It is not that the government hasn't had some success. But it has not been straightforward or simple, and various voices would express disappointment.

"A lot of those people who are criticizing are the people who don't feel we've done much or enough on reconciliation," Trudeau says, speaking in late January 2019 about the criticism of Wilson-Raybould's move. "But the facts of what we actually have done and the people who know how much we've done, recognize that we've been moving in the right direction harder, faster, stronger than anybody ever has."

By the government's own count, it has made twenty-nine commitments related to Indigenous peoples. The public tally of those commitments, maintained by the Privy Council Office, indicates that eleven of those commitments are "facing challenges." Though that does leave eighteen areas in which progress has been somewhat smoother.

The annual budget for Indigenous services and programs is currently set to increase from $11.4 billion in 2015–16 to $17.1 billion in 2021–22, including new money for education and housing. Eighty-two Indigenous communities have signed new ten-year funding commitments. Between November 2015 and April 27, 2019, eighty-five long-term drinking water advisories for Indigenous communities were lifted.

Three new bilateral forums were established to provide for direct talks between the prime minister and each of the Assembly of First Nations, Inuit Tapiriit Kanatami and the Métis National Council. The former American embassy in Ottawa, directly across from Parliament Hill, has been set aside as a national space for Indigenous peoples. The name of Sir Hector-Louis Langevin, the Confederation-era cabinet minister who became associated with residential schools, was removed from the building that houses the Prime Minister's Office. And, in one of her last acts as justice minister, Wilson-Raybould issued a new directive to guide the government's handling of civil litigation involving Indigenous peoples.

But the challenges have been significant.

As promised, the government convened a national inquiry into missing and murdered Indigenous women and girls. But the investigation struggled with staff departures, complaints about its progress and a dispute over its time frame. The commission's final report, released in June 2019, initiated a difficult debate about whether Canada's treatment of Indigenous women and girls constituted a "genocide." It may yet also inform meaningful government actions and reforms.

In response to a ruling by the Canadian Human Rights Tribunal about the treatment of Indigenous children, the government committed $382.5 million in immediate funding to address Jordan's Principle, a standard that says every Indigenous child should receive equal treatment in public services without denial or delay, regardless of jurisdictional disputes between levels of government. But Cindy Blackstock, the Indigenous advocate who pushed for that ruling, and the federal government continued to wrestle over the full implementation of the tribunal's broader orders.

The Liberals put their support behind a bill, sponsored by NDP MP Romeo Saganash, that calls for the alignment of Canadian laws with the United Nations Declaration on the Rights of Indigenous Peoples. But when the government later suggested that it remained committed to building the Trans Mountain expansion, even while it embarked on another round of consultation with Indigenous communities, Saganash blasted Trudeau in the House. "Why doesn't the prime minister just say the truth and tell Indigenous peoples that he doesn't give a fuck about their rights?" Saganash asked, employing an expletive for maximum impact.

A few months later, RCMP officers dismantled a blockade and arrested fourteen people to enforce a court injunction allowing for the construction of a natural gas pipeline through Wet'suwet'en territory in northern British Columbia. The Indigenous writer and columnist Tanya Talaga wrote that reconciliation was now "officially over."

In the spring of 2018, Trudeau pledged to pursue a framework for the recognition and implementation of Indigenous rights, with legislation to follow that fall. It would have been—and could still be—a landmark achievement in the advancement of reconciliation. But concerns were soon raised about the process for drafting that legislation and how quickly the government wanted to move. By December, the government had agreed to step back and re-evaluate.

As the SNC-Lavalin affair would lay bare, the framework was also a significant source of conflict between Carolyn Bennett and Jody Wilson-Raybould. "[Trudeau] was concerned that we were losing momentum and traction heading into the last year of the mandate on the rights recognition framework," Michael Wernick, the clerk of the Privy Council, told the justice committee, explaining the circumstances of a meeting between himself, Trudeau and Wilson-Raybould in September 2018. "He was aware, because he'd been briefed, both by the Privy Council Office and his political staff, that there was something of a policy standoff among his ministers. There were different views on a very significant thing, and we were trying to find a way . . . Essentially, I'd call it a form of conciliation or mediation to bring people together."

According to sources, a week after that meeting with Trudeau and Wernick, Wilson-Raybould sent a long memo to the ministers on the cabinet committee on reconciliation in which she criticized Bennett's approach. Wilson-Raybould declined to comment on any such memo, citing cabinet confidentiality.

Though the rights framework was delayed, the government did move forward in the fall of 2018 with two other significant initiatives: legislation to allow for the transfer of child welfare services to Indigenous communities and a new Indigenous Languages Act. Both bills were co-developed with Indigenous groups. Meanwhile, the government says it is engaged in self-determination discussions with over five hundred Indigenous communities.

"I believe that the government has done a lot on the Indigenous file," says Wilson-Raybould in an interview for this book. "There has been a significant amount of money invested in Indigenous communities, there's been significant work to address the day-to-day issues that Indigenous peoples face. And that's really important and nobody should take that away from the government."

But, she says, there still needs to be the structural change to empower Indigenous communities.

"I wanted to be able to have two tracks. One track is, yes, of course, we need to invest per capita the same amount we invest in other Canadians, solve the day-to-day issues. But in order to change the reality we have to create the space or the mechanism for Indigenous peoples to be self-determining," she says. "That's the rights framework. That's being able to enable Indigenous communities, if they're First Nations, to move away from the Indian Act, at their own pace and at their own time. Because until that happens, and this is proven, Indigenous communities will not thrive."

She says she has imagined that Justin Trudeau could be for Indigenous rights what his father was for official bilingualism. It's a tempting comparison. Pierre Trudeau's government passed the Official Languages Act in 1969, just a year after Trudeau became prime minister. But that legislation was informed by the recommendation of a royal commission—the Royal Commission on Bilingualism and Biculturalism—that had been struck by Lester B. Pearson in 1963. It was also preceded by Pearson issuing an official statement on his government's language policy in 1966. So the lesson of that comparison might be that nothing moves particularly fast.

For Justin Trudeau, the work of pursuing a rights framework could be completed with a second term in office. But winning that second term could depend, in part, on making the case that his government has made a decent amount of progress so far. Ultimately, he looks into the future and believes this period will be regarded as a turning point.

"It's a massive transformation, both internal to government and in the way we behave as a federation and as a country," Trudeau says. "It's messy, it's not easy. But we are really and genuinely moving in the right direction, and I am confident that fifty years from now, one hundred years from now, when Canada finally gets to the place where we need to get with Indigenous peoples, in our relationship—because we're not getting it in my time, that's guaranteed, just because there's so much to do—we will look back and say, for all the things that in hindsight we see they could've done differently or better, that was when it started. This is where true reconciliation actually got started."

———

THE FIRST HINT FOR Trudeau's advisors that something might be coming was the sight of Robert Fife, the *Globe and Mail*'s bureau chief in Ottawa, approaching Jody Wilson-Raybould after a meeting of cabinet in early February 2019. That afternoon, Wilson-Raybould messaged Butts. "Bob Fife seems to be doing a story on SNC," she wrote. "I did not say anything—have convo recorded. He seemed to know a great deal. Not sure how this could be . . . anyway felt compelled to let you know."

Two days later, on February 7, 2019, Fife's story appeared in the *Globe*, under the headline, "PMO pressed Wilson-Raybould to abandon prosecution of SNC-Lavalin." Citing unspecified sources, the *Globe* reported that members of Trudeau's office "attempted to press Jody Wilson-Raybould when she was justice minister to intervene in the corruption and fraud prosecution of Montreal engineering and construction giant SNC-Lavalin Group Inc." According to the *Globe*, "she refused to ask federal prosecutors to make a deal with the company."

This would become one of the most remarkable dramas in the history of Canadian politics and the most damaging crisis to confront the Trudeau government. For nearly two months it would dominate the political conversation, as a prime minister and his office struggled to make their way through to the other side. The minister who was too big to fail would fall, and the tremors would shake the foundation of Trudeau's government.

The story had actually begun in February 2015, when fraud and corruption charges were laid against SNC-Lavalin. It was alleged that employees of the company had bribed government officials in Libya between 2001 and 2011, when the country was under the rule of

Muammar Gaddafi. Importantly, a conviction on those charges would result in a ten-year ban from bidding on government contracts. Such a sanction could have serious ramifications for a company that did large amounts of public work.

But, in 2018, there had also been a significant change to the legal regime around such prosecutions. The Trudeau government, following the lead of the United States and the United Kingdom, had introduced into the Criminal Code a legal mechanism known as a "deferred prosecution agreement," or DPA.

Under a deferred prosecution agreement, a company accused of economic offences could avoid the harshest consequences of a criminal conviction if it met a series of conditions, including accepting responsibility for the wrongdoing, relinquishing any benefits derived from the inappropriate act, demonstrating that it had taken steps to ensure future compliance with the law and making reparations to the victims of its wrongdoing. If such an agreement was offered and successfully negotiated, there would be no criminal conviction and, thus, no ban on bidding for government contracts. In theory, this would hold a company to account, while also protecting innocent employees and shareholders from being harmed as a consequence of a guilty verdict. (Prosecutors would also avoid the cost of a trial and the risk of a not-guilty verdict.)

SNC-Lavalin, among others, had lobbied the government to introduce such a provision, and it had then hoped to be able to negotiate such an agreement. But, in October 2018, the federal director of public prosecutions decided against offering such an agreement to SNC-Lavalin. The company responded with a public plea for mercy. "While we had hoped that this new law would permit us to put this long journey behind us, we remain open and committed to negotiating such an agreement in the interest of our 52,000 employees," SNC's chief executive, Neil Bruce, wrote in an open letter that appeared as an advertisement in four newspapers. Nine thousand of those employees worked in Canada, including 3,400 in Quebec and 3,000 in Ontario.

The Public Prosecution Service of Canada—an independent agency established in 2006 to handle investigations under a number of federal statutes—was empowered to decide when a deferred prosecution agreement can be used. But the attorney general of Canada also retained the power to issue a directive to the director of public prosecutions. In December 2018, for instance, Wilson-Raybould issued a directive setting out how the public prosecutor should deal with cases concerning the non-disclosure of HIV. Under the law, such directives must be publicly published.

So, in the case of SNC-Lavalin, Wilson-Raybould could have instructed the public prosecutor to pursue a deferred prosecution agreement. She did not. But now Trudeau's office was accused of pressuring her to do so.

That mattered because of the principle of prosecutorial independence and what is known as the "Shawcross doctrine," so named for Sir Hartley Shawcross, the U.K. attorney general from 1945 to 1951.

As minister of justice and attorney general, Wilson-Raybould had effectively occupied two related, but distinct, roles. Since Confederation, the federal justice minister has always filled both roles, and the difference between the offices is perhaps not generally appreciated. But the distinction is important.

The justice minister sits as a member of cabinet, takes part in its deliberations, abides by its decisions and answers to the prime minister. But the attorney general is expected and entitled to make independent decisions when it comes to her office's powers to direct federal prosecutions. As laid out in the broadly accepted Shawcross doctrine, the attorney general can consult with cabinet colleagues and take advice on such decisions, but he or she should not be pressured or directed to take a particular decision.

If the *Globe*'s version of events was correct, Trudeau's office had potentially violated that principle. What's more, the article cast Wilson-Raybould's move to Veterans Affairs in a different light: the *Globe*'s report suggested officials in Trudeau's office were furious with Wilson-Raybould, and that her replacement, David Lametti, might be more amenable to pursuing a remediation agreement.

As would become clear over the ensuing two months, there had been some kind of friction between Wilson-Raybould and Trudeau's office over the handling of SNC-Lavalin. But it would also later be revealed that this was not the first time someone had raised SNC-Lavalin in the context of Wilson-Raybould's departure from Justice. In early January, when the cabinet shuffle was being finalized, Trudeau met with Jane Philpott, a close friend of Wilson-Raybould's. In that meeting, Trudeau told Philpott that he wanted to move her to Treasury Board, and Wilson-Raybould would then take her place as minister of Indigenous services. According to Butts's testimony to the justice committee, Philpott told Trudeau that Wilson-Raybould might see that as a demotion and might think she was being moved because of the "DPA issue."

Trudeau says he was taken aback at the suggestion. "The choices of who's in cabinet, who does what in cabinet, are always multi-faceted, and there's always all sorts of different factors, positive and negative, in any decision that you make. Disagreement over one specific modest-sized issue in terms of the scale—and I [want to be] careful about saying that because I don't want to minimize the potential impact on thousands of workers, because we take all those situations seriously—but this point of divergent perspectives was a minor-ish one in the grand scheme," he says, in a conversation that took place in late March 2019. "There was a lot of different reasons. If I were to list a number of reasons why we felt this was the right thing to do and the right move to make, it would not have been in the top five or ten reasons for that."

Butts later testified that he told Trudeau "he had to factor into his thinking the possibility that the assertion she had made would be made publicly, however far-fetched it seemed." According to Butts, Trudeau said he knew SNC-Lavalin wasn't the reason for moving her and he would not change his mind.

At his first opportunity to respond to the *Globe* story—an infrastructure announcement in Vaughan, Ontario—Trudeau said the report was "false" and that "at no time" did he or his office "direct the current or previous attorney general to make any particular decision in this matter." Other Liberals would eventually add that Wilson-Raybould had not been "pressured" to make a decision. For her part, Wilson-Raybould said she was bound by solicitor-client privilege and could not comment.

"I began to hear through various connections that she was kind of worried about that statement that I had made, that she didn't agree with it," Trudeau says. "And that maybe I wasn't being fully forthright."

The prime minister was due to be in Vancouver for another infrastructure announcement, and plans were made for him to meet with Wilson-Raybould while he was there. Before that meeting, Trudeau spoke with Philpott, who told him that Wilson-Raybould had concerns about what had transpired.

The prime minister and the former attorney general then met privately at the Vancouver airport, just after noon on February 10. "She expressed concerns about how I was being served by the people around me and the team around me," Trudeau says. This was, the prime minister says, the first time she had told him that she believed she'd been inappropriately pressured. "My first question was, 'Why now? Why are you telling me this now and not months ago?'" he says. The prime minister told her that he needed to reflect on what she had told him.

According to multiple sources, the prime minister later recounted that the former attorney general raised concerns about her interactions with officials in his office, including conversations with Gerry Butts and Michael Wernick. Though it would later be reported that Wilson-Raybould had demanded that certain people be fired, the prime minister says no such demands were made in Vancouver. (Though it's possible that some may have inferred that that was what the former attorney general wanted.)

"There was no absolute ultimatum; there were no names associated with it directly in terms of expectations," Trudeau says. "But she wasn't feeling that I was well-served by the top folks around me."

Wilson-Raybould did suggest that she would resign as minister of veterans affairs if a directive was issued to the public prosecutor. "She mentioned that she was watching very closely to see the *Canada Gazette* and if there was a DPA admitted then she would step down," Trudeau says.

In a conversation for this book, before Wilson-Raybould was expelled from caucus, Trudeau declined to comment on the appropriateness of that comment. But according to two sources, Trudeau said privately after the meeting that, if the issue in this dispute was undue pressure, he found Wilson-Raybould's suggestion that she would resign to be problematic.

In her own appearance before the justice committee in February, Wilson-Raybould said that she would have resigned as veterans affairs minister if a directive had been issued, but she did not say whether or not she had said as much to Trudeau.

Trudeau and Wilson-Raybould met for a second time the next morning, February 11, at the hotel where the prime minister was staying. "I said, 'Okay, I hear you on [the concerns about staff]. I'm going out to a press conference at a housing site in about an hour, I'm not going to be making massive changes in the way my office operates between now and then but I take that seriously,'" Trudeau recalls. "'Obviously there was a process problem here where you feel that something wrong happened. I don't. But we will do more work on this and we'll figure this out and we'll learn through this process.'"

At that infrastructure announcement in Vancouver, Trudeau disclosed he had met with Wilson-Raybould twice since arriving in British Columbia and that she confirmed for him "a conversation we had this fall where I told her directly that any decisions on matters involving the director of public prosecutions were hers alone." He also said that "her presence in cabinet should actually speak for itself."

Trudeau's office and Wilson-Raybould's office had discussed beforehand what Trudeau would say at that announcement. Initially, Trudeau was to say that nothing "untoward" had happened, but the minister's office was not in favour of that wording. It seems no objection was raised by Wilson-Raybould in regards to Trudeau's comment about Wilson-Raybould's presence in cabinet.

Then the SNC-Lavalin affair took the first of several twists. Shortly after Trudeau's announcement, Wilson-Raybould requested a third meeting with the prime minister. There she told Trudeau that she would be resigning from cabinet.

Her precise reasons for resigning are still unclear. Trudeau himself seems not to fully understand her reasoning. "The next morning I said that I was surprised and disappointed, and I was," he says. "These are delicate conversations, and I don't want to mischaracterize them or speak for anyone else—but I continued to not entirely understand why. I think she felt part of it [was] that I wasn't being well-served by my office in general. And that she didn't feel that she could continue to serve as part of the government."

Wilson-Raybould says she will not publicly discuss what was said in those meetings or why she resigned. "Conversations that I have had with the prime minister are subject to strict confidences. There has been no waiver of the relevant duty of confidentiality to the Government of Canada," she says when asked to comment. "It is deeply unfortunate—indeed frustrating—that I am prevented from telling what was actually said in various conversations that are the subject of strict confidentiality. This is especially so since it appears, based on your questions to me regarding these conversations, that others do not feel equally constrained and that you are receiving, as a result, false, self-serving/one-sided and inaccurate accounts of relevant events. This is not fair."

The morning of February 12, Wilson-Raybould released a statement to announce her departure from cabinet. She said she was doing so with a "heavy heart," but she did not offer any explanation. She did refer to "matters that have been in the media over the last week," but only to explain that she was seeking legal advice—from former Supreme Court justice Thomas Cromwell—as to what she could say publicly.

Several hours later, Trudeau appeared before cameras at another infrastructure announcement, this time in Winnipeg. He said he was "frankly, surprised and disappointed" by Wilson-Raybould's resignation. "This resignation is not consistent with conversations I had with Jody weeks ago when I asked her to serve as Canada's minister for veterans affairs and associate minister of national defence. Nor is it consistent with the conversations we've had lately," Trudeau said. "In regards to the matter of SNC-Lavalin, let me be direct: the government of Canada did its job and to the clear public standards expected of it. If anybody felt differently, they had an obligation to raise that with me. No one, including Jody, did that."

This was now a crisis. It would go on for another forty-nine days, until the evening of April 2, when Trudeau made the decision to expel Wilson-Raybould and Philpott from the Liberal caucus.

Less than a week after Wilson-Raybould's resignation, Butts announced his own departure. He had, in fact, made several attempts to resign before Trudeau finally accepted. "I was very confident that he had not done anything wrong," Trudeau says of why he did not immediately accept Butts's resignation, "that he had continued to serve me and this government and Canadians with the integrity and brilliance that was his bread and butter, his core."

Butts himself insisted he had done nothing wrong. But he said that anonymous sources were suggesting he had pressured the former attorney general. It was, he wrote in a statement, "in the best interests of the office and its important work for me to step away."

The close and well-known friendship between Butts and Trudeau might have made it particularly awkward for the prime minister to defend his principal secretary. By stepping away, Butts could also take responsibility for the relationship between Wilson-Raybould and the PMO. And being on the outside might have put Butts in a better position to contest whatever allegations were about to be levelled. But his departure did not end the story.

A day after Butts's resignation was announced, Wilson-Raybould sought and was granted extraordinary permission to address a meeting of cabinet. The next day, she spoke at a meeting of the Liberal caucus. Leaks to reporters suggested it had been a positive discussion. At that caucus meeting, and then publicly, Trudeau apologized to Wilson-Raybould for not being quicker to condemn some of the critical comments and depictions of her that had appeared in the media.

From afar, it was possible to think the Liberals might have been working toward some kind of resolution. But then, after Liberal MPs voted against an NDP motion calling for a public inquiry, Wilson-Raybould rose on a point of order in the House. "I understand fully that Canadians want to know the truth and want transparency," she said. "Privilege and confidentiality are not mine to waive, and I hope that I have the opportunity to speak my truth." Conservative and NDP MPs applauded her. According to one Liberal source, Liberal MPs had not been expecting Wilson-Raybould to make that intervention.

Under immense pressure to remove restrictions on Wilson-Raybould to speak publicly, the cabinet agreed on February 25 to waive cabinet confidentiality and solicitor-client privilege so that she might testify before the justice committee, which had moved to hold hearings on deferred prosecution agreements, the Shawcross doctrine and SNC-Lavalin. The authorizing order-in-council allowed her, and others, to discuss the exercise of her authority under the Director of Public Prosecutions Act relating to SNC-Lavalin while she held the office of attorney general.

Two days later, Wilson-Raybould spoke her truth. "For a period of approximately four months, between September and December of 2018, I experienced a consistent and sustained effort by many people within the government to seek to politically interfere in the exercise of prosecutorial discretion in my role as the Attorney General of Canada in an inappropriate effort to secure a deferred prosecution agreement with SNC-Lavalin," she said.

Between the testimony of Wilson-Raybould and Butts, who would testify on March 6, two basic narratives would take shape.

In Wilson-Raybould's account, officials within the government hounded her and her office about the fate of SNC-Lavalin and ignored her warnings that what they were saying to her was inappropriate. She refused to co-operate and was soon thereafter relieved of her duties as justice minister and attorney general.

In Butts's account, officials within the government were worried about the potential job losses if SNC-Lavalin was found guilty of criminal charges and wanted to be sure the government had fully done its due diligence around that possibility, while respecting the attorney general's right and duty to make that decision independently.

"When 9,000 people's jobs are at stake, it is a public policy problem," Butts said. "It was our obligation to exhaustively consider options the law allows and to be forthright with people in explaining the attorney general's decision, in order to be able to demonstrate that the decision was taken with great care in careful consideration of their livelihoods."

That Wilson-Raybould was shuffled to a different portfolio, Butts testified, was the end result of a decision by Scott Brison, president of the Treasury Board, to resign. Trudeau's office had tried to convince Brison to stay, but when his decision did not change, the prime minister decided to move Philpott from Indigenous Services to fill that vacancy. Wilson-Raybould would have replaced Philpott, but she refused. Instead, she was moved to Veterans Affairs instead.

According to Wilson-Raybould, she had received a notice from the director of public prosecutions on September 4, 2018, indicating that SNC-Lavalin would not be offered a deferred prosecution agreement. From there, she detailed a series of interactions involving herself, her office, the chief of staff to Finance Minister Bill Morneau, advisors to the prime minister, the clerk of the Privy Council and the prime minister himself. Some of these interactions, she felt, had been inappropriate. She said, for instance, that SNC-Lavalin had been raised during a meeting with the prime minister and the clerk on September 17. Trudeau, she said, had referenced the fact that there was going to be an election in Quebec and that he was an MP for a Quebec riding. Such things would not have been appropriate considerations for the attorney general.

Trudeau says his reference to the election in Quebec was motivated by a sense of wanting to "make sure that anything federal doesn't end up fodder for attacks back and forth" during the campaign and that he mentioned he was a Quebec MP to make the point that his understanding of the importance of SNC-Lavalin was informed by a connection to the people he served.

Testifying before the justice committee in March, Wernick offered a similar explanation for why he had referenced the election in Quebec. "It is a long-standing convention for the federal government to try to stay out of the fray of provincial election campaigns, and that the people of each province decide for themselves who they want to govern," he said. "In mid-September, based on the company's public-disclosure obligations, I was concerned that a purely federal issue could surface in the last two weeks of that rather heated campaign. It is my job to remind elected officials about those conventions."

According to Wilson-Raybould, she had decided at some point between September 4 and September 16 "that it was inappropriate" for her "to intervene in the decision of the director of public prosecutions in this case." But, in that meeting with Trudeau and Wernick, she did agree to meet with the clerk and the deputy minister of justice to discuss it further.

"She said that she had reflected on this and it was her decision to make and I think I knew going in that she was not planning on, or not particularly open to, issuing a directive," Trudeau says. "But I asked her if she could look into it again and really see about this because I knew that there was no immediate timeline on her making a decision or not. And I asked her to look at it and that's what she did. It was sort of the one check-in I had. I said, 'Look, this is an issue that's going to have an impact in a whole bunch of different ways. We need to make sure we're doing everything we can, so please look into it again.'"

That Wilson-Raybould was unhappy with what was said in her meeting with Wernick and Trudeau was seemingly corroborated by the deputy minister of justice, Nathalie Drouin, who met with Wilson-Raybould the next day and recalled for the justice committee that the former attorney general "expressed to me that she was not comfortable with the content of this conversation."

In his own testimony, Butts questioned whether Wilson-Raybould could have responsibly made a decision in twelve days and said he was unaware until she testified that her decision had been final as of September 16. He also suggested Wilson-Raybould's willingness to further consider the matter indicated her decision was not final. "If the attorney general had made a decision and communicated it to the prime minister and the clerk, why would there be a next step at all? Why would the attorney general take and solicit meetings on a closed matter?" he asked. "Moreover, why would the attorney general not communicate her final decision in writing to the prime minister?"

In the fall, officials in the PMO raised the possibility of seeking an external legal opinion. According to Butts's testimony, such an option was included in a memo drafted by lawyers at the Department of Justice. The government's operating assumption, he said, was "that the decision wasn't made, and that we were free to inform it with advice. In the end, it was the attorney general's alone to make, and it would be for all of us to explain. Most important, it would be for many thousands of people to live with."

Butts said that "when you boil it all down, all we ever asked the attorney general to do was to consider a second opinion.

"This was a novel law. It was the first time it had ever been used, so we thought the bare minimum we needed to do in order to look people in the eye who stood to lose their jobs was to make sure we had a good reason and to build process around that," Butts explained. "It's absolutely a bare minimum to get the best advice you can when a decision affects that many people."

Wilson-Raybould was apparently not inclined to pursue such an opinion. "I had made my decision as the attorney general. I did not need external legal counsel," she explained at the justice committee. "I did not need people in the Prime Minister's Office continuing to suggest that I needed external legal counsel. That's inappropriate."

In an interview for this book, Wilson-Raybould questioned the objective of seeking that second opinion. "Was it to back up that we've done everything we can? Well, I'm confident that I did everything I needed to do to make a decision," she says. "And if the relationship between the director of public prosecutions and the attorney general is now going to be subject to review from the Prime Minister's Office then we have a problem." She subsequently declined to detail what steps she had taken before making that decision.

In his own testimony, Butts said Wilson-Raybould would have been free to accept or reject whatever the external counsel advised. "It was not about second-guessing the decision," he said, "it was about ensuring that the attorney general was making her decision with the absolute best evidence possible."

On December 5, Butts and Wilson-Raybould met for dinner at the Château Laurier. Wilson-Raybould said she made clear then that Trudeau's staff needed to stop approaching her on the subject of SNC-Lavalin. "Towards the end of our meeting . . . I raised how I needed everybody to stop talking to me about SNC, as I had made up my mind and the engagements were inappropriate," she told the justice committee.

But, in his appearance before the committee, Butts said he did not remember her saying this. "I have no memory of her asking me to do anything or to speak with staff about any aspect of this file," he said.

Finally, two weeks after that meeting with Butts, Wilson-Raybould and Michael Wernick spoke by phone. Appearing before the justice committee on February 27, Wilson-Raybould recounted the call in detail. It had apparently been a contentious conversation. Wernick said Trudeau was determined to do something on the file, though he did not want to do anything improper. Wilson-Raybould warned the clerk that they were "treading on dangerous ground." Wernick said he was worried about the prime minister and the justice minister being at loggerheads. Wilson-Raybould invoked the Saturday Night Massacre—an infamous moment from the Watergate scandal when the attorney general and the deputy attorney general of the United States resigned in succession after refusing President Richard Nixon's demand that they fire a special prosecutor who was investigating the affair.

What Wilson-Raybould did not disclose on February 27 was that she had recorded that call. In her supplementary submission to the justice committee, she not only acknowledged recording the conversation but also provided the committee with an audio file. She conceded that recording the call was "extraordinary and otherwise inappropriate," but she said she had wanted to ensure she could accurately recall the details of the conversation. She was releasing the audio, she said, because Wernick had subsequently said he did not threaten her, could not recall specifics of the call and had questioned her account of it.

On the recording, the conversation is tense. The clerk sounds less threatening than concerned, but Wilson-Raybould also seems to hear a threat. Wernick says Trudeau "does not want to do anything outside the box of what is legal or proper," but the prime minister wants to understand why a deferred prosecution agreement is not being pursued. Wernick suggests Wilson-Raybould could ask the public prosecutor to explain her decision. Wilson-Raybould says the conversations on the issue have been "entirely inappropriate" and amounted to "political interference."

Wilson-Raybould tells Wernick the official notice from the public prosecutor, which apparently explained the reasons for not pursuing a deferred prosecution agreement, was forwarded to the Prime Minister's Office. Wernick is apparently unaware of this. Wilson-Raybould reiterates her concerns about inappropriate interference. Wernick says he doesn't see "anything inappropriate." At a few points, Wernick remarks that "people are talking past each other." He says he's worried about a "collision" between Trudeau and Wilson-Raybould because "he is pretty firm about this." Wilson-Raybould concludes the call by saying she is waiting for "the other shoe to drop." Wernick does not engage with her on that comment or on her reference to the Saturday Night Massacre.

During one of his own appearances before the justice committee, before the audio was made public, Wernick said, "I was worried, as a secretary of cabinet, that frustration was building, that colleagues and the prime minister had not been provided an explanation for why the DPA route, or option, was not being chosen or exercised, and why seeking outside counsel to do due diligence on the first use of a DPA was not being chosen. There was building frustration at the time, and I was concerned about that."

Trudeau says "frustration" might have been putting it too strongly. "Maybe it was a little hiccup we had to work through, a little irritant that was ongoing," he says. "But there were bigger files I was working on with her and trying to get through than this one."

In Wilson-Raybould's narrative, the call was a prelude to the cabinet shuffle: less than three weeks after that conversation with Wernick, she was told she would no longer be the justice minister. Trudeau says that, during their first meeting in Vancouver, Wilson-Raybould pointed to her conversation with the clerk when he asked her why she had not brought her concerns to his attention. But Wernick does not seem to have relayed to the prime minister or his advisors that the call was particularly tense or worrisome. In retrospect, this was a crucial moment.

In a discussion about the call for this book, Trudeau points to the fact that one party to the call knew it was being recorded and the other didn't. "When you make a decision to record a call and you know you're recording a conversation that you are potentially going to use later to prove a point, it affects what you say and how you characterize and how you engage in the conversation," he says. "And you do see two kind of different streams in the conversation where Michael is thinking one thing and she was making explicit some points that might not have registered if you didn't think, well, this is a call that is going to frame a whole thing. So I'm wary about even criticizing Michael for not filling me in on it because from his perspective it was the continuation of a kind of conversation that we'd had various times in various ways throughout the fall. And it wasn't particularly notable."

After Butts's testimony, Trudeau called a news conference at the National Press Theatre and stated his conclusion that an "erosion of trust" had taken place. He was quickly criticized for not apologizing. But the belief within Trudeau's office was that he had nothing to apologize for, that he and his advisors had not done anything inappropriate. The Liberal members of the justice committee opted to conclude the hearings after Butts and Wernick had responded to Wilson-Raybould's testimony, leaving it to the ethics commissioner to conduct a full investigation. The Conservatives and New Democrats cried cover-up.

Regardless, the crisis would carry on. In fact, in between the committee appearances of Wilson-Raybould and Butts, it had only deepened: on March 4, Jane Philpott resigned, explaining that she could not support the government's handling of the issue.

Two weeks later, at a meeting of Ontario Liberal MPs, Philpott's colleagues vented their frustrations. They had helped her get elected, stood by her during the controversy over her transportation expenses and trusted her on issues like medical assistance in dying even when they disagreed with her. Now she had publicly aired her own disagreement and taken a side against the government. There was anger and a sense of betrayal. They were frustrated that she would not tell them what more she knew about what had happened. "The treatment from my Liberal caucus colleagues was extremely harsh," Philpott says.

A day earlier, Philpott had given an interview to *Maclean's*. It had not yet been published, and she did not tell her colleagues that she had spoken to the magazine. A day later, the interview landed. In it she said, "There's much more to the story that should be told." For the sake of Philpott's status in the Liberal caucus, the timing was not ideal. Both she and Wilson-Raybould had been saying they could not speak fully because of their cabinet oaths, but now Liberals were apparently running out of patience.

"It's one thing to take a hit from the Opposition or circumstances beyond caucus or cabinet. It's another thing to take political hits from your own people," John McKay, a veteran Liberal MP, told reporters. Judy Sgro, another veteran Liberal, told reporters that either of the former ministers could stand in the House of Commons and speak freely because of parliamentary privilege. "It's either put up or shut up," she told CBC Radio's *The House*. "If you've got something to say, you've had two months to get out there and say it."

Beyond the particulars of the Shawcross doctrine, there was great speculation about Wilson-Raybould's "end game" and where the whole affair was leading. The community around Parliament Hill—the politicians, staff, journalists and lobbyists—is sustained by gossip and conjecture, and this was rich material. In mid-April, Conservative MP Lisa Raitt went so far as to tweet that she was not the source of Robert Fife's original *Globe* story, shooting down a convoluted version of events that had been circulating around Ottawa. At least one intriguing conversation does seem to have occurred: at some point, Patty Hajdu approached Ralph Goodale to warn him that his name had been floated as a possible interim leader, in the event that Trudeau had to step aside. The origin of that speculation is disputed, but Goodale was unaware of it and not at all interested in entertaining it.

Meanwhile, Wernick's two combative performances before the justice committee—during his first appearance he condemned the "vomitorium of social media"—were seized upon by Conservatives and New Democrats who accused him of being too political, even partisan. That might not have necessarily required Wernick to resign as clerk, but, as the most senior civil servant in the federal government, he was also part of a panel of top civil servants that the government had created to inform the public of any attempts to interfere in the fall election. Given the sensitivity of that task, the objections of the Conservatives and New Democrats were potentially profound. After nearly thirty-eight years in the public service, Wernick was also already thinking about retirement. So, on March 18, he announced his intention to step down before the summer.

That same day, Trudeau announced that Anne McLellan, a former Liberal minister, would be advising him on whether any policies or procedures needed to change around the minister of justice and attorney general, including whether the two roles needed to be separated. More interesting was the revelation that Trudeau had personally briefed Wilson-Raybould about his intention to enlist McLellan before announcing it.

"I said, 'Look, just so you know, we're bringing in Anne McLellan to give us external advice on the two roles. The clerk has chosen to step down, Gerry's already stepped down. We're making lots of changes. You know, I've admitted that I regret this whole thing and I've said that I believe you truly believe that you went through this. Is there not a path forward here?' And she was noncommittal," Trudeau recalls.

Jody Wilson-Raybould says it is "untrue that I was ever noncommittal in response to the kinds of comments reported to you." Again, she considers herself prevented by strict confidentiality from going further to describe her conversations with Trudeau.

During her appearance before the justice committee, Wilson-Raybould had noticeably declined to say whether she still had confidence in Trudeau. But both she and Philpott remained members of the Liberal caucus. And, for all the intrigue and frustration, there were apparently efforts being made to arrive at some kind of mutually acceptable resolution.

In that conversation in late March, Trudeau framed it as a matter of doing politics differently. "Speaking with some of my predecessors who've sat in this office, [they've] expressed a certain amount of bewilderment that there is even a question or a path about them remaining as part of the team or remaining candidates," he says. "And I think one of the things that I certainly have tried to highlight is I do believe in doing politics differently. And that means bringing together people from different perspectives, different backgrounds and trying to work it out. I mean, people are different in their styles and approaches as politicians, and we want to be doing politics differently and I think that part of that is showing a willingness to work things through, and being a strong leader doesn't mean imposing or being rigid but actually trying to leave lots of room for different perspectives . . . this is not a straightforward situation; it's a situation that requires openness to engaging in different ways and that's what I'm trying to do."

These efforts apparently came down to a proposal for a joint statement by Trudeau and Wilson-Raybould. "There was an exchange of proposals in terms of language of things that we could agree to . . . recognizing that the former attorney general did feel that there had been inappropriate pressure and was looking to protect the government, but that, on our side, we genuinely believed we were doing the right kinds of things. But there's a lot to learn on this, we've already changed some of the processes, and trying to find language that really sort of validates that on this issue there was a disagreement, but on the big picture we agree on reconciliation, on the environment and on all sorts of big things."

In Trudeau's telling, those discussions ended with Wilson-Raybould's side proposing a statement only from Trudeau that would have had him admitting to wrongdoing. "I can't apologize for something that I don't fundamentally think we did wrong. And that was really sort of the key of it. I'd say there's lots of things that we needed to learn from, and I really regret it . . . But that fundamental admission that we were wrong isn't something that I believe and therefore couldn't accept."

Wilson-Raybould says she "wanted the prime minister to acknowledge that something seriously wrong happened and to seek to remedy that situation to insure that it never happened again. And I wanted him to, in some way, apologize to Canadians and trust Canadians to believe that, yeah, something inappropriate happened, there were attempts at political interference, and that was inappropriate or wrong and this is what we're doing to remedy it."

That such effort and time were expended on Wilson-Raybould and Philpott could be viewed as a reflection of how important such figures were to the idea of who Trudeau was as a leader: two impressive, accomplished women, one of them a celebrated Indigenous leader. Public and media sympathy had quickly swung to Wilson-Raybould after the *Globe*'s initial report. She became a hero. And as the SNC-Lavalin affair dragged on, it became a story about so much of what Trudeau was supposed to be about: not only reconciliation but transparency, openness, doing politics differently, sunny ways, feminism. At a minimum it was a controversy concerning the government's ethics, one that raised questions about the government's competence and disposition. From any number of other angles, it could be used to question so much more.

Trudeau concedes that politics could have been part of his search for a happy ending. But he insists it was more than that. "I think there was a real sense that having strong, thoughtful people as part of a team that is doing things differently and doing things in a positive way really is worth fighting for. And putting the personal ego or vendettas or stuff aside. I mean, there are people who within caucus [were] starting to say, 'Well, she can't come out and say clearly, yes, I continue to have confidence in the prime minister, in the leader of the Liberal Party, then she doesn't get to run.' I said, 'You know what? You're making it personal and for me it's not about personal. It's about can we continue to function as a team.' And it took time to work through to the point where we could say, 'Yeah, we actually can't continue to function as a team anymore because that bond of trust is broken with cabinet,' and that was really a piece of it—with caucus as well as cabinet."

Liberal MPs were perhaps ahead of their leader on this. And the release of the Wernick tape on March 29 seemed to exacerbate concerns.

"My hope is that caucus will meet quickly and that caucus will, I suspect, be of one mind that we don't want people in the caucus who don't have confidence in our government," Liberal MP Rob Oliphant told the CBC in an interview on April 1.

In a letter to Liberal MPs on April 2, Wilson-Raybould said that the choice before the Liberal caucus was "about what kind of party you want to be a part of, what values it will uphold, the vision that animates it, and indeed the type of people it will attract and make it up." Once again, she declined to say that she had confidence in Trudeau and his government. Philpott did come forward to say she had confidence in the prime minister, but by then it was possibly too late.

Meetings of Liberal MPs were convened and the overwhelming view was that both Wilson-Raybould and Philpott should be expelled. Party politics is, for better or worse, a team sport, and the members of the Liberal team were apparently not convinced that Wilson-Raybould and Philpott could still be counted on as committed and trustworthy teammates. To that, it might be argued that neither of them did anything wrong: that they merely stated their objections on a matter of significant principle. But perhaps they didn't seem to be doing enough to limit the damage while doing so.

On the evening of April 2, Trudeau met with both of the former ministers to tell them he was ordering their expulsion. "The trust that previously existed between these two individuals and our team has been broken," Trudeau explained in a televised speech to the Liberal caucus. "Whether it's taping conversations without consent or repeatedly expressing a lack of confidence in our government and in me personally as leader, it's become clear that Ms. Wilson-Raybould and Dr. Philpott can no longer remain part of our Liberal team."

Philpott and Wilson-Raybould were informed individually, in meetings with Trudeau and caucus leadership. Philpott says she told Trudeau that she thought the whole situation was sad and regrettable and preventable and that she was sorry it had come to this.

On that, perhaps everyone could agree.

EVEN THE FRIENDLIEST ANALYSIS would have to conclude that something went wrong here.

In Wilson-Raybould's telling, officials within the Trudeau government cavalierly disregarded the principles of the Shawcross doctrine and put inappropriate pressure upon the attorney general—a charge Trudeau has categorically rejected. In the alternative, the concerns of a particular minister weren't fully grasped, a relationship broke down and the government stumbled unwittingly into an incredible crisis. A minister who was supposed to be too big to fail ended up becoming the greatest threat Trudeau's leadership has so far faced.

It is potentially worth noting that the original events in question played out through a fall in which Trudeau, his office and his government were dealing with NAFTA negotiations and the future of the Trans Mountain expansion. Maybe an office with fewer things to worry about would have been quicker to realize it had a problem. It perhaps didn't help that the Indigenous rights framework was also a source of significant conflict. And a strained relationship between the prime minister and the minister of justice might have set the stage for some kind of breakdown. But if you are convinced something inappropriate happened here, such context might not matter.

It is a rote tendency of political punditry to blame "communications" and "issues management" whenever a government finds itself mired in such unpleasantness, but the fact the government was unable to contain the controversy was another issue. In hindsight, it is tempting to wonder why everything wasn't fully aired within a week of the *Globe and Mail*'s report on February 7. But then, maybe no one could have imagined the story would still be going nearly two months later.

The vomitorium of social media seemed to be a significant force in the middle of it all. Twitter, a platform that encourages and rewards outrage, was a frenzy for politicians and journalists to feed and feed on. Some of the leading voices staked strident positions early. For three weeks, the *Globe*'s report was not substantially challenged. Then Wilson-Raybould testified and then another week passed before Butts offered the first detailed account from another perspective. By then, the popular narrative had set.

Trudeau did not shut things down as some of his predecessors might have—it's somewhat hard to imagine Stephen Harper allowing committee hearings to proceed—but he also didn't do things as differently as he could have. He might have been more proactive, transparent and open, putting more of his staff forward to explain themselves or encouraging Liberal MPs to allow the justice committee's hearings to continue. But he also might not have ever satisfied his critics or rivals. The ethics commissioner's inquiry may eventually provide a full airing of who said what to whom.

To some, Trudeau may have just looked weak. Not until he finally expelled Wilson-Raybould and Philpott was there a flash of anger or fight in him. And it is perhaps notable that his support among men dropped precipitously in the spring of 2019.

In the middle of it all, Bill Morneau tabled a budget—a moment the government should have been able to use to begin framing its offer for the fall election.

Each spring, when the budget is tabled, the Liberals play the finance minister's speech for a set of focus groups to gauge which elements make the best impression. But on March 19, when Morneau stood to deliver his remarks, the Conservatives responded by shouting and banging on their desks—a cacophony meant to protest the end of the justice committee's study. Morneau's remarks were rendered inaudible. The focus groups could not hear him above him the noise. Sometimes the metaphors write themselves.

In lieu of Morneau's dulcet tones, the moderators of the focus groups read the budget speech aloud. Those select groups of Canadian voters did like what they heard. The budget of 2019—built on new assistance for first-time home buyers, a new training benefit, steps to reduce prescription drug prices, pension reforms and a rebate to purchase electric vehicles—scored higher in some metrics than any of Trudeau's previous three budgets. Unfortunately for the Liberals, the SNC-Lavalin affair had obscured all that.

The whole affair is said, perhaps unexpectedly, to have had a galvanizing effect on the Liberal caucus and cabinet. In another attempt to bring attention to the end of the justice committee's investigation, the Conservatives forced a long series of votes in the House of Commons that ran through one night and into the next day. Trudeau made sure to be present with his colleagues, taking a shift in the House and hanging around the MPs' lobby. The experience became a team-building exercise.

Flying back to Ottawa to take part in that voting marathon, after an infrastructure announcement in Mississauga, Trudeau was joined by Omar Alghabra, a Liberal MP he has known since they were young backbenchers together from 2008 to 2011. Trudeau told Alghabra that Canadians expected to see their prime ministers get knocked down, but wanted to see whether they could get back up.

At that moment—March 21—the next federal election was exactly seven months away.

CHAPTER 13

HOLDING THE HILL

G erry Butts is fond of saying that governing is an essay question, while an election is multiple choice. One of his mentors, David Axelrod, once put it slightly differently "For three and a half years as president of the United States, every day is a referendum on you," he said in 2011. "The last four months of the campaign is a choice."

Within Axelrod's description is a tidy way of framing an incumbent's re-election campaign, a frame that has become popular among Liberals in 2019: "it's not a referendum, it's a choice."

In 2012, Axelrod's candidate was a leader who had been elected on promises of "hope" and "change." Great expectations had, perhaps inevitably, been followed by an imperfect reality. In Barack Obama's case, the U.S. economy was also still only slowly recovering from the Great Recession. His campaign's response was to remind voters that the 2012 presidential election was still a contest between two different choices.

"More than any other race, people measure not just the views but the qualities of two candidates and make very sophisticated judgments about who they want to lead them," Axelrod later said. "We obviously looked at the last re-election, in 2004. While there were fundamental differences, there was one large similarity: a president in a difficult situation ultimately won a race that many thought at the beginning that he might lose because the race was put in a context of a choice. When

317

people were faced with that choice, they resolved [it] in favor of President Bush in 2004. There were some lessons to be gleaned from that."

This idea of a choice also had the virtue of being true. American voters couldn't simply decide they weren't perfectly satisfied with Obama's presidency: they would have to choose between sticking with Barack Obama and replacing him with Mitt Romney. But this framing also likely pushed voters to get beyond any disappointment they had with the president. This was not a contest between the reality of an Obama presidency and some imagined ideal of what an Obama presidency could have been like. This was a choice between one president or another, and everything that choice entailed.

"When all is said and done, when you pick up that ballot to vote, you will face the clearest choice of any time in a generation," Obama said in his speech to the Democratic convention in September 2012. "And on every issue, the choice you face won't just be between two candidates or two parties. It will be a choice between two different paths for America, a choice between two fundamentally different visions for the future."

"Choice" was a word Trudeau used that night at Brébeuf, when the testimony of Jody Wilson-Raybould seemed to endanger his government. Though his explanation of what that choice would be about was, perhaps understandably, a bit unfocused.

Six weeks later, in April 2019, he went to Mississauga to address a convention of the Liberal Party of Canada's Ontario wing. Even then, he still felt it necessary to acknowledge the mess that had dominated the early spring. "My friends, we have a very big six months ahead of us. It is so, so important that we stay focused on the task at hand," he said. "Internal disputes only tell Canadians that we care more about ourselves than we do about them. You know, and I know, that that couldn't be further from the truth . . . Let's learn from our mistakes. Liberals fighting Liberals only helps Andrew Scheer."

The rest of his twenty-minute address was about shaping the choice.

Trudeau leaned heavily on his government's climate policy, on the economic and climatic reasons for acting, the mounting evidence of a real problem and the necessity of having a plan. Public concern about climate change had increased of late, and the Liberals apparently saw a useful point of contrast. Trudeau reminded Liberals of the federal rebate—the "Climate Action Incentive"—and he sought to frame the opposition. "Conservative politicians like Doug Ford and Andrew Scheer believe it should be free to pollute in this country," he said.

Scheer's Conservatives had yet to release their proposed plan for climate policy. So Trudeau went after Ford's actions: firing Ontario's chief scientist, repealing the province's cap-and-trade system, cancelling emissions testing for vehicles, scrapping energy efficiency programs and "wasting taxpayer dollars fighting federal leadership in court."

Back when Trudeau was sworn in as prime minister in November 2015, just one province was represented by a conservative premier: Saskatchewan, with Brad Wall. By this time, there were six. And within a week of Trudeau's appearance in Mississauga, there'd be a seventh: Dennis King in Prince Edward Island. At least three of those premiers—Alberta's Jason Kenney, Saskatchewan's Scott Moe and Doug Ford—were happy to oppose Trudeau. But no one was ever more enthusiastic about it than Ford. The Ford government was preparing to force every gas station in the province to put anti-carbon-tax stickers on gas pumps, a remarkable incursion on private businesses for the purposes of a political campaign. Meanwhile, public funds were also being used to air official Government of Ontario ads that attacked the federal policy. Such provocations at least gave Trudeau more latitude to attack Ford's policies in Ontario.

All things being equal, Trudeau might have preferred to have an ally at Queen's Park—someone like Kathleen Wynne, a premier who openly campaigned for Trudeau in 2015. But Ford could still be a useful belligerent, not least because he was both the most well-known conservative in the country and also one of the most unpopular politicians in Canada. When Abacus Data surveyed voters in late April, it found Trudeau's personal ratings had tumbled: 32 percent of respondents still had a positive view, but 46 percent were now negative. That was not great. But it was still significantly better than Ford. According to the same survey, the premier of Ontario was viewed positively by just 15 percent of respondents and negatively by 53 percent.

Ford could also be used to fill in a picture of what an Andrew Scheer government might look like. Scheer was still relatively unknown to the Canadian public, and his platform was yet to be detailed. But Ford was now in government, and so he was having to actually do things.

"But that's not all Doug Ford's done," Trudeau continued. "Yesterday, he announced his first budget, loaded with cuts. Cuts to services for farmers. Cuts to services for Franco-Ontarians, for seniors, for post-secondary students, for Indigenous peoples, for children, and for those who rely on community social services. And Andrew Scheer takes his cues from the Ontario premier, so Canadians can expect much of the same if he ever gets elected."

If Scheer hoped to campaign on balancing the federal budget, he would have to contend with such comparisons. Ford had campaigned on the idea that it would be easy to balance the budget in Ontario. But each week now brought some new example of a program that was being diminished or eliminated.

That the younger and milder Scheer might "takes his cues" from the older and louder Ford was something else. As much as it might help Scheer to have a few premiers making the same arguments and criticizing Trudeau in the same ways, there was another potential opportunity for Trudeau here: that is, that a significant number of Canadians might actually now be looking for someone to stand up to the likes of Ford, Kenney and Moe. Federally, his father had to fend off the challenges of Robert Stanfield and Joe Clark, but it was René Lévesque, the separatist premier of Quebec, who most animated Pierre Trudeau's time in power. Perhaps in Ford or Kenney, or some combination thereof, Trudeau could find a similar figure.

From budget cuts and climate change, Trudeau segued to an attempt to place Scheer and Ford within the context of a larger conflict. "Andrew Scheer and Doug Ford have decided to take the easy route. To divide people and spread hatred rather than finding real solutions," he said. "Around the world, right-wing parties are frightening and trying to exploit people's anger for electoral gains . . . And they've been some-what successful in turning anger into political support."

To some extent, the 2015 election in Canada, with its talk of banning the niqab and rooting out "barbaric cultural practices," now seems like a precursor to some of the populist politics that emerged globally in 2016. Having won that debate, Trudeau entered an era that seemed defined by such stuff, at least elsewhere in the world. Now the spectre of populism seemed to hang over every major election. And Trudeau seemed willing to invoke it.

Of course, Andrew Scheer and Donald Trump are rather unalike in disposition. But the Liberals have not been averse to noting any similarities in rhetoric or policy. In Mississauga, Trudeau referred to the fact that Scheer had recently failed to confront a member of the public who questioned him about a far-right conspiracy theory at a town hall (Scheer claimed he hadn't heard the question). Scheer had then spoken to a rally that included members of the so-called yellow vest movement. Trudeau also noted that, two years earlier, the Conservatives had opposed a motion in the House of Commons that condemned Islamophobia.

This was not quite a new theme for Trudeau. In a speech at the Liberal convention in Halifax in April 2018, Trudeau said that the Conservative Party had lately been "been emboldened by successful campaigns elsewhere in the world to divide people against one another." Two months later, at an event to nominate the first Liberal candidate for the 2019 campaign—Navdeep Bains in Mississauga–Malton—Trudeau had made a direct appeal. "We've seen it around the world, the politics of division, of polarization, of populism are taking more and more hold," he said, "and we have to demonstrate, here in Canada, for ourselves, for our communities, for our kids, but also for the world, that those don't always work."

There was a hint in that message of something Barack Obama once said to Trudeau: "Justin, hold the top of the hill." At first, Trudeau thought the idea was too defensive. "At that moment I sort of disagreed with him," Trudeau recalls. "I was like, 'No, it's not enough to just hold—we gotta get out there.'" In time, though, the value and the challenge of holding the hill seems to have become more apparent.

Scheer's Conservatives would no doubt balk at being described as a populist incursion. It would, for that matter, be altogether too much to say that the fate of global liberal democracy depends on a Canadian general election. As Trudeau himself notes, Canada is not alone at the top of the hill—in addition to Emmanuel Macron in France, Trudeau has found allies like Pedro Sánchez in Spain and Jacinda Ardern in New Zealand. But it would also be wrong to say Canada does not matter. And that Canada might stand as a certain kind of example for the world is a powerful idea, particularly at this moment.

Even still, Trudeau himself acknowledges that elections tend to turn on more immediately tangible concerns. "Ultimately the decisions Canadians make in an election are not around how we're positioning ourselves in the world," he says in a conversation in January. "It's, you know, how's my job looking? How're my kids' jobs looking? Am I able to pay my mortgage? Am I able to [afford] my retirement?"

These were the practical matters that bookended Trudeau's speech in Mississauga. He led with the most flattering data points: the lowest unemployment rate in forty years, 900,000 new jobs created and nearly 300,000 kids lifted out of poverty. He closed with a list of Liberal answers to contemporary concerns. To deal with the disruption of artificial intelligence and automation, the government had invested in skills training. For those who were worried about affording a house, the Liberals were offering new assistance. For those who weren't sure they could afford retirement, the Liberals had reformed the Canada Pension Plan and Old Age Security.

The Conservatives would have their own ideas about those things. But Trudeau was also building a contrast based on vision.

"If you do not have plan for the environment, then you do not have a plan for the economy," he said of climate change. "In fact, you do not have a plan for the future."

"Why worry about tomorrow, they say, when you're worried about today?" he said of conservatives. "What these parties don't realize, though, is that we have to work hard for the middle class today and give them hope for the future."

This would seem to be a frame he has been thinking about.

"It's a choice between . . . being afraid of the future or saying that we should be confident about our own abilities to take on the future," he says in a conversation in his Wellington Street office in April, a week after his speech in Mississauga. "I mean, Make America Great Again—it's basically, we're going to go back to the way it used to be in the idyllic postwar boom years in the suburbs. This idea of looking backwards, saying no, no, we can hold onto the way things were, return to those values and that way the country used to be. Versus what we're trying to say, which is, yeah the world's changing, there's lot to be worried about—but we got this. We got this as Canadians. We're going to invest in AI. We're going to fight climate change and develop the next kinds of solutions. We're going to continue to export our natural resources but we're going to do it better and smarter. We're going to make sure that there are jobs for you that will keep you through to retirement and jobs that will be there for your kids to have an even better quality of life. We see the changes coming, we've got a plan for them, and the past four years has demonstrated not just that we have a plan for that but it's working. . . . Or there's a 'We can fight the future, we can hold onto what it is, keep the outside world at bay, and just, you know, hang onto the way Canada was for a little longer.' I don't think that's the way to build a real future, I don't think that's a long-term vision, and I think Canadians need and will respond to a long-term vision. And that is the choice at the heart of this election."

That, at least, is the choice Trudeau sees, or the one he wants Canadians to see.

Of course, it's also not always easy to see what an election will be about. The 2015 campaign wasn't going to be about the niqab and Syrian refugees until suddenly it was. But the basic parameters of 2019 might be set. The Liberals will sell a testament to what they have done and a vision of where the current path leads. From the right and the left, their opponents will try to pull that vision apart, offering some combination of less or more.

By the spring of 2019, the Conservatives, seizing on the insecurities that the Liberals had focused on in 2015, were beginning to compile a package of tax breaks, matched with some kind of reduction in federal spending. Scheer was promising to make it easier to proceed with major resource projects, presumably to be accompanied by some lesser commitment to reducing greenhouse gas emissions. Other Liberal priorities would presumably be open to question—Scheer's Conservatives had, for instance, said little about reconciliation since he became leader.

Of course, it is rather easier to frame a choice in a two-party system. Unlike Obama, Trudeau will have to fend off the New Democrats and Greens as well, each of whom will likely promise to do more than the Liberals have done on issues like climate change and social programs, while forswearing non-renewable resource development.

So Canadians will have options. But a complicated choice is still a choice.

———

HISTORICALLY, CANADIANS ARE NOT quick to dump their national governments: once a party has won power, it usually has to work very hard to lose it. Not since R.B. Bennett, prime minister from 1930 to 1935, has a government come to office with a parliamentary majority and then been tossed out of power at the next opportunity. In that case, Bennett's mistake was winning power just as the Great Depression was taking hold (and then not moving fast enough to deal with it). The only other prime minister to arrive with a majority and leave after a single term was Alexander Mackenzie, the forgotten Liberal who governed from 1873 to 1878.

Pierre Trudeau, though, came perilously close to blowing it in 1972. In 1968, with Trudeaumania in full swing, the Liberals won 154 of the 264 seats in the House of Commons, more than double the total for Robert Stanfield's Progressive Conservatives. Four years later, after a disappointing first term and a listless re-election campaign, Trudeau's Liberals won 109 seats, just two more than Stanfield's PCs. The line between greatness and failure is sometimes that thin. The Trudeau government spent the next two years governing with the support of the New Democrats and then came back in 1974 to win another majority. Another comeback was needed after 1979 to achieve the grandest of Trudeau's successes: patriating the constitution and enshrining the Charter of Rights and Freedoms. The lesson perhaps being that durability and resilience are more important than any other quality a prime minister might wish to possess.

The spectre of '72 is easy to raise as Justin Trudeau's re-election hangs in the balance. The prime minister himself has invoked it, if only for the sake of getting a laugh. In April, a group of former officials in Pierre Trudeau's government gathered in Ottawa for lunch. Justin Trudeau stopped in to say hello and then announced that he and his advisors had settled on a slogan for the 2019 campaign: "The Land Is Strong," the infamously ponderous message that his father took to voters in 1972.

The election of 2019, though unwritten as of this writing, will have its own peculiarities. On the left, the Green Party has shown signs of life—maybe not enough to sweep Elizabeth May to power, but enough to make predictions that much harder. Eschewing the entreaties of May and the Greens, Jody Wilson-Raybould and Jane Philpott chose to run as independents, at least ensuring that they would remain characters in the story of the 2019 campaign. Jagmeet Singh, the first non-white party leader in federal history, has struggled mightily as leader of the New Democrats, but could now benefit from low expectations (to borrow a phrase: if he shows up to the first debate wearing pants, he might be declared the winner). On the right, Maxime Bernier's aggressively right-wing People's Party is at least a theoretical threat to Andrew Scheer's base of support. The Bloc Québécois, however dysfunctional, still lurks.

The most interesting contests seem likely to take place in a trio of potentially pivotal battlegrounds: in British Columbia, where opposition to a pipeline still lurks; in the suburbs of Ontario, where Conservatives and Liberals will compete to address cost-of-living concerns; and in Quebec, where Liberals (and Conservatives) might benefit from the NDP's decline.

Underneath all of that run the volatile currents of democracy in the second decade of the twenty-first century: the use of social media to wage political campaigns, the distorting speed and polarization of online discourse, the easy spread of disinformation, the threat of foreign interference and hacked emails. And then there is simply the world as it is. So long as Donald Trump is president, a wide range of disturbances must be considered highly possible: from a downturn in the global economy to the outbreak of military conflict.

That the Liberals, who can boast of presiding over the lowest unemployment rate in forty years, might enter the fall trailing the Conservatives could be evidence of a restless electorate or a testament to how much the Liberals have done to make things difficult for themselves. That Trudeau would wrestle Trump to a draw and still be in danger of losing the next election was probably not the plan.

In May, federal prosecutors dropped the breach of trust charge against Vice-Admiral Mark Norman, the former commander of the navy, who had been accused of leaking confidential cabinet information related to a shipbuilding procurement in 2015. Conservative MPs tried to frame the charge against Norman as another "scandal" for Trudeau. At the very least, it was another excuse to reference that other legal matter, the SNC-Lavalin affair.

While Trudeau continued to carry the weight of that episode, the spring of 2019 was not all bad. Four days before the charge was dropped against Norman, Saskatchewan's court of appeal ruled against the Moe government's challenge and upheld the constitutionality of the federal carbon price. A few weeks later, Trump agreed to drop his tariffs against Canadian steel and aluminum, thus clearing the way for the Trudeau government to put the new NAFTA before Parliament for ratification.

That agreement landed in Parliament amid a final rush of legislation, including bills on Indigenous child welfare and languages, and a rewrite of energy regulation. And then, days before Parliament adjourned for the summer, Trudeau announced that cabinet had re-approved the Trans Mountain expansion, clearing the way for construction to resume before the election. Burnishing his green cred ahead of any such announcement, Trudeau announced his government's intention to pursue a ban on single-use plastics, with one of Canada's most prominent environmentalists, Steven Guilbeault, standing beside him. Such developments could pull Liberal support back upwards. Or the Liberals could still be trailing when the official campaign begins in September.

Justin Trudeau has been somewhere like that before. For more than a year after he became party leader, the Liberals enjoyed a sizeable lead in public polling. Then, beginning in the fall of 2014, Liberal support began to erode. By the summer of 2015, it had dropped precipitously. Trudeau went into that year's election running third. A few months later, the Liberals were decisive winners.

"What we did in the run-up to 2015 was be confident in what we were talking about, be confident in what we had to offer, and keep our heads down and work really hard and do the work of connecting with people. And that's exactly what we're doing now, and it's certainly what we're going to be doing over the next six months," he says in late March. "I mean, we'll let our opponents talk about what they want to talk about and try and push the narratives that they will. We'll obviously see the media do what they want to talk about . . . We are doing things regardless of whether we're at this point able to properly communicate it to people. We keep doing the things that matter. And ultimately that's what this is about."

In 2015, he ultimately made the case that he was the right kind of change. In 2019, he has to make the case that he's still the best choice.

═══════

In May 2019, the Conservative Party released a series of new television ads, all aimed at the prime minister, each with the same tagline: Justin Trudeau, the Conservatives said, was "not as advertised." The slogan was cast in a red-and-white logo that resembled the "as seen on TV" mark that is sometimes slapped on packages for the gimmicky products that are sold in late-night commercials.

It was a slightly odd argument for the Conservative Party to be making. In 2015, Justin Trudeau had presented himself as a real change from Stephen Harper. Now the Conservatives were saying he had failed to be different enough, while their own leader was promising to be Stephen Harper with a smile. But it was also not hard to imagine the charge resonating with some number of skeptical Liberal voters, perhaps even driving support to the New Democrats or Greens, and thus leading to the sort of splits that the Conservatives would benefit from.

Trudeau, of course, is someone who was seen on TV. Much of his life has played out onscreen. He looks, and perhaps sometimes sounds, like the sort of person you would expect to see there. And for the entirety of his political career he has dealt with expectations, both good and bad.

"One of the first things I said when I won my nomination [in 2008] is, look, there's people out there who have incredibly high expectations, there are people out there who have incredibly low expectations," he recalls. "I'm fairly certain I'm going to disappoint everybody by being somewhere in the middle between the stratosphere and the depths."

He has since been everything from an international star to a beleaguered prime minister. The reality that exists beyond the TV commercials is complicated like that.

That he might fail to fully meet expectations as prime minister was a story waiting to be written from the moment he stepped onstage in Montreal four years ago to accept his victory. Four years later, those who expected a great deal might wish he had done better, even if they might also have to admit that he has been preferable to another four years of Conservative government. Those who expected very little, or worse, have no doubt found things in the last four years to confirm their suspicions (those outfits in India, for example). Though even those who still take a dim view of him might have to concede that he has done better at a few things (dealing with Trump, for instance) than they would have imagined.

He has surely also done one or two things that no one would have predicted, like buying a pipeline. That the world would go as it has gone was rather unexpected.

In many other ways, he has been exactly as advertised. He has been enthusiastic and eager, a bit audacious and periodically a little theatrical. He has been a very public figure. He has been proudly idealistic. He has pursued an ambitious agenda. His priorities have remained relatively consistent, however much the details of the follow-through might be debated. It has not always been smooth and tidy. His imperfections have been apparent. And he has been able to find the sort of trouble that should have been avoidable.

It is, at the time of this writing, too early to draw simple conclusions or start framing a legacy. If the Liberals lose power in the fall of 2019 and Trudeau resigns as leader, he will be spoken of in terms of disappointment and what was squandered. If the Conservatives are returned to power, it will seem that the Harper years were something other than an interregnum and Trudeau will be condemned by progressives for wasting the opportunity. If Trudeau remains prime minister, the story goes on. An election can endorse everything that occurred in the previous four years, or it can be an indictment of every shortcoming and failure.

In either case, there will be plenty of time to talk about that later.

There are some things, though, that endure beyond the whims of electoral politics and human fallibility. The unresolved work of reconciliation. The need for economic security. The promotion and acceptance of pluralism and diversity. The pursuit of equality. The practice of politics and the value of public institutions. The reality of resource development. The global and generational imperative of climate change and everything that is to come or might be avoided.

These are big things, the defining challenges of this particularly fraught and perilous moment. These four years have been about all those things. One way or another, so will the next four years, and the forty years after that.

Near the end of a conversation in late January 2019, Trudeau is asked if there's anything he wants to say that hasn't already been covered, anything else that's necessary to understand him or his government. He slowly builds to his own summation.

"What we are trying to do here matters. And it matters to me that

Canadians understand or that Canadians sense that this is about trying to do right by this country that has given us all so much, and it can sound corny or schmaltzy, but I mean that's been the story of my life, of opportunities given to me that weren't given to my classmates at Rockcliffe Park Public School. Opportunities given to me that weren't there for the kids I was in university with or my fellow river guides or snowboard instructors. These opportunities to think about things, to carry a certain amount of ideals and hopes for this country in me and to gather around me an amazing team of folks who step up to put their names on billboards and posters and say, 'Yeah, I think we can actually be idealistic in this time of cynicism and work our asses off to try and build something real.'"

Any time you do that, he says, it is the nature of human institutions that some things won't work out the way you would have liked. But he'll stack up the capacities and thoughtfulness of those in his government who "try and do right in their time here."

And then he is talking about paddling.

The image of Pierre Trudeau in a canoe is one of the more iconic of the first Trudeau era. In 2003, three years after Pierre's death, Justin and his friend Gerry retraced Pierre's canoe trip along the Nahanni River in the Northwest Territories, part of a campaign to expand environmental protection for the waterway. Twelve years later, in the midst of the election campaign, Trudeau got in a canoe and paddled along the Bow River in Calgary. Possibly he just needed to burn off some energy before that night's leaders' debate. It also made a nice photo.

In January 2017, he was lightly roasted for saying at a town hall that Indigenous youth wanted canoes and paddles to help them reconnect with the land. Six months later, he got in a kayak and paddled along the Niagara River, part of an event that Trudeau used to restate Canada's commitment to the Paris Agreement, just days after Donald Trump announced his intention to withdraw.

Getting in a canoe and paddling the rapids near the prime minister's cottage at Harrington Lake was said to be a rite of passage for Pierre's boys. And the metaphor apparently left a mark.

"The opportunity to steer Canada through these rough waters of the first decades of the twenty-first century is amazing," Trudeau says. "The way the world is changing, the way our economies are changing, this time of transition is so anxiety-wrenching for so many people. But I go back to one of the first things that my dad taught me, which is how to paddle down rapids. How to paddle down the river. You know, look for the V. You keep moving faster than the water, you realize there's going to be rocks and waves and things along the way, and you don't try and paddle against the current, but you try and use the forces that you are caught in to get through as dry and as safe as possible at the end of the day. And that idea that we are in this sweep of history, like the sweep of rapids in a river, and all we can do is try and steer around the rocks and prevent ourselves from wrapping our canoe around a big old boulder, and keep everyone paddling in sync and responding to everything going on around you, but with a clear sense of purpose and direction and a plan. That's what this is."

AUTHOR'S NOTE

THE REPORTING AND WRITING for this book was done between June 2018 and June 2019, though it is also informed by my previous work for the CBC and *Maclean's*. What is reported and written here was aided by a number of interviews and conversations, some conducted on the record, some not. For the book, the prime minister agreed to participate in a series of interviews, from which I have quoted extensively.

ACKNOWLEDGEMENTS

THROUGHOUT MY CAREER, I have been blessed with great editors, but there are five who deserve particular credit for getting me this far: Christina Vardanis, Dianne de Fenoyl, Ken Whyte, Jim Bray and Rob Russo. Whatever success I have had is mostly their doing. The failures are my own.

Two people are primarily responsible for turning a vague notion into this book: Jennifer Lambert and Martha Webb. Their guidance was exemplary.

My thanks to everyone at HarperCollins, particularly Noelle Zitzer and Melissa Nowakowski, for their support and efforts on my behalf, to Linda Pruessen for copy editing, to Stephen D. Cook for transcription, to Alison Woodbury for legal matters, to Sarah Wight for proofreading, and to the friends who offered their thoughts on early drafts of the chapters here.

My eternal gratitude to the friends and family members whose support and patience, throughout the writing of this book and in all the years leading up to this, have been limitless.

INDEX